A Critical Look at Institutional Mission

WRITING PROGRAM ADMINISTRATION
Series Editors: Susan H. McLeod and Margot Soven

The Writing Program Administration series provides a venue for scholarly monographs and projects that are research- or theory-based and that provide insights into important issues in the field. We encourage submissions that examine the work of writing program administration, broadly defined (e.g., not just administration of first-year composition programs). Possible topics include but are not limited to 1) historical studies of writing program administration or administrators (archival work is particularly encouraged); 2) studies evaluating the relevance of theories developed in other fields (e.g., management, sustainability, organizational theory); 3) studies of particular personnel issues (e.g., unionization, use of adjunct faculty); 4) research on developing and articulating curricula; 5) studies of assessment and accountability issues for WPAs; and 6) examinations of the politics of writing program administration work at the community college.

BOOKS IN THE SERIES

Labored: The State(ment) and Future of Work in Composition edited by Randall McClure, Dayna V. Goldstein, and Michael A. Pemberton (2016)

A Critical Look at Institutional Mission: A Guide for Writing Program Administrators edited by Joseph Janangelo (2016)

A Rhetoric for Writing Program Administrators edited by Rita Malenczyk, 2nd ed. (2016). First ed., 2013.

Ecologies of Writing Programs: Program Profiles in Context edited by Mary Jo Reiff, Anis Bawarshi, Michelle Ballif, & Christian Weisser (2015)

Writing Program Administration and the Community College by Heather Ostman (2013)

The WPA Outcomes Statement—A Decade Later, edited by Nicholas N. Behm, Gregory R. Glau, Deborah H. Holdstein, Duane Roen, & Edward M. White (2012). *Winner of the CWPA Best Book Award*

Writing Program Administration at Small Liberal Arts Colleges by Jill M. Gladstein and Dara Rossman Regaignon (2012)

GenAdmin: Theorizing WPA Identities in the 21st Century by Colin Charlton, Jonikka Charlton, Tarez Samra Graban, Kathleen J. Ryan, and Amy Ferdinandt Stolley (2012). *Winner of the CWPA Best Book Award*

A CRITICAL LOOK AT INSTITUTIONAL MISSION

A GUIDE FOR WRITING PROGRAM ADMINISTRATORS

Edited by Joseph Janangelo

Parlor Press
Anderson, South Carolina
www.parlorpress.com

Parlor Press LLC, Anderson, South Carolina, USA
© 2016 by Parlor Press
All rights reserved.
Printed in the United States of America on acid-free paper.

S A N: 2 5 4 - 8 8 7 9

Library of Congress Cataloging-in-Publication Data

Names: Janangelo, Joseph, editor.
Title: A critical look at institutional mission : a guide for writing program administrators / edited by Joseph Janangelo.
Description: Anderson, S.C. : Parlor Press, [2016] | Series: Writing Program Administration | Includes bibliographical references and index.
Identifiers: LCCN 2016031965 (print) | LCCN 2016055314 (ebook) | ISBN 9781602358409 (pbk. : alk. paper) | ISBN 9781602358416 (hardcover : alk. paper) | ISBN 9781602358423 (pdf) | ISBN 9781602358430 (epub) | ISBN 9781602358447 (ibook) | ISBN 9781602358454 (Kindle)
Subjects: LCSH: Writing centers--Administration--Handbooks, manuals, etc. | Writing centers--Research--Methodology. | English language--Rhetoric--Study and teaching (Higher)--United States | Report writing--Study and teaching (Higher)--United States | Academic writing--Study and teaching--United States | Universities and colleges--Aims and objectives--United States. | Universities and colleges--United States--Administration.
Classification: LCC PE1405.U6 C74 2016 (print) | LCC PE1405.U6 (ebook) | DDC
808/.042071173--dc23
LC record available at https://lccn.loc.gov/2016031965

2 3 4 5

Writing Program Administration
Series Editors: Susan H. McLeod and Margot Soven

Cover image: Patrick Schöpflin. Unsplash. Used by permission.
Copyeditor: Jared Jameson.
Cover design: David Blakesley

Parlor Press, LLC is an independent publisher of scholarly and trade titles in print and multimedia formats. This book is available in paper, cloth and eBook formats from Parlor Press on the World Wide Web at http://www.parlorpress.com or through online and brick-and-mortar bookstores. For submission information or to find out about Parlor Press publications, write to Parlor Press, 3015 Brackenberry Drive, Anderson, South Carolina, 29621, or email editor@parlorpress.com.

Contents

Acknowledgments   *ix*

Introduction: Of Provocations and Possibilities   *xi*
    Joseph Janangelo

Part I: Connecting and Contending   1

1 Community Engagement and Authentic Writing: Institutional Mission as Centripetal and/or Centrifugal Force   *3*
    Dominic DelliCarpini

2 Transcending Institutional Boundaries and Types: Undergraduate Research   *24*
    Joyce Kinkead

3 Strategic Assessment: Using Dynamic Criteria Mapping to Actualize Institutional Mission and Build Community   *40*
    Nicholas N. Behm

4 Creating a Program of Success for Underrepresented Students at Research Institutions   *59*
    Farrell J. Webb and Anita R. Cortez

Part II: Designing and Discerning   75

5 Out of the Ivory Tower and into the Brand: How the New Two-Year College Mission Shapes the Faculty-Manager   *77*
    Jeffrey Klausman

6 The Pen and the Drone: Manumotive Writing Programs and the Professional Imagination at West Point   *92*
    Jason Hoppe

7 The BYU English Department's Future Scholars Program: Planning for a Faculty to Match the Institutional Mission   *112*
    Kristine Hansen

8 Designing and Delivering General Education Curriculum at a Small Liberal Arts College   *130*
   Anita M. DeRouen

Part III: Relating, Reflecting, and Resisting   149

9 When Fantasy Themes Collide: Implementing a Public Liberal Arts Mission in Changing Times   *151*
   Rita Malenczyk and Lauren Rosenberg

10 Negotiating Institutional Missions: Writing Center Tutors as Rhetorical Actors   *169*
   Andrea Rosso Efthymiou and Lauren Fitzgerald

11 People Make the Place: Using an Evolving Mission as a Secondary School Teacher and Program Development Tool   *186*
   Andrew Jeter

12 Same-Sex Marriage at a Jesuit University: Institutional Integrity and Social Change   *203*
   Joseph Janangelo

Afterword   *223*
   Steve Price

Contributors   *231*

Index   *235*

About the Editor   *243*

For Yola C. Janangelo and Peter Janangelo

and

Farrell J. Webb

Acknowledgments

I am very grateful to David Blakesley, Colin Charlton, Jared Jameson, Michael Limón, Susan H. McLeod, and Margot Soven for their guidance and direction. All the contributors deserve gratitude for their hard work and generosity. Thanks to Carmella Fiorelli, Nicholas Grosso, Yola C. Janangelo, John Lincoln Schilb, and Farrell J. Webb for responding to a draft of the proposal. Special thanks to Jacqueline Long, Arthur Lurigio, Lester Manzano, Jane Neufeld, and Thomas J. Regan, S.J. at Loyola for their fine character and collegiality.

Introduction: Of Provocations and Possibilities

Joseph Janangelo

On May 13, 2013, *The Chronicle of Higher Education* published David Evans's blog "Chairs and the Big Picture." Explaining "the chair's role in advocating for and articulating the institution's mission at the departmental or divisional level," Evans argues that institutional mission is both undervalued and underexplored. He writes,

> I am certainly aware that many academics think mission statements and their attendant missions are a piece of corporate nonsense, but let me tell you: Accreditors and others who control institutional fates care deeply about them. Our regional accreditor, the Higher Learning Commission, has "Mission and Integrity" as its first criterion for accreditation, and expects its member institutions to pay serious attention to mission in their operations and planning. Boards of trustees, similarly, often come from corporate settings where organizational mission is a key component of operations and, in my experience, expect an administration to put mission at the center of its priorities.

The term *institutional mission* (hereafter IM) has become central to contemporary academe. On the positive side, it represents markers of identity and hallmarks of accomplishment. Those words denote distinctive institutional history and intellectual heritage, including important traditions of learning and service. IM also evokes a legacy of scholarship and pedagogy that contemporary stakeholders (e.g., faculty and administrators) can use to steward their departments, programs, and initiatives forward.

At many academic institutions, mission connotes vision and purpose. It also reflects philosophy and integrity of practice. As such, IM is a motor for action. By that, I mean mission tells us *why* we do what we do. As the biggest why, mission can guide institutional action by asking everyone to work together for a shared purpose. Mission is also something of a "universal adapter." It is designed to work comprehensively, for example in the capacious wording of mission statements, to direct and serve every unit at the school. As a further contribution, IM also signifies something purposively specific: the high-quality education a particular school offers its students. At its best, IM can set an institution apart from others, giving it a distinctive identity and competitive edge for recruiting and retaining high-caliber and dedicated students, faculty, and staff. In this sense, IM can become a rhetorical tool that trumpets a school's deliverables. It can help an institution argue that what it is doing is distinctive and purposeful. Consider *Arizona State University: Design Aspirations for a New American University*, which seeks to prepare students for a competitive job market and responsible citizenship. Consider also the *National Standards and Benchmarks for Effective Catholic Elementary and Secondary Schools*, which promises to develop a student's intellect and character.

If mission can convey meaningful assay marks, it can also issue a mandate for institutional work. Of course, such work occurs in a marketplace. Almost any institution is one of *some* (e.g., Historically Black Colleges and Universities, religiously affiliated or Ivy League schools). More often, it is one among *many* two- and four-year schools seeking to attract and retain students. Students have choices about where they will enroll (e.g., recruitment) and where they will remain (e.g., success, satisfaction, and retention) until they earn their degrees. As potential future donors, they will have more choices about which schools they support and promote, as well as where they will pay to send their children. Given that many schools are engaged in vigorous competition for students, IM has earned considerable cachet among administrators, some of whom may draw on IM as a mandate and "unique selling proposition" ("USP" is business parlance) for institutional practice. This is understandable because, in addition to any school's past accomplishments, there is current and long-term work left to be done in the future. Yet for that work to occur, it must be desired and demanded. People must find that work valuable, and be willing and able to pay for it. That is where schools are challenged to steward their futures by translating their missions into what students, parents, accreditors, and the workplace deem visionary and viable institutional practice.

Such work can involve institutional branding and, perhaps, rebranding and revitalization. Whether reflecting aspiration or accomplishment, IM can be called upon to help a school retain, augment, redirect, or resurrect its ethos, reputation, and status. From a leadership perspective, such activities raise important questions:

- How can institutions remain distinctive and desirable in an evolving and competitive academic marketplace?
- What happens when accreditors' mandates differ from what students, faculty, or alumni want for their schools?
- How do institutions negotiate the creative tension between contemporary professional best practices and local, legacy practices?
- How can institutions honor, and perhaps revive, past traditions without appearing ossified, insular, or change-averse?
- How can an institution ensure that its new programs and initiatives, designed to serve the needs and desires of millennial students, are in close harmony with its central commitments and values? This pertains to pedagogical practice, curricula, course delivery, degree programs, civic engagement initiatives, internship experiences, faculty hiring processes, and administrative structures.
- How can institutions build on past success? Institutional achievement can be daunting because it is something to contend with and keep proving, therefore a constant challenge.
- How do institutions successfully address, or at least responsibly manage, the expectations of invested stakeholders, including current and prospective faculty, as well as program and central administrators and alumni donors, who may have different and differing visions of what *their* institution should (not) do, support or become?
- How do institutions maintain their "integrity" while evincing an openness to change? Things to consider include student recruitment, satisfaction, and retention. Other topics include institutional ranking and the perceived value of the degree and campus experience.
- In moving forward, what rubrics can institutional leaders and other stakeholders use to discern principled decision-making from commercial pandering or compromise?

- What is the role of nostalgia (e.g., recalling the institution as it was and what it stood for) in moving forward? Ideally IM is about enduring values, but evoking the past can be tricky. It can make an old school look too . . . old school. Excessive evocation of past achievements and traditions can make an institution appear to be about *then and there* rather than *here and now*. Although institutional stewards may wish to strategically reference the aura of an accomplished yesterday, they should understand the importance of building forward (Brand) to enhance their school's contemporary presence and sharpen its competitive edge.
- In stewarding change, how can institutions best promote and protect their brands? The work of institutional revitalization (e.g., "to up one's brand") needs an effective marketing strategy to generate and maintain the desired public attention (Lanham) and buzz. That necessitates procuring a responsive, and even an anticipatory, social media presence. It also means making hard, controversial choices. In all likelihood, whatever institutions showcase as their signature (e.g., prestige, vanguard, or service) initiative, that initiative may have to compete strenuously with other campus efforts, which may struggle for comparable resources and recognition.
- Are there limits or test cases for treating mission as a kind of universal adapter that can work successfully anywhere on campus?
- Finally, are we willing to imagine honorable and valuable places or activities at our institutions (e.g., departments, programs, initiatives, course delivery systems, and campus life) where mission does not fit, serve, or even really pertain?

Responding ethically and critically to these questions offers opportunities for philosophical scrutiny and intellectual creativity. It also presents challenges for ethical, impactful, and sustainable practice.

The contributors to this book have met such challenges with ingenuity and perspicacity. This volume features chapters by accomplished faculty and administrators from a range of institutions, including two-year colleges; land-grant, state, and faith-based schools; liberal arts colleges; secondary schools; and the United States Military Academy. These scholars labor in complicated concert with their institutions. They understand that where they work impacts their work. Separately and together they explain that, while serving and stewarding IM can sometimes be a vexed and vexing project, it is also a stimulating and worthy one. Describing both motor and mandate, these authors challenge the idea that "What is omnipresent is imperceptible" (Todorov 67). They interrogate the site-specific contours of where they work and what they are "asked" (e.g., invited, compelled, tempted and exhorted) to do. Moreover, they examine the competing investments and compelling imperatives that can fuel and forestall institutional health, development, and change. Forsaking pacific narratives of celebratory alignment and innovation, these scholars eschew tales of "success" or "failure." Rather, as experienced (and sometimes distanced) insiders, they offer a nuanced look that is critical *of* and critical *to* institutional practice. They delineate the provocations and possibilities of institutions striving to live out—and sometimes struggling to live up to—their inherited, tacit, conflicting, and even evolving mission(s).

This book has three sections. Part I is called *Connecting and Contending*. This section discusses current high-profile practices. Authors link IM to civic engagement, undergraduate research, assessment, and academic advancement programs. They show how engaging in such activities can help institutions increase their visibility, while fueling student and faculty preparedness and satisfaction. Authors bring a critical note to their arguments by explaining how those popular and participatory initiatives can involve stakeholder resistance and critique.

In chapter 1, "Community Engagement and Authentic Writing: Institutional Mission as Centripetal and/or Centrifugal Force," Dominic DelliCarpini examines the ways that institutional mission statements interact with the learning goals of writing programs that aspire to foster community and civic engagement. He provides both a theoretical and practical basis for the use of mission statements as a tool for localizing engagement efforts. In chapter 2, "Transcending Institutional Boundaries and Types: Undergraduate Research," Joyce Kinkead describes what undergraduate research can mean and become at a variety of schools. She explains that "a broad range of missions can exist within these institutional types," and helps us understand how undergraduate research must compete for institutional attention and resources. In chapter 3, "Strategic Assessment: Using Dynamic Criteria Mapping to Actualize Institutional Mission and Build Community," Nicholas N. Behm explains how an assessment experience applying dynamic criteria mapping strengthened institutional mission by cultivating collegiality among colleagues, privileging faculty expertise, and clarifying expectations for students. Behm argues that assessment can be employed strategically to accomplish political objectives, such as faculty ownership of assessment and institutional accountability to academic mission. In chapter 4, Farrell J. Webb and Anita R. Cortez describe challenges to "Creating a Program of Success for Underrepresented Students at Research Institutions." They also suggest strategies for supporting faculty and staff engaged in such work.

Part II is called *Designing and Discerning*. In this section, authors show how stakeholders move their institutions forward in thoughtful and intentional ways. With a focus on strategy and action, these scholars discuss how institutions work to secure their futures by looking forward and planning ahead. Such planning tests institutional pliancy by raising questions like: how much should institutions change and how much should they retain from past legacies and traditions? Whether rebranding a two-year college, designing a writing center in accordance with a military academy's holistic goals, securing an institutional future by mentoring graduate students' success, or working with colleagues to design and deliver a new general education curriculum, this section shows stakeholders moving forward by careful deliberation and design.

In chapter 5, "Out of the Ivory Tower and into the Brand: How the New Two-Year College Mission Shapes the Faculty-Manager," Jeffrey Klausman offers a candid, philosophical appraisal of how his "college mission has become leaner, harsher, and more corporate than ever." He describes the implications for two-year college faculty and the preparation of graduate students interested in two-year college work. In chapter 6, "The Pen and the Drone: Manumotive Writing Programs and the Professional Imagination at West Point," Jason Hoppe describes the work of establishing, and explaining the value of, a writing center at the U.S. Military Academy. Hoppe shows how change agents can work creatively and persistently within pressing institutional constraints. In chapter 7, "The BYU English Department's Future Scholars Program: Planning for a Faculty to Match the Institutional Mission," Kristine Hansen shows how a faculty mentor stewards graduate student success at Brigham Young University while advancing its institutional interests and future. In chapter 8, "Designing and Delivering General Education Curriculum at a Small Liberal Arts College," Anita M. DeRouen helps us understand the complications and intellectual value of aligning "curricular reform with a campus's mission and overarching strategies." Describing the attendant "outlay of resources," DeRouen offers us "learning points" we might follow to steward change and reform.

Part III is *Relating, Reflecting, and Resisting*. In this final section, authors discuss the complications of teaching and administrating within specific institutional cultures. They document the project of working within and against vaunted traditions and compelling (sometimes compulsory) exigencies. Reflecting on the restrictions and opportunities they face, these scholars help readers understand that our work is rarely ours alone. These authors throw into relief the fact that we work in community with others, for others, and within institutional imperatives.

In chapter 9, "When Fantasy Themes Collide: Implementing a Public Liberal Arts Mission in Changing Times," Rita Malenczyk and Lauren Rosenberg theorize how faculty and administrative work can involve "forwarding institutional fantasies which collide" and sometimes elude fulfillment. In chapter 10, "Negotiating Institutional Missions: Writing Center Tutors as Rhetorical Actors," Andrea Rosso Efthymiou and Lauren Fitzgerald present narratives of undergraduate writing center tutors at a Jewish institution with a religious-driven mission. The authors find that identifying undergraduate tutors' rhetorical activity and listening to tutors' reflections on their work within the institution offers writing program administrators models of productive engagement with institutional mission. In chapter 11, "People Make the Place: Using an Evolving Mission as a Secondary School Teacher and Program Development Tool," Andrew Jeter shows how he and his colleagues turned genre on its ear by redrafting their writing center's mission statement again and anew to build community and ensure that the center's defining document accurately expressed its designers' evolving work. In chapter 12, "Same-Sex Marriage at a Jesuit University: Institutional Integrity and Social Change," Joseph Janangelo analyzes a fidelity test case in which a school's faith-based mission is brought into campus and public conversation concerning institutional identity and student need. The author describes what can happen when an institution feels it must, in adherence to mission, disappoint and perhaps alienate some of its community members. In the Afterword, Steve Price reflects on the book's chapters and offers his own thoughts about mission.

I hope you enjoy this book and that it offers worthy provocations for reflection, conversation, and purposeful stewardship of your writing programs and writing centers.

Works Cited

Arizona State University: Design Aspirations for a New American University. Web. 4 August 2014.

Brand, Stewart. *How Buildings Learn: What Happens after They're Built.* Viking: New York, 1995. Print.

Evans, David. "Chairs and the Big Picture." *The Chronicle of Higher Education.* 13 May 2013. Web. 5 August 2014.

Lanham, Richard A. *The Economics of Attention: Style and Substance in the Age of Information.* Chicago: U of Chicago P, 2006. Print.

National Standards and Benchmarks for Effective Catholic and Elementary Schools. 2012. Web. 5 August 2014.

Todorov, Tzvetan. "Reading as Construction." *The Reader in the Text: Essays on Audience and Interpretation.* Ed. Susan R. Suleiman and Inge Crosman. Princeton,: Princeton UP, 1980. 67-82. Print.

PART I: CONNECTING AND CONTENDING

1 Community Engagement and Authentic Writing: Institutional Mission as Centripetal and/or Centrifugal Force

Dominic DelliCarpini

Institutional Mission, while primarily an attempt to define and articulate the core values of an organization—why it exists—also defines an organization's relationships with external constituencies and stakeholders. Among those stakeholders is the community that surrounds, and often has expectations of, the institution. For those programs that embrace civic rhetoric, service learning, or other forms of community engagement and/or authentic writing, that wider community also becomes a key site for student learning. As such, sustainable, civically-oriented writing programs live at the intersection of college mission and community need. This chapter explores the rhetorical entry-points in college missions that can help to define, limit, and—ideally—support community-based writing initiatives. After discussing the role of mission as a unifying force for individual programmatic initiatives and reviewing recent thought on "authentic" public writing, I demonstrate ways that elements of institutional mission can authorize, validate, and make sustainable such programs by alignment with college mission.

INSTITUTIONAL MISSION AS CENTRIPETAL FORCE

In physics, centripetal force is defined as the "center-seeking force," that which combats the tendency of a body to move in its original path along a straight line due to inertia and constant acceleration (see Figure 1).

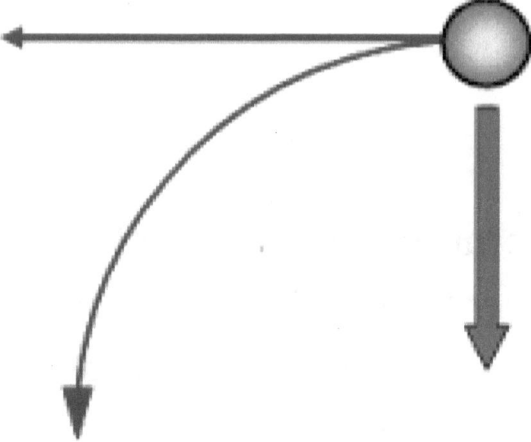

Figure 1. Effects of Centripetal Force

The physics of an institution, and in particular, an institution of higher learning, is similar. While there are many forces that tend to drive specific facets of an institution in straight lines, toward specific goals—goals driven by the many thinkers that comprise a college or university—mission provides a counter force that pulls each initiative toward a common center. Institutional mission, then, can be seen as the centripetal force that attempts to keep individual initiatives balanced between innovation and "mission creep" (Kinkead, this volume). It pulls individual and programmatic work into concentric orbits around the central aims of an institution of higher learning (see Figure 2).

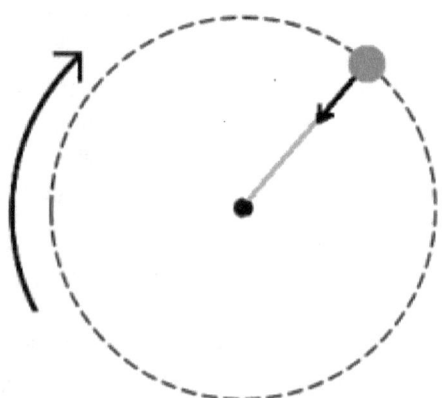

Figure 2. The Centripetal Force of Mission Keeps Individual Programs within the Institution's "Orbit."

Centrifugal force, as it is commonly called, is *not* a true force in nature. Rather, it might be more properly termed the "centrifugal effect," an effect caused by the tendency of an object to move in a straight line outward from the center. Metaphorically, then, we might see the college mission as a counter-balance to the tendency of individual thinkers or sub-groups to move in directions solely motivated by personal or programmatic goals. Mission, as centripetal force, pulls those individual acts into the orbit of the overall intended ethos of the institution.

While this seems like a fortunate physics for an institution in that it allows for individual initiatives while keeping them from losing their core connection to the larger institution, resultant relationships can be fraught. This is especially true when a new outward force—the pull of community needs—is added to the equation: Is the goal of civic engagement—actualized by community involvement, service learning, and other acts of citizenship—centrally driven by the larger, common good, or is it an act meant to serve the mission of the institution? Are curricular efforts driven by a program's pedagogical beliefs or research interests, or by the authentic attempt to effect positive community change? And is authenticity determined by the work's achievement of goals determined by external stakeholders, or by student learning goals?[1] Drawing from these core theoretical questions about authenticity, I will explore ways that this institutional physics might allow for a material and intellectual system that mirrors these forces of nature. Can the centripetal force of a college mission allow programs to push away from the institutional center (into the community) without losing essential connections to the institution that supports them in intellectual and tangible ways? While this type of productive tension may be idealized, I explore ways that such an ideal might be approximated by drawing upon specific elements of college mission—elements that authorize external engagement while also keeping acts of engagement within the orbit of institutional values.

This rhetorical act—the inclusion of wider citizenship goals in a mission—is (like most rhetorical acts) real and tangible; it carries responsibilities and consequences. In this case, claims to civic engagement or citizenship very publicly create demands for programming, funding, and sustainability of engagement activities, while at the same time requiring that such activities are demonstrably nested in college, program, and community missions. As a former Writing Program Administrator, and current Chief Academic Officer, I am also keenly aware that current exigencies complicate the attainment of this ideal balance, as both civic and educational units face unprecedented challenges. That is, unlike the pure physical system that keeps centripetal force balanced with acceleration and inertia (which have centrifugal effects), the world we now face can create imbalances that may 1) limit and in some cases render inauthentic civic elements of a college mission, as centripetal forces such as budget cuts can cause us to discard any mission element seen to constitute "mission creep" and, at the same time, 2) increase the external expectations exerted upon colleges who claim to community engagement, as community needs increase due to similar financial and social exigencies. In sum, we face times that test, and will continue to test, the authenticity of mission elements that lay claim to community engagement. The first question, then, is what "authentic" looks like in this physical, rhetorical, and pedagogical space.

In "Writing Program Assessment and the Mission-Driven Institution," Kristine Johnson argues that "institutional missions may aim to do more than can reasonably be expected from an undergraduate education, and indeed this expansiveness is inherent in the concept of mission" (72). Johnson's assertion reveals one of the many places where the centrifugal effect—the desire to define an institution's mission as "expansive" and broadly based—has the potential to make the actual work of community engagement expressed there, like other element of mission, "vague or functionally meaningless" (72). Instead, Johnson suggests, "WPAs must negotiate not only the pressure to provide comparative evidence but also the challenges of teaching and assessing intrinsic educational ends" (73). Returning to mission elements more directly related to the pedagogical core of higher learning, Johnson goes on to assert the primacy of teaching students "to reveal or demonstrate their habits of mind, attitudes, beliefs, and worldviews in writing" (83). At the same time, she contends that "shifting this discussion to mission gives WPAs a fuller way to think about what institutions do in the world" and what we "offer to society and the world" (87)—that is, to make more authentic promises about what a college can offer to its community: reflective and active citizens. So, while acknowledging the "inescapably indirect" methods of assessment that are needed to align writing programs with institutional mission, she argues for the richness of such assessments, as they can demonstrate mission achievement. By this measure, authentic writing is writing that demonstrates the kinds of "expansive" student learning to which missions lay claim, rather than more tangible effects upon the community.[2]

Likewise, in "We Don't Need Any More Brochures: Rethinking Deliverables in Service Learning Curricula," Kendall Leon and Thomas Sura suggest that the "elevation of deliverables" (deliverables which are metonymically represented by the omnipresent brochures produced for community organizations in service learning courses) has neglected "the goal of critical consciousness" that should be at the center of this work (62). The "engagement portfolios" they recommend as an alternative to the more common deliverables are meant to involve students—and in turn, community organizations—in the construction of a rhetorical memory for organizations, a habit of mind that could then serve to inform future writing by and for the organization. This more rhetorical, more expansive understanding of what colleges and college writers (including both students and faculty) can do in the world is also asserted by David Coogan, who argues that service learning "offers rhetoricians a unique opportunity to discover the arguments that already exist in the communities we wish to serve" (668) and so to produce more viable forms of argument for and with them. Drawing upon Susan Wells's key reminder that the public is not a "neutral container" for students to fill, and that it has "its own history, its own vexed constructions, its own possibilities of growth and decay" (qtd in Coogan 668), Coogan illustrates ways that "discovering the arguments that already exist in the communities we wish to serve means listening closely to our community partners and corroborating what they have to say" (689).

This turn toward habits of mind as the "deliverable" of service learning and community engagement initiatives complicates the notion of authenticity by reminding us of the mission of an institution of higher learning. That is, it suggests that the impulse to produce "authentic" writing in service learning programs—deliverables with an immediate impact upon the organizations they serve—may at the same time be pulling programs further away from their pedagogical center. Dipping into community affairs by college faculty and students that makes community partners' needs central, but which lacks ties to mission, can pull efforts out of the orbit of pedagogical mission. Expressed another way, using writing for and with the community as keys to authenticity can, when not tied to mission, neglect key learning goals. When the production of deliverables that may or may not do lasting good is "elevated" to the status of outcome, as Leon and Sura seem to suggest; or when a "vague" sense of mission (as Johnson suggests) drives small forays into the larger world; or when, as Coogan suggests, we miss the larger arguments being made in the community in favor of isolated moments; then perhaps we have slipped away from the centripetal pull of our identities as institutions of higher learning (and in the case of writing programs, from the higher-level rhetorical knowledge we claim to), and have instead moved again toward the volunteeristic impulse to simply do good. That is, both the inertia of the urge to serve and the acceleration of those needs to serve in times when governmental and non-governmental agencies lack resources, can pull us away from the mission of higher learning. In so doing, they also can threaten the sustainability of programs that, after all, must demonstrate their worth by aligning with college mission (Behm, DeRouen, this volume).

This most recent theorizing on service learning, and the public engagement it represents, offers possible new definitions of authenticity, definitions that are not measured by the nature or utility of a document produced, but rather *by the authenticity of the learning associated with the production of writing motivated by public work.* If we are seeking to align civic writing with college mission, perhaps the centripetal pull of mission, rightly understood, can be an ally in that it serves as a consistent reminder of the complex nature of the rhetorical knowledge necessary to bring our students into the realm of public argument.

RHETORICIANS AS AGENTS OF CHANGE AND/OR AS TEACHERS

In 2000, the *New York Times* published a story about Elaine Scarry, "a Harvard English Professor known for her interpretive daring" who had "focused her deconstructive powers on explaining airplane crashes." In that story, Emily Eakin writes of Scarry:

> In academic circles, this wide-eyed woman with a girlish voice and unruly blond locks is mostly known for her unflinching investigations of war, torture and pain. These are grim and very unlikely subjects for a Harvard English professor. But Scarry, 54, has long tested the boundaries of literary criticism, devoting the same analytical energies to reading a naval weapons manual as she does to reading Thomas Hardy. She has ventured even further afield with her current obsession: airplane crashes. This latest fixation has led her outside the ivory tower and into the fray of public debate.

As this narrative of an English professor who has escaped the gravitational pull of the "Ivory Tower" to take on an investigation of the infamous crash of TWA Flight 800 unfolds, Scarry is quoted as follows: "There is nothing about being an English professor that exempts you from the normal obligations of citizenship. . . . In fact, you have an increased obligation, because you know how to do research." As I noted in an earlier essay, this dictum has stayed much on my mind in my own work (especially given memories of Dr. Scarry in her role as my former undergraduate English professor). But while the *New York Times* story saw this moment as the strange (and temporary) escape of an English teacher from the Ivory Tower into the messy marketplace of ideas, I continue to see—as did Dr. Scarry—this entry into public debate as a natural use of analytical and deliberative habits of mind.

But that is not what the public sees, nor expects, from professors (and especially "English professors") whether teachers of literature or teachers of writing—a distinction that, despite efforts to distinguish Rhetoric and Composition, is still lost on much of the public.[3] And those analytical habits also may not be what community partners think they need from local colleges.

For that reason, when we reach out beyond the traditional, imposed, and expected roles that define us in the eyes of the public, even for the sake of authentic public writing, we risk a panoply of consequences (both internal and external)—especially if we do so in ways that are not demonstrably tethered to the mission of higher learning. And, perhaps, rightly so. While "there is nothing about being an English professor that exempts you from the normal obligations of citizenship" in private acts such as Scarry's investigation of TWA Flight 800, teaching is a public act and one that comes with obligations—to the institution, program, and students that we serve. As such, we are obligated as citizens of our institution—even when acting as authentic agents of change—to find those rhetorical entry points that can unify mission and civic engagement. Doing so can make us better *public* citizens as well, as education is the primary good we bring to that wider public.

Indeed, as Susan Wells characterizes "what we want from public writing":

> The difficulty of constructing a public is not an accident attached to our cloistered academic status. We are not uncertain in our treatment of public writing because we have been sheltered from a vibrant public sphere. Our public sphere is attenuated,

> fragmented, and colonized; so is every else's. All speakers and writers who aspire to intervene in society face the task of constructing a responsive public. Nobody, even the president speaking on national television, enters it without difficulty. (328-29)

Wells goes on to present four viable ways that public work can be directly tied to programmatic outcomes, all of which fit institutional models and exigencies, and three of which can be performed in our classrooms; the fourth is tied to external spaces (such as internships within political organizations) but also has demonstrable curricular connections.[4]

Ellen Cushman's "The Rhetorician as an Agent of Social Change," finds less value in such classroom-based simulations, since "the very power structure of the university makes it difficult to establish and maintain [authentic] dialogue" since "there's only so much we can get to know about our students within the sociological confines of the academic composition classroom" (19). Indeed, she offers justifiable concern about the vagaries of institutional settings and the potential for unreflective teaching practices that would have us (perhaps unwittingly) serve the hegemony of the Ivory Tower. She thus argues for "the give-and-take established in activist research" (20) that would move us, as teachers of rhetoric, out into the public sphere without shedding our scholarly eye:

> In the opening of *The Pedagogy of the Oppresssed*, Freire evaluates the oppressors in society: "To affirm that men are persons and persons should be free, and yet to do nothing tangible to make this affirmation a reality is a farce" (35). If we let *tangible* be synonymous with activism, then to what extent is promoting critical consciousness in our classrooms "activist"? My sense is that we're not doing enough because we're acting within the role of teacher that has been perpetuated by the institution, and thus keeps us from breaking down the barriers between the university and the community. In fact, many critical pedagogues have betrayed their activist agenda in their classrooms by characterizing their students as "dull," "numb," "dumbly silent," "unreflective," "yearning," and/or "resentful." They place themselves in the oppressive position by relegating students to the category of the "unfortunates." (24-25)

Despite their differences, what Wells and Cushman share is an understanding that abandoning the academic or scholarly in favor of perceived public need—or in the case of Leon and Sura, elevating "deliverables" to the role of an outcome—can be counterproductive.[5] In the case of Cushman, the underlying point may be that as pedagogues (which she reminds us is only "two letters shy of becoming demagogues"), we risk enacting the same kind of *noblesse oblige* upon our students as we do upon or community partners.

I would add to, and slightly revise, that contention: Such a treatment of both the community and our students as "unfortunates" can be exacerbated when we pull too far from mission and attempt to assume the role of community expert or activist. Indeed, not only does the abandonment of elements of our educational mission *not* enrich public discourse; it further undermines the efficacy and perception of the university as a community institution, rather than an institution that exists separately, and perhaps even sees itself as above, the public sphere. We would be shortsighted to ignore the fact that undermining our own critical space, in the context of an increasingly skeptical public, would be unwise. Even if it was advisable for us to maintain the rarified space of higher education that we once occupied (and it is decidedly *not* advisable), were we to try, we would find that it has gone the way of Brigadoon. John Dewey's chickens, as I have argued on several other occasions, are coming home to roost. Over a century ago, Dewey reminded us that "while there still is, and probably always will be, a particular class having the special business of inquiry in hand, a distinctively learned class is henceforth out of the question. It is an anachronism . . . . Academic and scholastic, instead of being titles of honor, are becoming terms of reproach" (17).

Thus, as we consider what "authentic" means, we must recall that we live now in a quite different environment than even the one into which Wells and Cushman made their arguments less than two decades ago. While their work implicitly acknowledges the omnipresent anti-intellectualism of the American public sphere, it did not face the more dangerous claims being made now about the value of higher education. The *Academically Adrift* syndrome that has been echoed in many other works plays into the hands of an already skeptical public, and draws further scrutiny upon any acts originating in the academy that can be perceived as "outside our mission": "Save the world on your own time," we will hear, as Stanley Fish has framed it (and us).[6]

While we may write off the growing wave of skepticism about higher education as a sensationalist enterprise, I would suggest that doing so would be unwise—and unrhetorical.[7] Not only would doing so further concretize the notion that we are disconnected from the world around us—certainly not the stance of engagement we seek—but it would likewise, to extend Cushman's argument, brand the public we seek to enter as "unfortunates": "dull," "numb," "dumbly silent," "unreflective," "yearning," and/or "resentful." Or perhaps it brands *us* as the misunderstood "unfortunates." Neither are subject positions we should seek to inhabit, to my way of thinking.

So, I now return to the role of institutional mission as a centripetal force, one that—framed and used wisely—can tether us to what it is we truly value as we enter public arguments.

"Deliverables" Revisited through the Commonplaces of Institutional Mission: Beyond Volunteerism to Deliberative Rhetoric

Let's return briefly to Johnson's sense that institutional mission can be characterized as either "vague or functionally meaningless," or "expansive," depending on one's perspective. While the expansiveness and vagueness of mission statements can indeed lead us (and our audiences) to treat those documents as "functionally meaningless," it would be shortsighted to treat missions as *rhetorically* meaningless. To the contrary, we might treat institutional mission as a set of rhetorical commonplaces or *topoi* from which we can invent the most reasonable and effective stance for our writing programs. Treated as a storehouse of available arguments, mission need not serve a hegemonic institutional role; it can instead bring forth the value of our "learning deliverables" and help us to articulate to the wider public what engagement means, why teaching deliberative rhetoric matters, and how that form of learning supports authentic civic actions.

Perhaps this has not been accomplished in the past because of the "corporate" feel of mission that is discussed in the introduction to this book. But this is but one of the myriad reasons why faculty sometimes look past institutional mission. The language sometimes seems trite, platitudinous, and clichéd. Mission statements across institutions can also seem interchangeable, at least in part. Language included sometimes feels more obligatory than committed. As noted above, there is always a vagueness that comes with any large, visionary, aspirational, or existential statement. And the language is often pathos- and ethos- rather than logos-centered. Those features of mission are especially non-effectual with the critical readers that are college faculty. We are not an easily moved bunch, after all. But perhaps we *should* let the *gravitas* of mission-based language move us. Perhaps there is value in those moments of large-minded thinking, allowing this genre to approximate what Joseph Janangelo calls (in the introduction to this book) the "universal adapter" that can work anywhere on campus.

If treated as rhetorical commonplaces—bits of discourse commonly shared by an audience or community—mission elements can provide a rhetorical entry-point to arguments that support outcomes-based engagement activities. In the physical model I am proposing, we might treat these commonplaces as authorizing the centrifugal impulse to venture out into community writing while also supplying the centripetal force that tethers us, usefully, to our institutional cores. They can also accelerate the impulse to reach beyond the institution into the wider community as a way of educating future citizens in deliberative habits of mind.

This rhetorical exercise of aligning college mission with the goals of civic engagement must be performed locally, of course, to be fully authentic. But what follows are some examples of ways that the store of commonplaces that exist within mission statements could help programs to move toward the ideal of nurturing the deliberative habits of minds that define strong citizenship skills. What I mean to stress in this exercise are ways that available rationales for public and engaged writing as part of a rhetorical education are often already nested within the college mission. Mission can also support the larger sense of "deliverables" described by Leon and Sura, and the educational purposes of public writing discussed by Wells, Cushman, Coogan, and a wide variety of others who have theorized the relationship between writing pedagogy and civic engagement.[8]

Consider for example the ways in which the mission elements in Eastern Connecticut State University's mission provides rhetorical entry-points for a wider understanding of how institutional goals can serve community goals and the teaching of deliberative habits of mind:

> Eastern's inclusive residential campus, outstanding faculty, emphasis on teaching excellence and exceptional facilities *raise students' aspirations and cultivate engagement, inquiry, integrity and social responsibility.* In the traditional arts and sciences, as well as in pre-professional programs that are grounded in the liberal arts, Eastern students apply theory in practical settings. *Faculty research, scholarship, creative work, and community engagement inform teaching and learning, advance knowledge and enrich the*

> *liberal arts curriculum.* The University is committed to serving the state of Connecticut and the nation by preparing its students for their future personal, professional and public roles, as leaders in both their communities and professional fields. (Eastern Connecticut, emphasis added)

Noteworthy here is that the ultimate goal of having an "outstanding faculty, emphasis on teaching excellence and exceptional facilities" is to "raise students' aspirations and cultivate engagement, inquiry, integrity and social responsibility." Further, the mission makes it clear that community engagement is also a means to a larger end—to advance knowledge and to enrich the liberal arts curriculum. By one measure of authenticity, such a perspective can be seen as self-serving—as using engagement as a means to educational mission. But in the context of the arguments made by recent authors discussed above, the larger goals of developing deliberative habits of mind justify such a perspective—and promise ultimately to offer to the wider public "leaders in both their communities and professional fields" that possess these habits.

This recalibration of the relationship between civic roles and institutional mission takes a longer view of our institutions as places where future citizens are educated through present actions. Of course, there are understandable concerns with such a perspective, as it could be perceived as treating community activism as a laboratory exercise used for educational, rather than civic, purposes. I would suggest, however, that such claims ignore institutional reality; after all, an institution *always* serves its own mission, even when it can simultaneously serve others. Drifting off from the centripetal forces in some cases is warranted, even admirable. But doing so also often leads to ineffectual and unsustainable efforts. Nesting student learning outcomes within civic goals, conversely, can allow for more mission-driven—and so more authentic and sustainable—efforts.

This is often accomplished by treating higher-level learning outcomes as a driver of authentic and engaged community action, as in the Mission of Wayne State University's College of Education:

> Out of the conviction that education is the means by which human circumstances can be improved, the College of Education prepares professionals who have the commitment and competence needed to help people acquire the knowledge, skills and understandings to enable them to participate in and contribute

to a complex, changing society. To achieve this mission, the college is committed to excellence in teaching, research and service.

In this mission statement, the goal of educating future educators is framed as enabling others to "participate in and contribute to a complex, changing society." Of special note is the subordination of "excellence in teaching, research, and service" to this larger, civic goal.

Equally interesting are mission elements that coordinate teaching and research with community engagement, rather than subordinate one to the other. For example, Oregon State's mission notes that

> As a land grant institution committed to teaching, research, and outreach and engagement, Oregon State University promotes economic, social, cultural and environmental progress for the people of Oregon, the nation and the world.

The syntactic act of coordination, one might argue, suggests that this institution sees equivalencies—and so equivalent value—among teaching, research, and outreach. It also suggests each of these priorities serve to increase citizenship skills.

Mission statements also often provide commonplaces that speak to the relationship between institution-specific priorities and community service that can then be used to frame the efforts of programs in institutionally authentic ways, as with the following elements in the missions of Evergreen State College and Muhlenberg College:

> *As an innovative public liberal arts college,* Evergreen emphasizes collaborative, interdisciplinary learning across significant differences. Our academic community engages students in *defining and thinking critically about their learning.* Evergreen *supports and benefits from local and global commitment* to social justice, diversity, environmental stewardship and service in the public interest.

* * *

> Muhlenberg College aims to *develop independent critical thinkers who are intellectually agile, characterized by a zest for reasoned and civil debate, committed to understanding the diversity of the human experience, able to express ideas with clarity and grace, committed to life-long learning, equipped with ethical and civic values,*

and prepared for lives of leadership and service. . . . All members of our community are committed to educating the whole person through experiences within and beyond the classroom. Honoring its historical heritage from the Lutheran Church and its continuing connection with the Evangelical Lutheran Church in America, Muhlenberg encourages, welcomes, and celebrates a variety of faith traditions and spiritual perspectives. (emphasis added)

Here, framed in secular (Evergreen College) and faith-based (Muhlenberg College) ways, mission articulates the liberal arts goals of the institution specifically as a form of community support and engagement. Of special note is the way that Evergreen College stresses a key habit of mind—metacognition (characterized as "defining and thinking critically about their learning") and that habit of mind's connection to the available synergy between college and community (characterized as "supports and benefits from local and global commitment"). Since these elements are placed side by side, much can be made of the connection between them in support of the kind of informed citizenship and critical pedagogies posited by Coogan's materialist perspectives as well as Leon and Sura's calls for "engagement portfolios" that might replace the more common community deliverables such as "brochures, posters, whitepapers, and so on" (60). Muhlenberg's mission likewise offers key commonplaces of value by nesting the ability to "express ideas with clarity and grace" amidst goals such as commitment to "understanding the diversity of human experience" and "ethical and civic values." No matter whether "clarity and grace" is the characterization of composing skills that we may find most apt, rhetorical education is clearly valued.

Expressing that value through alignment with institutional mission is important for a number of reasons—including integrity. So when Lynchburg College includes in its mission the development of "students with strong character and balanced perspectives and prepar[ing] them for engagement in a global society and for effective leadership in the civic, professional, and spiritual dimensions of life" or when it promises to "extend its reach beyond the campus through experiential learning, cultural opportunities, and service by sharing the expertise and commitment of faculty, staff, and students with the broader community," programs that wish to focus upon civic and community programs can demonstrate their participation in those goals. When the Community College of Philadelphia notes that "the College serves Philadelphia by preparing its students to be informed and concerned citizens, active participants in the cultural life of the city, and enabled to meet the changing needs of business, industry and the professions," its writing program can find in that mission a tether to institutional support—and perhaps resources—that will allow it to move out into the community. Or when Lafayette College aspires in its mission to "foster the free exchange of ideas" and "to nurture the inquiring mind and to integrate intellectual, social, and personal growth," and then goes on to note that "The College strives to develop students' skills of critical thinking, verbal communication, and quantitative reasoning and their capacity for creative endeavor; it encourages students to examine the traditions of their own culture and those of others; to develop systems of values that include an understanding of personal, social, and professional responsibility; and to regard education as an indispensable, lifelong process," the syntax itself suggests a correlation between key habits of mind and skills—critical thinking, verbal communication, and creativity—and behavioral civic outcomes: examining "the traditions of their own culture and those of others" and developing "systems of values that include an understanding of personal, social, and professional responsibility."

Even in the missions of more selective institutions, one can find commonplaces and rhetorical entry-points that support service-oriented programs, and that also can articulate a wider understanding of rhetorical education's role in developing a deliberative citizenry. Consider, for example, the mission of Franklin & Marshall College, a "residential college dedicated to excellence in undergraduate liberal education," whose mission articulates its aims

> to inspire in young people of high promise and diverse backgrounds a genuine and enduring love for learning, to teach them to read, write, and think critically, to instill in them the capacity for both independent and collaborative action, and to educate them to explore and understand the natural, social and cultural worlds in which they live. In so doing, the College seeks to foster in its students qualities of intellect, creativity, and character, that they may live fulfilling lives and contribute meaningfully to their occupations, their communities, and their world.

Similarly, Gettysburg College articulates "the power of a liberal arts education" as helping

> students to develop critical thinking skills, broad vision, effective communications, a sense of the inter-relatedness of all

knowledge, sensitivity to the human condition, and a global perspective, all necessary to enable students to realize their full potential for responsible citizenship.

While a skeptical eye might, as noted by Kristine Johnson, find these mission statements "vague" and so "functionally meaningless," a more generative rhetorical perspective can mine a good deal of raw material from which to build substantial arguments toward community-based writing. As the examples of above illustrate, the commonplaces embedded in mission statements can help to redefine what we mean by authentic writing, including the transferrable habits of citizenship that are promised in many institutional missions, and to which we can add pith and detail in programmatic learning outcomes. This act of alignment with institutional mission is more than an empty semantic exercise, and such efforts to bring this work into the orbit of institutional priorities need not feed hegemony. To the contrary, it can help to bring to the center of the work of higher education its very real obligation to educate students in the habits of mind that inform a deliberative citizenry.[9] More specifically, these statements provide entrée to the deliberative "habits of mind" identified in the *Framework for Success in Postsecondary Writing*, and so carry with them the promise of both civic and educational engagement.[10]

DRAWING DOTTED (BUT BOLD AND TWO-WAY) LINES: COMMUNITY ENGAGEMENT AS MISSION-DRIVEN DELIBERATIVE RHETORIC

While my purpose in this chapter has been largely to suggest ways that college mission can inform and support the work of writing programs that seek public and/or civic outcomes, I must conclude with a few important caveats and items for further consideration.

Mission statements offer many inroads for civically-engaged programs that wish to locate themselves within the goals of the larger institution; and that is especially true when the authenticity of public writing is defined in ways that draw upon deliberative habits of mind, i.e., habits that are likely to lead to rich civic participation. They also, as Wells argued many years ago, help us to "take up directly the possibilities and problems of the university's location in relation to the public and the professions" (340). But, as she also notes, such a strategy always requires "serious and sustained organizational work" (340).

Of this, there is no doubt; it would be Pollyannaish to perceive connections to College mission as a panacea that can seamlessly connect a program's efforts in civic engagement to the larger goals of the college. Still, institutional mission can provide rhetorical entry points that bring individual programs into the conversations about our institutions' aims for public writing. It can also localize and contextualize those arguments, helping programs and their administrators to create learning outcomes that align with college-level goals. In this way, mission can serve as a type of rhetorical *exordium* for our arguments, grounding the goals about which we care most deeply within the words that publicly define our institution. As Weiser and Rose have argued, "As engagement work emerges as an expectation for faculty work and institutional commitments, writing program faculty need to understand and be prepared to locate their writing programs in relationship to these efforts" (4).

While there is a long and appropriately complex debate about what constitutes authenticity in public writing, I am suggesting that one possible definition might look to alignment with college mission. After all, the mission is not merely a document meant to define the work we do as college faculty; it is also the set of promises we make to our students and the wider public. When we suggest that our work will prepare them for acts of citizenship, we need to make explicit efforts in that direction, and to demonstrate the fulfillment of those outcomes. One of those explicit efforts can be fostered by exposure to public arguments, where authentic deliberation takes place, and where students might engage in rhetorical exercises that are authentic precisely because they serve our institutional mission, precisely because they give students experiences that can educate them for future acts of citizenship. Whether simulated or real, whether affecting change or not, one measure of authenticity in public writing is whether it serves the stated mission of the college students attend. In that sense, the centripetal force of a college mission, in conjunction with the centrifugal pull of a wider public, create a system that can be authentic for both.

Notes

1. The notion of what constitutes "authentic writing" is a vexed one. Brian Gogan's "Expanding the Aims of Public Rhetoric and Writing Pedagogy: Writ-

ing Letters to Editors" explores various definitions of authenticity, and complicates Petraglia's notion that "any writing pedagogy 'encourages inauthentic writing.'" Gogan suggests that Petraglia's notion of "authenticity-as-location" is not an adequate measure. He asserts that an understanding of "authenticity-as-legitimation" restores the place of public rhetoric and writing pedagogy within the notion of authenticity. In this chapter, I extend that argument, suggesting that when we align pedagogies that encourage habits of mind essential to civic engagement with institutional mission and goals, authenticity can also be measured by mission fulfillment.

2. Clearly, this notion of authenticity is quite different from that which would suggest that direct benefit to the community and achievement of social change is its true point of measurement. It does not define authenticity, with Deans, as a type of "writing for the community," or "writing with the community," nor does it exclude "writing about the community," which was central in an earlier wave of service learning methodologies, or the vexed notions of "volunteerism" that are discussed at length by Candace Spigleman. While this notion does not contradict Deans's seminal discussions on service learning, it does argue for an expanded definition of authenticity, suggesting that in the context of institutional mission, authenticity can also be measured by the learning and growth in habits of mind that can inform the future acts of students-as-citizens.

3. See "Coming Down from the Ivory Tower: Writing Programs' Role in Advocating Public Scholarship," in Rose and Weiser for an extended discussion of the ways in which the imposed role and expectations has created a double-bind for the professoriate: they have framed acting more fully in the public sphere as outside the purview of professors, while denigrating the isolation of "Ivory Tower." This is the conundrum faced when civic engagement is not connected to mission as well.

4. Wells suggests that "the classroom itself can be seen as a version of the [Habermasian] public sphere" (338). While this notion that has met with some resistance by later theorists of public writing, her suggestions for teaching strategies that enact this simulated public sphere still inform a great many classroom pedagogies, both in first-year writing and advanced writing/WAC initiatives. I would argue that this notion of public writing, while problematic in ways detailed by Cushman and others, continues to offer useful intersections with elements of larger college missions and learning outcomes.

5. Cushman, in her later "Sustainable Service Learning Programs," seems to place more value on not only civic impact but demonstrable academic learning outcomes: "Service learning programs that have sustained themselves have incorporated reciprocity and risk taking that can be best achieved when the researcher views the site as a place for teaching, research, and service—as a place for collaborative inquiry—with the students and community partners" (43).

6. See, for example, *Academically Adrift: Limited Learning on College Campuses* and *We're Losing our Minds: Rethinking American Higher Education.*

The latter begins with this direct indictment of the work of higher education—and one that ties to the specific goal of preparation for civic engagement: "Our colleges and universities are failing to deliver true higher learning—learning that prepares graduates to meet and excel at the challenges of life, work, and citizenship" (1).

7. For responses to recent critiques of higher education, see reviews of *College: What It Was, Is, and Should Be* by Andrew DelBanco and *We're Losing Our Minds: Rethinking American Higher Education* by Richard P. Keeling and Richard H. Hersh by DelliCarpini, Malenczyk, and Miner. Malenczyk views these critiques as part of a "continuous loop of jeremiad and response" (553) whereas Miner sees value in the potential of these critiques of higher education—when placed in dialogue with one another—to help us to "reconsider education in more expansive ways" (557). I, like Miner, argue in "Rhetoric Matters" that we can benefit by participating in, rather than simply defending ourselves against, these and other current critiques of higher education.

8. For a useful overview of the interactions of writing programs and community engagement activities, see Jaclyn M. Wells's "Writing Program Administration and Community Engagement: A Bibliographic Essay" in Rose and Weiser.

9. For a full discussion of ways that academic writing can foster deliberate habits of mind, see my "Coming Down from the Ivory Tower: Writing Programs' Role in Advocating Public Scholarship," where I argue for ways that "scholarship can serve both academic and civic interests," and that "legitimate the academic research done in first-year composition as crucial preparation for the work of the larger polis" (195).

10. Consider, for example, how this mission could be aligned with the habits called out in the *Framework for Success in Postsecondary Writing*: *curiosity* ("explore and understand the natural, social, and cultural worlds"); *openness* ("sensitivity to the human condition" and "global perspective"); *engagement* ("capacity for independent and collaborative action"); *creativity* (stated directly); *persistence* ("realiz[ing] their full potential); *flexibility* ("sensitivity to the human condition"); and, *metacognition* (reflective learning and "critical thinking"). Alignment of mission with findings of the National Survey of Student Engagement might also provide a worthwhile way to draw dotted lines between high-impact practices and key learning goals. See Rose and Weiser, "Introduction: The WPA as Citizen Educator" for a discussion of how "engagement . . . becomes an underlying principle of higher education, not simply a contribution to student success" (2).

Works Cited

Coogan, David. "Service Learning and Social Change: The Case for Materialist Rhetoric." *College Composition and Communication* 57.4 (2006): 667–93. Print.

Council of Writing Program Administrators, National Council of Teachers of English, and National Writing Project. *Framework for Success in Postsecondary Writing*. Council of Writing Program Administrators. 2011. Web. 14 June 2014.

Cushman, Ellen. "The Rhetorician as an Agent of Social Change." *College Composition and Communication* 47.1 (1996): 7–28. Print.

—. "Sustainable Service Learning Programs." *College Composition and Communication* 54.1 (2006): 40–65. Print.

Deans, Thomas. *Writing Partnerships: Service Learning in Composition*. Urbana: NCTE, 2000. Print.

DelliCarpini, Dominic. "Coming Down from the Ivory Tower: Writing Programs' Role in Advocating Public Scholarship." *Going Public: What Writing Programs Learn from Engagement*. Eds. Shirley Rose and Irwin Weiser. Logan, UT: Utah State UP, 2010. 193–215. Print.

—. "Rhetoric Matters: Why Denial May Not Work This Time." *College Composition and Communication* 64.3 (2013): 545–50. Print.

Dewey, John. "The School and Society." *John Dewey: The Middle Works, 1899–1924*. Ed. Jo Ann Boydston. Vol. 1. Carbondale, IL: Southern Illinois UP, 2008. 4–113. Print.

Eakin, Emily. "Professor Scarry Has a Theory." *New York Times Magazine*. The New York Times Company, 19 Nov. 2000. Web. 10 June 2014.

Gogan, Brian. "Expanding the Aims of Public Rhetoric and Writing Pedagogy: Writing Letters to Editors." *College Composition and Communication* 65.4 (2006): 534–59. Print.

Johnson, Kristine. "Beyond Standards: Disciplinary and National Perspectives on Habits of Mind." *College Composition and Communication* 64.3 (2013): 517–41. Print.

Leon, Kendall and Thomas Sura. "'We Don't Need Any More Brochures': Rethinking Deliverables in Service-Learning Curricula." *Writing Program Administration* 36.2 (2013): 59–74.

Malenczyk, Rita. "Jeremiad and Insularity." *College Composition and Communication* 64.3 (2013): 549–53. Print.

Miner, Marlene R. "Asking the Right Questions." *College Composition and Communication* 64.3 (2013): 554–58. Print.

Spigleman, Candace. "Politics, Rhetoric, and Service-Learning." *Writing Program Administration* 28.1/2 (2004): 95–114. Print.

Rose, Shirley and Irwin Weiser. "Introduction: The WPA as Citizen Educator." *Going Public: What Writing Programs Learn from Engagement*. Eds. Shirley Rose and Irwin Weiser. Logan, UT: Utah State UP, 2010. 1–14. Print.

Wells, Jaclyn. "Writing Program Administration and Community Engagement: A Bibliographic Essay." *Going Public: What Writing Programs Learn from Engagement*. Eds. Shirley Rose and Irwin Weiser. Logan, UT: Utah State UP, 2010. 237–55. Print.

Wells, Susan. "Rogue Cops and Health Care: What Do We Want from Public Writing?" *College Composition and Communication* 47.3 (1996): 325–4. Print.

2 Transcending Institutional Boundaries and Types: Undergraduate Research

Joyce Kinkead

As Director of Writing Programs, I did not really understand the full weight of the institutional mission of my university until I began moving to college and central administrative positions. Then, the importance of the land-grant university became much clearer as I watched candidates for a humanities dean position queried on their position on topics such as multiple land use policies. In retrospect, the land-grant institution where I landed was a perfect match, as the Morrill Act that established these new institutions in 1862 provided a liberal and practical education to the working classes, particularly the sons and daughters of farmers. People like me.

My institution is one of 75 US land-grant institutions, of which 23 are Historically Black institutions (HBCUs). The nation's 33 American Indian tribal colleges are also members of this group. The overarching organization is the Association of Public and Land-Grant Universities (APLU), which has an overall membership of 235.

My time in central administration influenced my scholarship and teaching. How might my work as a faculty member in a department of English reflect the institutional mission? One of the ways that I drew on the institutional mission was to create a new course in the upper-division area of our Universities Studies (general education) program: The Farm in Literature and Culture. Students explore a range of texts, beginning with ancient works such as Virgil's *Georgics*, continuing through pivotal early American readings such as Crevecoeur's *Letters from an American Farmer*, reading realistic fiction such as Hamlin Garland's *Main-Traveled Roads*, and extending to contemporary interpretations such as Novella Carpenter's *Farm City*. A textbook, *Farm: A Multimodal Reader* (Kinkead, et al), was a natural outgrowth of this course. Other land-grant institutions have adopted it where sustainability is a theme in its lower-division writing courses. In essence, this approach is an exploration of the *culture* of agriculture that embraces our institutional mission.

This chapter investigates the intersections among institutional mission (IM), undergraduate research, and literacy education—with particular attention to writing. Undergraduate research has been termed "the pedagogy of the 21st century" ("Joint Statement") and has been deemed as one of a few demonstrably high-impact practices (Kuh).

INSTITUTIONAL TYPE AND MISSION

Institutions of higher education embrace three basic missions: teaching, research, and service. More precisely, colleges and universities engage in student learning, discovery and application of knowledge, and service to the community. And it is largely through the faculty that these missions are accomplished.

The Carnegie Classification System offers an eye-opening look at the diversity of institutions possible, identifying the range of degrees offered, as well as specialized foci:

* * *

Doctoral Universities

- R1: Doctoral Universities—Highest research activity
- R2: Doctoral Universities—Higher research activity
- R3: Doctoral Universities—Moderate research activity

Master's College and Universities

- M1: Master's Colleges and Universities—Larger programs
- M2: Master's Colleges and Universities—Medium programs
- M3: Master's Colleges and Universities—Smaller programs

Baccalaureate Colleges

- Baccalaureate Colleges: Arts & Sciences Focus
- Baccalaureate Colleges: Diverse Fields

Baccalaureate/Associate's Colleges

- Baccalaureate/Associate's Colleges: Mixed Baccalaureate/Associate's Colleges
- Baccalaureate/Associate's Colleges: Associate's Dominant

Associate's Colleges

- Associate's Colleges: High Transfer-High Traditional
- Associate's Colleges: High Transfer-Mixed Traditional/Nontraditional
- Associate's Colleges: High Transfer-High Nontraditional
- Associate's Colleges: Mixed Transfer/Career & Technical-High Traditional
- Associate's Colleges: Mixed Transfer/Career & Technical-Mixed Traditional/Nontraditional
- Associate's Colleges: Mixed Transfer/Career & Technical-High Nontraditional
- Associate's Colleges: High Career & Technical-High Traditional
- Associate's Colleges: High Career & Technical-Mixed Traditional/Nontraditional
- Associate's Colleges: High Career & Technical-High Nontraditional

Special Focus Institutions (a high concentration of degrees is in a single field or set of related fields)

Two-Year

- Special Focus Two-Year: Health Professions
- Special Focus Two-Year: Technical Professions
- Special Focus Two-Year: Arts & Design
- Special Focus Two-Year: Other Fields

Four-Year

- Special Focus Four-Year: Faith-Related Institutions
- Special Focus Four-Year: Medical Schools & Centers
- Special Focus Four-Year: Other Health Professions Schools
- Special Focus Four-Year: Engineering Schools
- Special Focus Four-Year: Other Technology-Related Schools
- Special Focus Four-Year: Business & Management Schools
- Special Focus Four-Year: Arts, Music & Design Schools
- Special Focus Four-Year: Law Schools

- Special Focus Four-Year: Other Special Focus Institutions

Tribal Colleges

* * *

In spite of what would appear to be an inclusive list, a broad range of missions can exist within these institutional types. For instance, my own land-grant institution is also a research university with high activity, but the land-grant designation is not a Carnegie classification. Consider that over 3,900 institutions exist, and each has a mission statement. And, there is also *mission creep*. Cuban documents how research trumped teaching in many institutions, "catering only to the most serious of students who worked closely with professors who conducted original research" (178). In my own state, I've watched one institution morph from a two-year technical college to community college to four-year comprehensive college to now being deemed a university. On the other hand, original research has been democratized so that students—undergraduates and graduates—may contribute to the making of knowledge and the solving of problems, no matter the institutional type.

All institutions look to the high-impact practices that Kuh (2008) defined through the data provided by the National Survey of Student Engagement (NSSE) as these speak to the importance of undergraduate education and influence recruitment and retention of students. Kuh's (2013) follow-up work on the percentage of students involved in high impact practices indicates that the incidence of student-faculty interactions on research do not vary significantly by institutional type. Senior students report participation in student-faculty research in a range of about 20 to 33 percent. The highest activity is in baccalaureate institutions, but research universities do not lag far behind. Primarily undergraduate institutions (PUIs) focus on teaching and learning, and experiential learning is an important component. PUIs are so defined as their undergraduate enrollment outweighs any graduate student numbers.

Research universities were famously taken to task for not paying sufficient attention to undergraduate education in the 1998 Boyer Report, *Reinventing Undergraduate Education: A Blueprint for America's Research Universities*, which called for these institutions to make "research-based learning the standard" for its students. That call was heeded, and one of the clearest indications was the designation of undergraduate research offices and programs so that students would engage in inquiry. (See Kaufman and Stocks for descriptions of NSF award-winning undergraduate research programs in both PUIs and research universities.) Not surprisingly, the emphasis on undergraduate research is strongest in STEM areas; Kuh's NSSE data reveals that about 20 percent of students in the arts and humanities have research activity in contrast to 42 percent of biological science students.

Mission statements are not set in stone. At times, institutions put themselves under the microscope and change direction (Efthymiou and Fitzgerald, Klausman, this volume). Such was the case with the University of Puget Sound, which strategically charted a course to become a national liberal arts university. To do so, they downsized, focused on academics, strengthened liberal arts, became more selective but also more diverse, and concentrated fundraising on its initiatives (Resneck). One result was a ramping up of undergraduate research activity. Elon University also revised its mission statement to emphasize its commitment to undergraduate education: ". . . provide a dynamic and challenging undergraduate curriculum grounded in the traditional liberal arts and sciences" (Levesque and Wise).

LITERACY EDUCATION—THE TEACHING OF WRITING

Mapping the undergraduate writing curriculum reveals that writing is pervasive in the academy. Notably, lower-division writing courses prove to be the one universal in any college curriculum. Purdy and Walker believe that these are the liminal places where students can begin to see themselves as researchers engaging in authentic inquiry. Sunstein and Chiseri-Strater were some of the first to engage students in this kind of research with their ethnographic-based approach in *Fieldworking*. More recently, the writing about writing approach advocated by Downs and Wardle features students entering the disciplinary conversation about writing and enacting research. Writing may appear in colleges and universities in the following places:

- Lower-division writing: first- and second-year courses (the latter occurring when first-year writing is extended developmentally over students first two years)
- Writing across the curriculum (defined here as *writing to learn*)
- Advanced composition courses
- Writing in the disciplines (defined here as learning the discourse conventions in a particular field)

- Writing Studies majors (e.g., rhetoric and composition, professional writing, technical writing, and communication studies)
- Capstone and/or portfolio experiences

Inquiry occurs in any and all of these sites. The research process itself reinforces communication skills, particularly in the dissemination stage when students present or publish the results of the work they've done. Undergraduate research celebrations occur in department symposia, campus showcases, undergraduate-specific conferences (e.g., NCUR, CUR's Posters on the Hill), and professional conferences. The Conference on College Composition and Communication (CCCC) has featured poster sessions by undergraduate researchers since 2010. The poster, a nontraditional format in the humanities, requires students to communicate their results in a highly visual format in which text takes a backseat to visuals (a 40 percent to 60 percent ratio). Increasingly, digital formats provide opportunities for students to share their work, and the trend in open access to scholarly knowledge supports such efforts. The *Journal for Undergraduate Multimedia Projects* (*JUMP*) is but one outgrowth. Traditional print venues such as *Young Scholars in Writing*, a high-quality peer-reviewed journal for undergraduate research in writing and rhetoric, offers students intensive editorial support.

The role of graduate students serving as instructors in composition programs also needs to be taken into consideration. While preparing to be future faculty, they also are mentoring undergraduates. Gonzalez argues that graduate students need to be advised on how to work with undergraduate researchers, and she suggests that undergraduates through postdoctoral appointments be thought of as one continuous learning community. Graduate teaching assistants may draw on their own undergraduate research experiences, or they may need to be reminded or educated about the transformative power of engaging in authentic research. The University of North Carolina at Chapel Hill developed a program whereby graduate students work with faculty to "turn course assignments into robust research projects" appropriate to a flagship research university (Pukkila, et al., 28). For instance, in a course on Reading and Writing Women's Lives, students gather archival biographical documents for particular women and then write their biographies.

Undergraduate Research

Kuh's influential work in high-impact education practices provides data-informed evidence that undergraduate research provides students with "actively contested questions, empirical observation, cutting-edge technologies, and the sense of excitement that comes from working to answer important questions" (*High Impact* 20). While it is not the province of this essay, undergraduate research is also embraced internationally. Jenkins and Healey are particularly prolific in advocating "undergraduate research for all" in their UK-based publications and through *CUR Quarterly's* "International Desk" section.

A group of writing scholars and teachers has advocated for undergraduate research as an important part of students' educational experience. Treating students as researchers is the theme of work by Kinkead ("Learning," "How," *Advancing*), Kinkead and Grobman, and Grobman and Kinkead, particularly in the illuminating examples shared in *Undergraduate Research and English Studies* (see also Behling). Grobman was also responsible for creating a peer-reviewed journal, *Young Scholars in Writing*, and more recently a journal that highlights students' projects in their communities, *Undergraduate Journal of Service Learning and Community-Based Research*. Notable is CCCC's establishment of a task force and then committee on undergraduate research.

Students are engaging in authentic inquiry in each of the writing areas noted earlier. *YSW* features a first-year writing section in which students may contribute. An ethnography on punk literacy in 1980s Waco (Pleasant) is but one fine example. Peer tutors present at regional conferences and the National Conference on Peer Tutoring in Writing and have been featured in a special issue of *The Writing Center Journal* devoted to undergraduate research (Fall 2012). *Kairos* 6.1 (2011) did the same. Technical writing students conduct usability studies and conduct digital research on the web. Methods texts have been published for such research (McKee and DeVoss; Hughes and Hayhoe).

Intersections: Institutional Mission, Writing, and Undergraduate Research

How does undergraduate research in writing intersect with institutional mission? Of course, this varies by institutional type, but some relationship may exist no matter the kind of college or university (DelliCarpini,

Hoppe, this volume). Vander Lei and Pugh say of enacting institutional mission in writing programs, "Despite the difficulties of understanding institutional mission, we are optimistic not only that WPAs can leverage institutional mission to enhance writing programs but also that WPAs can contribute to the continuing evolution of the mission of their institution" (107). It is slightly more complicated to add undergraduate research to the mix. One of the reasons why this is the case is that the humanities have been slow to join the national conversation about undergraduate research. Traditionally, humanists see scholarly research as a solo enterprise; however, writing studies generally has been more open to embracing collaborative work and the work of students. It is still a game of catch-up when compared to sciences, social sciences, and engineering.

In this section, various institutional missions will be used to illustrate how undergraduate research and writing may build upon their principles.

While research may not seem a part of the two-year college, there has been an increasing presence. This is due in part to "the significant size and natural diversity of the community college student body," coupled with more faculty with research backgrounds and a student-centered pedagogy. Four-year institutions have also reached out to these campuses to promote "seamless articulation" for transfer students (Brown et al. 27).

Sample Community College Mission Statement

> Community College X is a public, open-access, comprehensive community college committed to serving the broader community. Its mission is to provide quality higher education and lifelong learning to people of diverse cultures, abilities, and ages, and to serve the needs of community and government agencies, business, industry and other employers.

Application: Responding to this mission, students in the writing center create a plan to open a writing center that serves the needs of "the broader community," whether that is writing a grant proposal or a memoir.

Sample Private Liberal Arts Coeducational College Mission Statement

> Education in all its forms is the central mission of College Y. The pivotal commitment of the Faculty, Administration, and

> Staff to the intellectual and personal development of students is the College's most important and enduring tradition. Teaching and learning link the classroom to other aspects of student life and contribute to an educational environment that supports civility, respect, and meaningful student-faculty interaction. Our students talk about "working with" rather than "taking courses from" their professors. Undergraduates spend time with their teachers identifying problems, clarifying questions, experimenting with solutions, and frequently doing collaborative research.

Application: Building on the tradition of strong faculty-student collaboration, a student uses creative writing as therapy for the developmentally disabled, a project funded through the undergraduate research office.

Sample Public Comprehensive Regional University Mission

> As the comprehensive teaching university, Regional State University has a responsibility to use its intellectual, scientific and technological resources to support and advance the economic and cultural life of the region and the state while maintaining its historic focus on the preparation of teachers. The university's growing number of innovative academic programs helps to ensure that Regional State University students are prepared to think critically, communicate effectively and act responsibly within a context of personal and professional ethics. The Program for Undergraduate Research represents an unparalleled opportunity for students to work closely with faculty mentors and to present research and creative work at regional and national conferences.

Application: Coordinators for core-curriculum seminars, first-year writing, and writing across the curriculum come together to offer faculty development by tasking them to revise courses to be more student-centered and research-focused. Drawing on Ballenger's work that posits research papers should be re-envisioned as primary rather than secondary research. Workshops on "Writing to Inquire" and writing for dissemination helped faculty re-focus course assignments. An on-campus undergraduate research journal is one place where students may publish their work (Brush et al.).

Sample Four-Year Public Regional Institution Mission

> Directional University is a four-year public institution established in 1970. Its purpose is threefold: to provide students with an excellent education, stimulate inquiry and research, and serve the region and the state. The University offers bachelor's degrees in a wide range of liberal arts disciplines, as well as in the health sciences, education, and business and professional areas. The University recognizes the importance of the out-of-the-classroom experience and offers opportunities for students to engage in activities that promote personal growth. Since our highest priority is excellence in teaching and learning, we believe that intellectual inquiry and analysis by students and faculty members are essential. We encourage all scholarly pursuits, including student research for courses and faculty research for presentation and publication and for use in the classroom. Our goal of an academic experience built on inquiry and research as well as the transmission of information allows students to develop their ability to think and communicate, to gain knowledge and skills, to pursue a career or further study, to appreciate the creativeness of the human mind, to be aware of the human and natural environment of the world, and to have the capacity to pursue a life of learning and understanding.

Application: Student teams in professional writing help local organizations by developing a variety of documents: reports, brochures, kiosk displays, presentations, and web pages. Projects might include developing a list of grant funding sources for local nonprofits; designing historical displays for guided tours through a former slave village; developing compliance documents for an accreditation visit (Johnson et al.).

Sample HBCU University Mission

> HBCU University, a culturally diverse, comprehensive, research intensive and historically Black private university, provides an educational experience of exceptional quality at the undergraduate, graduate, and professional levels to students of high academic standing and potential, with particular emphasis upon educational opportunities for Black students. Moreover, the University is dedicated to attracting and sustaining a cadre of

> faculty who are, through their teaching, research and service, committed to the development of distinguished, historically aware, and compassionate graduates and to the discovery of solutions to human problems in the United States and throughout the world. With an abiding interest in both domestic and international affairs, the University is committed to continuing to produce leaders for America and the global community.

Application: HBCU University's mission is evident in this description of a class within the writing program: One of HCU University's missions is to equip students with the skills essential for leadership and service. Preparing students to promote and defend issues of concern, English 003 emphasizes argumentation and, as a tool in argumentation, the research process. Argumentation is a discourse that seeks to change attitudes or to bring about action. This course will enable students to argue effectively by stressing critical reading, logical thinking, research techniques, and an awareness of contemporary issues.

Sample Jesuit Private College Mission

> Spiritual University is an exemplary learning community that educates students for lives of leadership and service for the common good. In keeping with its Catholic, Jesuit, and humanistic heritage and identity, Spiritual U models and expects excellence in academic and professional pursuits and intentionally develops the whole person—intellectually, spiritually, physically, and emotionally. The Spiritual U experience fosters a mature commitment to dignity of the human person, social justice, diversity, intercultural competence, global engagement, solidarity with the poor and vulnerable, and care for the planet.

Application: Students tutor, mentor, and teach in the city's public school system and come to understand America's education inequality crisis. One participant notes, "It has helped me understand poverty and racial inequality in my city, across America, and around the world."

Application: Students in technical writing help design communication pieces in print and on the web for community projects that focus on helping the homeless.

Sample Research University Mission

> The mission of Research University is to advance knowledge that will best serve the nation and the world in the 21st century. RU is committed to generating, disseminating, and preserving knowledge, and to working with others to bring this knowledge to bear on the world's great challenges. RU provides its students with an education that combines rigorous academic study and the excitement of discovery with the support and intellectual stimulation of a diverse campus community.
>
> The primary goal of the research university is to produce new knowledge and share it. The organization reflects this mission with infrastructure that encourages proposal writing for grants and contracts, manages risk, ensures the responsible conduct of research, and rewards success. First-year students may need assistance in learning how to navigate such a complex organization and engage in the opportunities offered (Andreatta).

Application: Writing is used as a vehicle to explore humanistic and scientific issues in a broad cultural context. Students produce a spectrum of work: autobiography, scientific essay games, and web-based hypertext projects.

Concluding Comments

Understanding institutional goals and mission can help those involved in literacy education. Some institutions also have developed statements on vision and goals. Those, too, can be interrogated so the writing administrators can see where their own goals intersect with those of the larger institution. It is not out of the question for a department or writing program to develop its own mission statement that draws on and reinforces the larger statement. In a book I wrote about advancing undergraduate research programs (2010), I demonstrated how the university mission statement led to creating one for our research office and also designing one for the undergraduate research program. These nested statements helped develop goals and objectives as well as a marketing plan.

Fitting the activity to the mission can be a good way to demonstrate the program's value to the institution. A Jesuit institution appreciates intellectual, spiritual, and moral growth, coupled with a dedication to service and social justice. A land-grant university values access and success, particularly for first-generation college students. Public institutions can show their significance to state and federal legislators through undergraduate research celebrations such as CUR's Posters on the Hill or similar events at the state level.

Still, challenges exist. Most notably is the perennial problem of resources. Competition for financial support may exist in any number of worthy programs. After all, undergraduate research is just one of several worthy high-impact practices. Don't service learning, internships, study abroad, and learning communities deserve robust funding? Revenue streams that may help support undergraduate research and writing studies initiatives may come from public or private sources depending on the institutional context. A research office may be convinced to use some of its F&A (facilities and administration) funds for instance. Or, the fundraising arm of the institution may get on board and help writing studies enhance its programs with named centers, professorships, and scholarships. Similarly, grants may be tapped for support. But these initiatives require time and energy on the part of writing program administrators on what most likely is a very busy schedule already. It also challenges the writing administrator to work within the chain of communication of the institution, beginning most likely with a department chair.

Resources are needed not only for faculty and staff but also for student support. Will there be space for students working on community-based research to come together? Are there grants available to students to conduct research that requires them to travel to archives? Is there support for students to present at professional conferences? Are there dissemination venues—print, electronic, symposia—for student work on campus?

The integration of writing, undergraduate research, and institutional mission also assumes administrators who are savvy and knowledgeable about each of these areas. It takes a mature faculty member to keep abreast of writing scholarship and research as well as to sign on to the literature of higher education. General periodicals such as the daily *Chronicle of Higher Education* or *Inside Higher Education* can provide insights.

Within any state, competition rather than cooperation may be the mode of operation. Some states' institutions have banded together to host undergraduate research conferences to provide lower-cost venues for student dissemination. Even then, elitism among the institutional types may arise: a research university that believes real research is possible only on its campus.

Yet another challenge is the current attack on the humanities and the perceived lack of value or marketability of its degrees. Can an undergraduate's research in writing studies compare favorably to the student who is working with a faculty mentor's NIH or NSF funded project on finding a cure for cancer? A writing specialist must be a rhetorician extraordinaire to make the case.

While undergraduate research had its origins in the sciences, it has expanded to encompass all disciplines, all students, and all institutional types. Interrogating the institutional mission can lead to valuable and rich work in writing and undergraduate research.

WORKS CITED

Andreatta, Britt. *Navigating the Research University: A Guide for First-Year Students*. NY: Wadsworth, 2006. Print.

Ballenger, Bruce. *Beyond Note-Cards: Rethinking the Freshman Research Paper*. Portsmouth, NH: Boynton/Cook, 1999. Print.

Behling, Laura. *Reading, Writing, Research: Undergraduate Students as Scholars in Literary Studies*. Washington, DC: Council on Undergraduate Research, 2009. Print.

Boyer Commission on Educating Undergraduates in the Research University. *Reinventing Undergraduate Education: A Blueprint for America's Research Universities*. Stanford, CA: Carnegie Foundation for the Advancement of Teaching, 1998. Print.

Brown, David R., Thomas B. Higgins, Penny Coggins. "The Increasing Presence of Undergraduate Research in Two-Year Colleges." *CUR Quarterly* 28.2 (2007): 24–28. Print.

Brush, Edward, Michelle Cox, Andrew Harris, and Lee Torda. "Undergraduate Research as Faculty Development." *CUR Quarterly*, 31.1 (2010): 11–16. Print.

Cuban, Larry. *How Scholars Trumped Teachers: Change Without Reform in University Curriculum, Teaching, and Research, 1890–1990*. NY: Teachers College Press, 1999. Print.

Downs, Douglas, and Elizabeth Wardle. "Teaching about Writing, Righting Misconceptions: (Re)Envisioning 'First-Year Composition' as 'Introduction to Writing Studies.'" *College Composition and Communication* 58.3 (2007): 552–84, 2007. Print.

Gonzalez, Christina. "Undergraduate Research, Graduate Mentoring, and the University's Mission." *Science* 293 (2001): 1624–1626. Print.

Grobman, Laurie, and Joyce Kinkead. *Undergraduate Research in English Studies*. Urbana, IL: National Council of Teachers of English, 2010. Print.

Hughes, Michael A., and George F. Hayhoe. *A Research Primer for Technical Communication: Methods, Exemplars, and Analyses*. 2nd ed. NY: Routledge, 2007. Print.

Jenkins, Alan, and Mick Healey. *Institutional Strategies to Link Teaching and Research*. Higher Education Academy, 2005. Web. 5 August 2014.

"Joint Statement of Principles in Support of Undergraduate Research, Scholarship, and Creative Activities." NCUR and CUR, 2005. Web. 5 August 2014.

Johnson, Christopher D., Lynn Hanson, and Jennifer L. Kunka. "De-centered Discovery: Advancing an Undergraduate Research Culture within the English Major." *Creative Inquiry in the Arts & Humanities: Models of Undergraduate Research*. Eds. Naomi Yavneh Klos, Jenny Olin Shanahan, and Gregory Young. Washington, DC: Council on Undergraduate Research, 2012. Print.

Kauffman, Linda, and Janet Stocks. *Reinvigorating the Undergraduate Experience: Successful Models Supported by NSF's AIRE/RAIRE Program*. Washington, DC: Council on Undergraduate Research, 2004. Print.

Kinkead, Joyce, Evelyn Funda, and Lynne McNeill. *Farm: A Multimodal Reader*. Silverlake, TX: Fountainhead, 2014. Print.

Kinkead, Joyce. *Advancing Undergraduate Research: Marketing, Communications, and Fundraising*. Washington, DC: Council on Undergraduate Research, 2010. Print.

—. "How Writing Programs Support Undergraduate Research." *Developing and Sustaining a Research-Supportive Curriculum: A Compendium of Successful Practices*. Eds. Kerry K. Karutsksis and Timothy E. Elgren. Washington, DC: Council on Undergraduate Research, 2007. 195–208. Print.

—. "Learning through Inquiry." *Valuing and Supporting Undergraduate Research*. Ed. Joyce Kinkead. San Francisco: Jossey-Bass, 2003. 5–17. Print.

—. "Undergraduate Researchers as Makers of Knowledge in Composition in the Writing Studies Major." *The Changing of Knowledge in Composition*. Eds. Richard Gebhardt and Lance Massey. Logan: Utah State UP, 2011. 137–160. Print.

Kinkead, Joyce, and Laurie Grobman. "Expanding Opportunities for Undergraduate Research in English Studies." *Profession 2011* (2011): 218–230. Print.

Kuh, George D. *High-Impact Educational Practices: What They Are, Who Has Access to Them, and Why They Matter*. Washington, DC: Association of American Colleges and Universities, 2008. Print.

Kuh, George D., and Ken O'Donnell. *Ensuring Quality & Taking High-Impact Practices to Scale*. Washington, D.C.: Association of American Colleges and Universities, 2013. Print.

Levesque, Maurice J., and Mary Wise. "The Elon Experience: Supporting Undergraduate Research across All Disciplines." *CUR Quarterly* 21.3 (2001): 113–16. Print.

Mack, Kelly M., Katherine M. McGraw, Kamilah M. Woodson-Coke, and Orlando L. Taylor. "Developing an Office for Undergraduate Research at Howard University." *CUR Quarterly* 27.2 (2006): 69–73. Print.

McKee, Heidi A., and Danielle Nicole DeVoss. *Digital Writing Research: Technologies, Methodologies, and Ethical Issues*. NY: Hampton, 2007. Print.

Pearce, Susan Resneck. "Mission Possible: Mission-Based Decisions Can Offer Immediate and Dramatic Benefits." *CUR Quarterly* 21.2 (2001): 117–121. Print.

Pleasant, William Eric. "Literacy Sponsors and Learning: An Ethnography of Punk Literacy in Mid-1980s Waco." *Young Scholars in Writing* 5 (2007): 137–145. Print.

Pukkila, Patricia J., Martha S. Arnold, Aijun Anna Li, Donna M. Bickford. "The Graduate Research Consultant Program: Embedding Undergraduate Research Across the Curriculum." *CUR Quarterly* 33.4 (2013): 28–33. Print.

Purdy, James P., and Joyce R. Walker. "Liminal Spaces and Research Identity: The Construction of Introductory Composition Students as Researchers." *Pedagogy: Critical Approaches to Teaching Literature, Language, Composition, and Culture* 13.1 (2013): 9–41. Print.

Sunstein, Bonnie Stone, and Elizabeth Chiseri-Strater. *Fieldworking: Reading and Writing Research*. Boston: Bedford/St. Martin's, 2006. Print.

The Carnegie Classification of Institutions of Higher Education (n.d.). About Carnegie Classification. 2010 Web. 26 April 2016.

Undergraduate Research/Creative Projects." *US News and World Report Education*. US News and World Report LP. 2014. Web. 5 August 2014.

Vander Lei, Elizabeth, and Melody Pugh. "What Is Institutional Mission?" *A Rhetoric for Writing Program Administrators*. Ed. Rita Malenczyk. Anderson, SC: Parlor Press, 2013. 105–17. Print.

Wardle, Elizabeth, and Douglas Downs. *Writing about Writing*. 2nd ed. Boston: Bedford, 2014. Print.

3 Strategic Assessment: Using Dynamic Criteria Mapping to Actualize Institutional Mission and Build Community

Nicholas N. Behm

Using dynamic criteria mapping (DCM) as an example, this chapter argues that assessment can be applied strategically to build a sense of community and rapport among colleagues, promote faculty ownership of assessment activities, and empower faculty to fulfill their cardinal role of strengthening and protecting the academic mission of their respective institutions. Central to that work is understanding how an institution's mission—that rhetorically dense public presentation of an institution's identity, sense of tradition, values, and academic focus—informs assessment practices. Equally critical is discerning how assessment possesses the power to initiate changes in a program's or a department's or an institution's mission, but also harnessing and exercising that power strategically to privilege institutional mission and faculty expertise, highlight ways in which institutions have lost focus on their institutional missions, and initiate critical conversations about changing those missions if necessary.

This chapter begins with a description of the institutional dynamics pervading Elmhurst College, and in the second section, explains my reasoning for choosing DCM as the methodology for the summer assessment workshop that I was charged to lead. The third section outlines the activities of that workshop, linking them to and describing how they exemplify institutional mission. The fourth section describes the results of the DCM exercise, and finally, the last section offers suggestions for applying DCM at other institutions.

Institutional Context

Elmhurst College, originally founded as a seminary in 1871, is now a four-year liberal arts institution in the tradition of the United Church of Christ that offers bachelor's and master's degrees, as well as select certificate programs. Located in Elmhurst, Illinois, which is just outside of Chicago, the college boasts an undergraduate and graduate student population of approximately 3,200. With about a third of its students living on campus, it serves primarily commuter students, marketing itself as "transfer-friendly" for students who complete coursework and associate's degrees at a variety of community colleges in the Chicago area. The college prides itself on cultivating the "Elmhurst Experience," an axiom that invokes the college's mission of engaging students' intellectual and professional self-formation and preparing them for life-long learning and work in a competitive and dynamic global society. Integral to this experience are the college's core values of intellectual excellence, community, social responsibility, stewardship, faith, and its institutional mission:

> Elmhurst College inspires its students to form themselves intellectually and personally and to prepare for meaningful and ethical work in a multicultural, global society. Working together with passion and commitment, we foster learning, broaden knowledge and enrich culture through pedagogical innovation, scholarship and creative expression. ("About")

With the advent of the Great Recession in 2008, the college has experienced difficult financial challenges, which have been precipitated by a decrease in traditional and transfer student populations. Like many institutions facing similar financial strains, Elmhurst College has recently emphasized a corporate model of administration, vesting power and authority with a privileged few administrators and reinforcing a top-down, authoritarian decision-making process that often rejects shared governance with faculty and other members of the institutional community. This has created a difficult campus environment in which faculty and administration engage in an internecine conflict of mutual suspicion, distrust, and aversion, a conflict that has only intensified as a result of administrative decisions that faculty perceive as violating the college's academic mission. For instance, in spite of significant faculty resistance, college administrators initiated the School for Professional Studies to create, coordinate, administer, and market accelerated undergraduate,

graduate, and certificate programs that primarily appeal to adult students, occur in nontraditional formats, and rely heavily on, if not exploit, adjunct faculty. Faculty balked at the for-profit, revenue-generating purpose of the School for Professional Studies, which was promoted to stakeholders as the solution to the college's financial woes. Faculty also expressed serious misgivings regarding how certificate and accelerated programs might diminish academic integrity across the institution and jeopardize the school's academic reputation and brand, which the school has diligently fostered and strengthened over its 143-year history.

The institutional dynamics have transformed intense faculty skepticism regarding assessment into disheartening cynicism, as many faculty presume that any assessment practice manifests menacing ulterior motives by administration, like the curtailment or termination of programs or consolidation of departments. Faculty cynicism regarding assessment poorly serves faculty interests and student learning, as it cedes authority for developing and facilitating assessment to administrators—who, unfortunately, often exhibit a propensity to purchase assessment from dubious corporations—and deprives faculty of tangible evidence that their teaching positively affects student learning. By rebuffing assessment, faculty only imperil their own positions, leaving them exposed to withering claims of inefficiency and unproductivity by administration, which faculty at Elmhurst find themselves currently combatting, and to captious critiques leveled by politicians and higher education policy wonks.

As a result, at Elmhurst College, "a culture of assessment" has been difficult to cultivate (Janangelo and Adler-Kassner). With the exception of departments, like Education and Nursing, that must fulfill state and legal mandates, assessment across the college has been hindered by poor coordination among programs, departments, and the institution; weak faculty ownership; and inconsistent follow-up in using data to facilitate necessary course, programmatic, and curricular changes that could benefit student learning. For instance, to assess courses within a previous general education curriculum, faculty members simply submitted reports that discussed how students fulfilled and/or exceeded objectives. Not surprisingly, that method of reporting proved unreliable and ineffective due to inconsistent submission of reports and the lack of valid, impartial data.

The purposeful indifference to assessment exhibited by faculty and administrators changed quite suddenly after the college was admonished by the Higher Learning Commission (HLC) during an accreditation visit in the fall of 2009. During that visit, the HLC review team cited the lack of empirical evidence of student learning and the many institutional challenges with assessment as requiring immediate improvement and mandated that the college submit a progress report in 2012 detailing the college's subsequent assessment initiatives. In response to this exigency, faculty and administrators consolidated assessment efforts under the purview of an assessment board, consisting of nine elected, interdisciplinary faculty members who coordinate assessment activities across the institution, maintain an institutional assessment plan, and utilize data to make recommendations for continuous program improvement. Though HLC's warning compelled the college to implement reasonable assessment initiatives, lessening stakeholder indifference, faculty cynicism of assessment remained prevalent, inhibiting faculty ownership of assessment and preventing them from conceptualizing it as a critical practice that strengthens their positions and actualizes institutional mission.

Rationale for Choosing DCM Methodology

In June of 2013, as an untenured faculty member and purported assessment expert on campus, a reputation ascribed to me by my colleagues because I dared champion it in faculty meetings, I agreed to develop and facilitate an assessment exercise that involved student final papers from the college's first-year seminar program. I was given significant discretion in designing an appropriate assessment exercise. The only requirements were that the exercise needed to provide insights that might secure a firmer foundation for future assessment of FYS and generate feedback that could be shared with faculty and students to improve teaching and learning.

I had additional, more politically ambitious motivations, though, viewing the charge to assess as an opportunity to work closely with my faculty colleagues in nurturing community and collegiality. Although supported by the college's mission statement and core values, community-building had been sorely dampened by the above mentioned financial woes, the administration's authoritarian leadership, and the anxiety of agonizing relentlessly about suspensions in hiring, cost-of-living-adjustments, benefits, and merit raises due to lower-than-expected student enrollment. I also hoped that in participating in a positive assessment experience, my colleagues could learn how assessment can be a generative, epistemic practice, one that, when it utilizes faculty expertise and experience and privileges student learning, aligns with and embodies college's institutional mission and core values, especially intellectual excellence. If my colleagues could conceptualize assessment as a scholarly enterprise that informs pedagogy and fosters learning, I thought, they could possibly soften their cynicism, making inroads into the long, arduous work of building a culture of assessment on campus. Lastly, I also hoped that an assessment exercise would work furtively, beyond the prying eyes of administrators, to make faculty realize how assessment could be used rhetorically and strategically to demonstrate the value of faculty, exercise our academic authority, and empower faculty to hold the college accountable to its academic mission. It is axiomatic in the disciplinary literature that assessment is a political technology that can be used for good or ill purposes. Faculty, at Elmhurst College and elsewhere, must assert ownership of assessment to ensure that it is being exercised in ways that explicitly align with and strengthen an institution's academic mission, genuinely inform teaching and foster learning, and carefully cultivate community.

In considering these myriad purposes and when reflecting on the college's mission and core values, I decided that dynamic criteria mapping (DCM) was the most appropriate methodology because it encourages intensive interaction among participants and privileges the discernment of how institutional dynamics inform evaluation criteria and influence pedagogy. As a qualitative assessment practice, DCM is intensely local and situational, challenging faculty to clarify their pedagogical values, identify evaluation criteria, develop appropriate learning outcomes for their courses, and understand how assessment functions within and should serve to strengthen an institution's mission (Broad, *What*). Since it is a site-based, locally controlled assessment practice that responds to the conditions, needs, and circumstances as they are demonstrated by or affect students, faculty, and other community members, it offers an inherently flexible and adaptable methodology that can be tailored to specific institutional contexts. For instance, it has been applied at community colleges (Alford), regional state institutions (Adler-Kassner and Estrem; Stalions), state flagship research-intensive institutions (Detweiler and McBride), urban universities (Harrington and Weeden), as well as other types and sizes of institutions. The primary purpose of DCM is to make explicit, through small and large group discussion and critical reflection, what a department, community, or program really values when assessing and evaluating student work (DeRouen, this volume).

The deliverables of the methodology are primarily qualitative, consisting of participant notes, marginal comments on sample essays, audio recordings of these discussions, pictures of notes that have been written on white boards, and sample visual representations of what a group values. I knew that DCM, with its emphasis on discussion and clarification, would encourage my colleagues to talk with and learn from each other, and feel the joy and satisfaction of collaborating on something that would not only inform their teaching and encourage learning but also align with the mission of the college by strengthening and improving the FYS program.

Indeed, the FYS program—by all appearances, at least, if not in execution—directly relates to the college's mission in that FYS serves as a developmental requirement, helping students develop the habits of mind of inquisitive, effective college students, understand the importance of a liberal arts education, and learn how to apply the liberal arts to the academic topic of their respective FYS courses, their major, and their future professional career. Students' respective FYS course, then, functions as *the* foundational course in their experience of working through the various critical processes that facilitate their personal, intellectual, and professional self-formation—the essential component of the Elmhurst Experience. As such, all incoming first-year students must enroll in FYS during the fall semester of their first year. Each course section studies a different academic topic based on a respective professor's disciplinary expertise, and students' FYS professors also serve as their academic advisor for their entire first year at the college—a component that, some feel, strengthens retention.

For all of its positive qualities, the FYS program, in its design and implementation, unfortunately manifests faculty's resistance to perceived administrative intrusions and skepticism of assessment, and reflects the dysfunctional institutional dynamics. During its design and multi-year pilot phase, for example, faculty and administrators wrangled considerably over the required programmatic components that each course section had to assign; the course and program goals, objectives, and learning outcomes; and faculty discretion with course assignments, grading, and assessment. Faculty, citing academic freedom, strenuously resisted common assignments and vigorously argued for autonomy in determining appropriate assignments for their courses.

As a result, no common FYS curriculum exists, and there are few common elements across FYS courses. Even with the common elements, like a final paper, there is no uniformity in how they are assigned, completed, and graded. What is more, since little oversight exists, FYS courses suffer from the lack of consistent implementation of program and course goals and objectives, making any legitimate assessment impossible. After several failed attempts by the college to assess the program, no one really knows with any certainty whether students accomplish the learning outcomes of the FYS program or their individual courses. No empirical evidence exists to suggest that FYS really helps students to think critically about self-formation or about the relationship between the liberal arts and professional preparation. The college, then, cannot confidently state that the FYS program facilitates and strengthens the institutional mission by providing the foundation for the Elmhurst Experience.

DCM Assessment Activities at Elmhurst College

Given my untenured status, I felt uneasy entering this fray involving intense interpersonal challenges. Yet, with the reputation of being a campus leader on assessment, I was charged to do something—anything that might effectively address any one or all of these challenges, and respond effectively to institutional dynamics, which provided a perfect crucible to test the merits of DCM as a methodology. All of the college's problems existed, and continue to exist, as a result of interpersonal conflict—the propensity for doublespeak, the inability to compromise, the lack of effective leadership, and the unwillingness to seek consensus on goals, objectives, and learning outcomes. In conflict with our institutional mission, we lacked, and in many respects still lack, community, collegiality, openness, transparency, and trust in each other, the very things that an assessment exercise, particularly DCM, can generate when done well.

Since the college had already collected student final papers from most sections of FYS, I saw an opportunity to design and facilitate an assessment exercise that moved inductively from specific student artifacts to intensive discussions of assignment and performance expectations for final papers to a broader discussion regarding programmatic and course goals, objectives, and outcomes. The student papers anchored and focused the discussion, requiring that participants diligently consider what they wanted students to demonstrate in the final papers and then work backwards to discuss how course and program outcomes might change to accommodate those expectations. Moreover, of the very few common assignments across the approximately thirty sections of FYS, the final paper assignment is critical in terms of programmatic assessment, as it serves as the artifact used to assess students' critical thinking, capacity to analyze ethical questions, and ability to synthesize secondary material. Previous assessment exercises using student final papers, though, had been frustrated by a lack of consensus regarding the assignment's purpose, learning outcomes, and genre, as FYS sections had fulfilled the final paper requirement differently, assigning an in-class essay exam or a short response paper or an intensive, thesis support essay.

In applying a modified version of DCM, I had hoped that the resulting clarity, consensus, and criteria map, as well as a stronger feeling of community and collegiality among the faculty participants, would address these myriad concerns, placing the FYS program in a stronger position to fulfill its purpose and thereby strengthen the academic mission of the school. The three-day DCM exercise consisted of nine faculty, including myself, and involved many steps, primarily alternating between intensive small and large group discussions as participants collaborated to generate consensus on expectations for the final assignment and a criteria map that captures the evaluative dynamics of those expectations as participants critically reviewed final papers.[1] In planning the exercise, I slightly modified DCM methodology to privilege primarily discussion among participants and generate qualitative data, like personal and group discussion notes, responses to guiding questions on worksheets, and maps. So, although student final papers were reviewed to springboard, anchor, and focus discussion, none of them were live-rated, and no quantitative data was generated or recorded. Also, I wanted to create conditions in which faculty would be free to make connections among assessment, the final papers, FYS, and institutional mission. After all, the intended deliverables of the exercise were a stronger sense of community and collegiality, a better understanding of assessment as a scholarly activity and its connection to institutional mission, a less cynical view of assessment, and agreement on expectations for the final paper component of FYS. Only the latter was rendered tangibly and visually in the form of a criteria map that could be distributed to students to clarify expectations for the final paper assignment (See Figure 1).

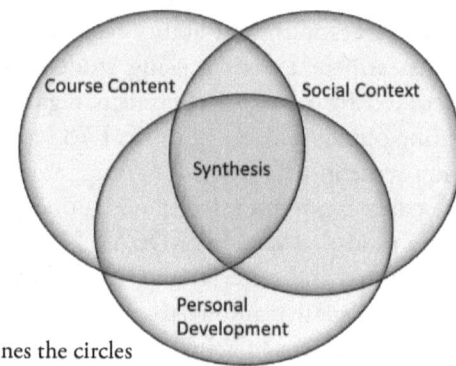

Writing intertwines the circles
- Identifiable focus
- Accessible
- Coherence and Cohesion
- Grammatically Correct

Figure 1. Expectation Map: Final Paper

    The first activity required that participants review and evaluate five sample essays individually, taking notes and responding to the following open-ended questions, which were distributed via a worksheet: Would you pass or fail this text? Why? What rationale can you provide for passing or failing the text? What aspects or characteristics of the sample text do you value? Why do you value those aspects/characteristics? What do they reflect, represent, and/or demonstrate? These questions were meant to prod participants to make explicit the hidden criteria and expectations with which they critically read student papers and to provide a rationale for why those criteria and expectations mattered, why they valued them so highly, and what their favored expectations represented or reflected within student writing. This step was critical not only in encouraging participants to make explicit their expectations but also in establishing the groundwork for making connections between FYS and the college's core values and institutional mission. Since its inception, the college has just assumed that FYS has fulfilled its role as the foundational course for students' self-formation. But, how can the college inspire students in FYS to begin the critical process of forming themselves as intellectuals and professionals if there is no consensus on and consistency regarding what students should aspire to demonstrate? How can faculty foster learning and demand intellectual excellence from students if no one agrees on what specific attributes demonstrate learning and intellectual excellence in student products?

After reviewing the student samples, participants engaged in a series of intensive small and large group discussions. The small group discussions consisted of three groups of three (i.e., trio groups) while the larger group discussions involved all participants. Here, because of space constraints, I discuss the steps collectively, relating how they generated community and collegiality, encouraged faculty participation in assessment, and connected to or aligned with institutional mission. The trio and large group discussions were equally critical for developing community and collegiality among participants, engaging participants in a rewarding and meaningful assessment experience, identifying faculty expectations of what students should accomplish in their final papers, and generating consensus on those expectations. In both the trio and large groups, participants were responsible for discussing their respective readings of each sample text, reaching consensus on expectations of what students should demonstrate in their final papers, and generating a visual rendering of how those expectations interrelated with each other. To do this, participants noted evaluative comments, identified specific textual features exhibited or not by sample texts, and referenced specific passages from sample texts. They labored to cluster synonymous expectations, comments, and criteria together; categorize those clusters; and construct a visual representation of clustered criteria and of the relationships among those clusters. The purpose of this process was to get the group to agree on the dynamics that affect the relationship among the favored expectations and to collaborate to draft a map that depicts those dynamics.

Essential to invoking, generating, and strengthening the institutional values of community and intellectual excellence, participants relied on their experiences teaching FYS and disciplinary backgrounds to provide context for, support, and defense for their readings and preferred criteria, listening to and validating each other's experiences and expertise as they engaged alternative readings generated by disparate disciplinary lenses and knowledges. Instead of claiming superior readings or marking disciplinary turf, though, participants reflected on their respective disciplinary backgrounds to enrich the group's work of negotiating perspectives on what students ought to demonstrate in these papers and what specific textual features demonstrate students' achievement of those expectations.

Results of DCM Exercise

Despite varying levels of teaching experience and different disciplinary backgrounds, participants reveled in this intensely generative process of collaborating to establish common ground, to articulate expectations of what students should be able to do at the end of their respective FYS courses, and to render those expectations intelligible to other community members, particularly other faculty and students. Even within the constantly shifting dynamics actuated by negotiation and the sharing of disparate disciplinary experiences and knowledges, what percolated to the surface of discussion most frequently and what resonated with participants most acutely was the concept of self-formation, a central component of Elmhurst College's institutional mission.

As an institution, the college commits itself to creating conducive conditions for providing rewarding and challenging learning experiences through which students endeavor to realize their potential, become ethical agents, and form themselves intellectually and personally. For participants in the DCM exercise, such intellectual and personal engagement was perspicuously described when students wrote about the interrelation and significance of FYS academic content, personal development, and social context. It was the synergy of these three overarching expectations that participants thought most closely reflected sophisticated critical and analytical thinking, and represented students' struggles with the larger intellectual and personal project of self-formation—the key to the Elmhurst Experience.

A distinguishing feature of FYS courses at Elmhurst College is that each course relates academic content unique to a professor's disciplinary expertise, so sections of FYS do not overlap in terms of academic content. Given this distinguishing feature of the FYS program, participants agreed that within their final synthesis essays, students should assiduously engage the academic content of their respective FYS courses. Such engagement could be exhibited by quoting, challenging, critiquing, questioning, or integrating course readings, lectures, activities, class discussions, and values of the college to support and develop claims, to serve as examples, to function as evidence, to springboard discussion, to develop a thesis, and/or to reflect critically on students' personal values, beliefs, and experiences. Participants felt that speaking to and reflecting on the academic content of students' FYS courses not only served as a springboard into larger discussions of personal development and social context but also enriched and complicated those discussions (DelliCarpini, this volume). It is essential to self-formation, participants thought, that students demonstrate the ability to reflect earnestly and insightfully on course content and note possibilities for the application of that content to personal and social situations. Such a move sets the stage for students to understand how academic content specific to their FYS courses, as well as other courses, transfers to public, political, and social arenas.

With regards to personal development, participants in the DCM exercise worked from the presumption that the academic content and activities of FYS courses were supposed to encourage students to think critically about their experiences, values, beliefs, and assumptions. As a result, during small and large group articulation sessions, it became clear that participants valued passages from student samples that exhibited some degree or kind of critical self-awareness, which they described with phrases like "awareness of self as other," "intellectual curiosity," "growth," "self-reflection," "personal growth," "personal journey," and "personal change." When reviewing these final papers, participants expected the student writer to discuss how s/he had progressed or matured or changed personally and to provide evidence to describe and support that movement to a more critically aware sense of self.

Participants also agreed that students ought to discuss the larger social significance of both the academic content of their respective FYS courses and their personal development (DeRouen, this volume). The institutional mission commits the college to provide learning experiences through and in which students form themselves personally and intellectually, and compels it to help students understand that their self-formation does not materialize within a proverbial vacuum but serves the purpose of "meaningful and ethical work in a multicultural, global society." In their FYS courses and other academic experiences at the college, then, students are not just involved in an intensive process of self-actualization and empowerment, but in the more intellectually challenging process of discerning how they can make crucial interventions within their communities, acting as agents of meaningful change and performing ethical work that contributes substantively to people's lives. In the student samples, participants saw students struggling to describe this component of self-formation in passages that made articulations among course content, personal development, and society at large, discussing the social implications and importance of what students learned and noting how they would act on that knowledge to make a difference in their communities. Participants primarily used the following words and phrases to describe students' connection to social context: "social implications," "bigger picture," "connection to world—outside course, outside student," "ethics," "global understanding," "engagement," and "personal connection to college and society." Participants valued highly students' essays that clearly demonstrated intellectual perspicuity and personal maturity by analyzing and synthesizing the academic content of their respective FYS course, reflecting on their personal development, and suggesting ways that, as a result of their FYS experience, they could engage their social context ethically and critically.[2]

Participants struggled to render the dynamics of these interrelated expectations, but for DCM methodology, a criteria map that visually represents the evaluative dynamics of criteria, expectations, and/or learning outcomes is a necessary deliverable. It was essential, too, that the assessment exercise produce some artifact that could close the assessment loop by providing clarity and guidance to faculty and students regarding expectations for the final paper, which would improve teaching and learning, make for a more rewarding educational experience for students, and align with and promote the college's mission and core values (DeRouen, this volume). After offering various ideas for visuals and considering ways to accurately represent the dynamics actuating the interrelation of personal development, course content, and social context, participants determined that a modified VENN diagram was most appropriate, as it not only allowed them to signify the importance of each expectation with individual large circles but also emphasized and privileged the synergy of the three (See Figure 1). Throughout the DCM exercise, participants noted that the most effective student samples strategically intertwined discussions of personal development, course content, and social context, noting their interrelation and showing, for instance, how course content enriched their knowledge and moved them to act on that knowledge to effect positive change in their communities.

Supporting Institutional Mission

I had hoped that the map limning faculty expectations for the final papers would serve several vital purposes related to institutional mission and programmatic assessment. For example, with the map in hand and after distributing it to students, FYS faculty could clarify expectations for the final paper, "foster learning," as the institutional mission notes, and understand how the assignment fits within the programmatic assessment structure for FYS. Students, too, could benefit from seeing the map and consulting it as they draft their final papers, generating products that fulfill the expectations of faculty and demonstrate programmatic and course outcomes, "broaden[ing] knowledge" of self and others, and enriching process of forming themselves intellectually and personally. Furthermore, with student artifacts that were drafted to meet clear and consistent expectations across sections of FYS, the college could possess material that might provide a stronger foundation for programmatic assessment of FYS, and that could be used to determine if, how, and what students are learning. It is the lack of this information that has engendered such skepticism of the ostensible merits of FYS among faculty. With legitimate data, the college could more accurately represent the benefits of the program to stakeholders, particularly students, parents, and accreditors, showing how the program promotes intellectual excellence, facilitates students' self-formation, and cultivates an ethic of lifelong learning.

The DCM exercise worked as intended; by employing DCM methodology, participants reached consensus on what they value when reviewing final synthesis essays, what students should demonstrate in those essays, what the final synthesis essays should consist of, and how their expectations could be visually represented to students and other stakeholders. During the debriefing session at the end of the DCM exercise, it became clear that participants gained and experienced other benefits, too, such as professional development consisting of a richer understanding of writing assessment and of the generative aspects of assessment in general. Assessment, when it is theoretically informed and responsive to local institutional dynamics, is a knowledge-making, scholarly enterprise that inherently exercises intellectual excellence and innovation. At least for these nine participants, then, the DCM exercise contributed to developing a culture of assessment. It was clear, too, that participants took great pride and felt a strong sense of satisfaction in cultivating collegiality and enriching our intellectual community. They also felt great satisfaction in collaborating to improve teaching and learning and make assessment work organically in response to the needs, expectations, and aspirations of faculty and students rather than the insecurities of administrators or the demands of accreditors.

Sadly, all did not go perfectly. Challenges emerged when the methodology and the map delineating expectations of what students should demonstrate in their final papers were presented during a pre-semester

FYS workshop to FYS faculty who did not participate in the DCM exercise. Since these faculty were not privy to the conversations that occurred during the DCM exercise, they lacked the shared foundation of knowledge of assessment and community that were developed, resulting in confusion about the methodology, the expectations, and the map. They lacked the experience of investing in the process and collaborating with colleagues to articulate expectations and to facilitate a DCM assessment experience aligned with the college's institutional mission. Unfortunately, I couldn't recreate that experience in a two-hour workshop.

Moreover, some faculty came to the pre-semester workshop with expectations that they were going to receive a rubric and be given clear directives regarding the final essay. They may have misread and misunderstood the map, then, because they might have tried to read it as a rubric rather than as a visual representation of expectations and the evaluative dynamics that constitute the interrelation of those expectations when applied critically to student samples. Expectations for a rubric and directives went unmet, as I preferred to facilitate the workshop using consensus-building strategies consistent with DCM methodology. Faculty cynicism regarding assessment, always an undercurrent in discussions of assessment on campus, percolated to the surface, generating a level of resistance that I, naively, failed to foresee given the success of the DCM exercise. I could neither dispel the confusion nor fulfill the expectations of this cadre of FYS faculty, so extending the work of the DCM participants to other FYS faculty experienced limited success. Though generating agreement from a larger group of FYS faculty proved challenging, I remain heartened by the rewarding experience of leading a DCM assessment exercise and linking it to institutional mission with the intent of employing assessment strategically and politically to generate consensus, cultivate community, and encourage faculty ownership of assessment.

If others were to attempt DCM at their institutions, they should consider the following suggestions: urge participation from all faculty teaching within a program or department, prepare participants for the process by providing background information about DCM as a methodology, and allow the group to pursue the various openings, ideas, and intuitions generated by the inherent dynamism of discussion. If I possessed the opportunity to recreate the assessment experience, I would have held the assessment exercise during the school year and lobbied energetically for participation from all faculty teaching FYS courses. If all FYS faculty would participate in a DCM assessment exercise, I suspect that much of the cynicism and resistance and many of the difficulties that I experienced in the pre-semester workshop could be assuaged and overcome. Though generating consensus with thirty participants, instead of nine, would present its own set of challenges, I know from the research and from this experience that DCM methodology is uniquely appropriate for situations in which ambiguity with expectations and/or learning outcomes exists, cynicism among stakeholders permeates discussions regarding assessment, and questions regarding the value of a program and its connection to institutional mission remain prominent (Broad, *What* and "Organic").

A critical component of how I facilitated the DCM exercise was a comprehensive explanation of the steps of the methodology as I modified it, the purpose of the process, and the underlying theory supporting the methodology. I had predicted that participants would possess any number of preconceptions about assessment that might dramatically influence their participation, and I purposely sought to challenge those preconceptions, especially the traditional impression of assessment as norming, reading, and rating with which so many faculty are familiar. I also provided background information on contemporary writing assessment scholarship, emphasizing how scholars of writing assessment have worked diligently to counteract positivistic assessment mechanisms—like multiple-choice, high-stakes exams—by developing assessment practices that capture the complexity of learning, the context-sensitivity of knowledge construction, and the diversity of learning and writing styles. Contemporary scholarship on composition theory, I explained, argues that writing assessment practices must be site based, locally controlled, contextually sensitive, accessible, and rhetorically based (Broad, "Organic"; Huot; Yancey). In other words, effective writing assessment develops organically out of the conditions, circumstances, curricula, and student needs that pervade a particular institutional context (Adler-Kassner and O'Neill; Broad, *What*; Huot; Moss). From my perspective as the facilitator, providing this necessary background information seemed to circumvent the immediate suspicion and visceral anxiety that often arises when people experience new situations and learning opportunities. It also provided participants with a foundation of knowledge with which they could situate themselves in the process and understand the critical importance of their collaborative efforts.

When conducting a DCM exercise, I believe that it is absolutely critical for a facilitator to resist the temptation to micromanage the process or participants' labor. Yes, a facilitator must have a plan, but a facilitator must also remain open to the creative potential of digressions, fits and starts, frustrations, and disagreements. As is the case with any situation in which people work together, during a DCM exercise, disagreements will occur, tension will amass, and tangents will alter or slow or enrich participants' efforts. If a facilitator believes in and engages their creative possibilities, these can beget positive outcomes, like insight, rapport, and the altering of perspectives—all of which are worth the risk of a little conflict and extra time.

It is essential that faculty conceive of assessment as central to institutional mission, engaging assessment sincerely and conceptualizing it as a political technology with which they can improve teaching and learning, reinforce and assert their academic expertise, build rapport with colleagues, and hold institutions accountable to their respective missions (DelliCarpini, Efthymiou and Fitzgerald, Kinkead, this volume). Situating assessment practices within and aligning them to institutional mission lends those practices and faculty participating in them focus, credibility with stakeholders, and kinship with the core values that have informed and invigorated the work of an institution throughout its history. In reflecting on the collaborative labor that occurred during the DCM assessment experience, I understand now that such work not only reflected the spirit of Elmhurst College's institutional mission but also actualized it and embodied its laudable core values. In collaborating "with passion and commitment," participants cultivated community, respect, and collegiality ("About"). In sharing their experiences and disciplinary knowledges, participants embodied intellectual excellence, finding common ground in spite of disciplinary differences. In articulating clear expectations and drafting a visual representation of the dynamics actuating those expectations, participants diligently worked to foster learning within FYS, a critical stage in students' rigorous and deliberate process of forming themselves intellectually and personally. Lastly, in genuinely engaging the DCM methodology, participants broadened and enriched their knowledge of assessment and learned how it might be applied in ways that respect and rely on practitioner expertise, exercise contemporary scholarship, promote collegiality, and strengthen institutional mission.

Notes

1. The DCM exercise consumed three days, during which participants worked from approximately 9am–4pm. The nine participants, including the author, represented a variety of disciplinary backgrounds, such as English, geography, library sciences, business, education, and art. All participants were paid a small stipend for their service.

2. Since FYS courses are not designated writing courses, participants felt uncomfortable evaluating the proficiency of writing exhibited by student samples. Participants recognized, however, that poor writing inhibited their review of student samples and significantly diminished the quality of those samples. As a result, participants agreed that the final papers should possess an identifiable focus, conform to usage and grammar rules, be accessible to a general audience, and demonstrate coherence and cohesiveness.

Works Cited

"About Elmhurst College: Mission, Vision and Core Values." Elmhurst College, n.d. Web. 29 July 2014.

Adler-Kassner, Linda and Peggy O'Neill. *Reframing Writing Assessment to Improve Teaching and Learning.* Logan, UT: Utah State UP, 2010. Print.

Adler-Kassner, Linda and Heidi Estrem. "The Journey is the Destination: The Place of Assessment in an Activist Writing Program—Eastern Michigan University." Broad et al. 14–36.

Alford, Barry. "DCM as the Assessment Program: Mid Michigan Community College." *Organic Writing Assessment: Dynamic Criteria Mapping in Action.* Logan, UT: UP of Colorado and Utah State UP, 2009. 37–51. Print

Broad, Bob. "Organic Matters: In Praise of Locally Grown Writing Assessment." *Organic Writing Assessment: Dynamic Criteria Mapping in Action.* Logan, UT: UP of Colorado and Utah State UP, 2009. 1–13. Print.

—. *What We Really Value: Beyond Rubrics in Teaching and Assessing Writing.* Logan, UT: UP of Colorado and Utah State UP, 2003. Print.

Broad, Bob, et al. *Organic Writing Assessment: Dynamic Criteria Mapping in Action.* Logan, UT: UP of Colorado and Utah State UP, 2009. Print.

Detweiler, Jane and Maureen McBride. "Designs on Assessment at UNR: University of Nevada Reno." *Organic Writing Assessment: Dynamic Criteria Mapping in Action.* Logan, UT: UP of Colorado and Utah State UP, 2009. 52–74. Print.

Harrington, Susanmarie and Scott Weeden. "Assessment Changes for the Long Haul: Dynamic Criteria Mapping at Indiana University Purdue University Indianapolis." *Organic Writing Assessment: Dynamic Criteria Mapping in Action.* Logan, UT: UP of Colorado and Utah State UP, 2009. 75–118. Print.

Huot, Brian. *(Re)articulating Writing Assessment for Teaching and Learning.* Logan, UT: Utah State UP, 2002. Print.
Janangelo, Joseph and Linda Adler-Kassner. "Common Denominators and the Ongoing Culture of Assessment." *Assessment in Writing.* Eds. Marie C. Paretti and Katrina Powell. Vol. 4. Tallahassee: Association of Institutional Research Press, 2009. 11–34. Print.
Moss, Pamela. "Can There Be Validity Without Reliability?" *Educational Researcher* 23.2 (1994): 5–12. Print.
Stalions, Eric. "Putting Placement on the Map: Bowling Green State University." *Organic Writing Assessment: Dynamic Criteria Mapping in Action.* Logan, UT: UP of Colorado and Utah State UP, 2009. 119–53. Print.
Yancey, Kathleen Blake. "Looking Back as We Look Forward: Historicizing Writing Assessment." *College Composition and Communication* 50.3 (1999): 483–503. Print.

4 Creating a Program of Success for Underrepresented Students at Research Institutions

Farrell J. Webb and Anita R. Cortez

This chapter examines the challenges and success of the Developing Scholars Program (DSP) at Kansas State University (K-State), a large land-grant university serving approximately 24,000 students in Manhattan, Kansas. The DSP, founded in 2000, is designed to help first-generation college students, including those designated as "underrepresented" students, make a successful transition from high school to a research institution. This chapter has four sections. In part one, we explain the difficulties some students face in entering the academy. In part two, we describe the steps the DSP takes to help students succeed. In part three, we explore the work that needs to occur if institutions of higher learning are to do a better job of mentoring these students. Finally, in part four we discuss the impact participating in student success programs can have on faculty careers.

CURRENT BARRIERS TO STUDENT SUCCESS

We begin with the conviction that traditional, lofty ideas about who a college student is or should be are at odds with the changing profile of student demographics. For example, recent data show that the number of women in higher education increased 49 percent compared to 42 percent for men for the period 1996-2010 (Husser and Bailey). The number of non-traditional students (those 25 and older) increased from 1996 to 2010 fueled in part by the need to have a college degree to obtain better employment opportunities. By the year 2010 the number for

25-34 year olds was 45 percent and 32 percent for those 35 and older (Husser and Bailey). Overall, there is a 14 percent projected increase for undergraduate students for the years 2010-2021 (Hussar and Bailey). Most salient for our purposes are the projections for the future. A conservative estimate indicates that approximately 15 percent of future students are projected to be first-generation students by 2020 (VanDerWerk and Sabatier). When race/ethnicity projections are considered, there are marked increases for each group for the same period. See Table 1 for the projections for each group.

Table 1. Projected US College Enrollment Increases 2010-2021 by Race/Ethnicity

Race/Ethnicity	Projected Enrollment Increase
White	04%
Black	25%
Hispanic	42%
Asian/Pacific Islander	20%
American Indian/Alaskan Native	01%

There is also some underreporting and non-reporting, so projected estimates might be slightly lower than actual numbers may bear out (Hussar and Bailey). In our view, such compelling demographic shifts reveal that changes in the student-body at institutions of higher learning are not only inevitable but unavoidable. This means that institutions will have to adapt their view on who their students may be and what the institution should do to attract, retain, and support this changing demographic.

Understanding the "New" Students in the Academy

It is incumbent upon institutions to develop an awareness of the future student population's socioeconomic backgrounds, race/ethnicity, and likely preparation and familiarity with the academy when developing student success programs. As mentioned, K-State launched the DSP with the goal of increasing access and facilitating enhanced academic achievement for underrepresented as well as first-generation college students by matching students with faculty research mentors. As noted on the DSP website, "To date the DSP has an impressive 83 percent 5-year graduation rate over its first 15 years." This rate is notable because it exceeds the general graduation rate of K-State which is about 68 percent for 5 years. Approximately 350 undergraduate students have participated in the DSP's mentoring, coaching, financial support, and peer community of scholars. The results have been greater than expected. Developing Scholars can count themselves among winners of both the Goldwater and Fulbright awards, some of the most selective and prestigious national scholastic awards available (kstate.edu). In addition, several DSP students have garnered admission to some of the nation's most recognized graduate and professional schools, including the following: the University of California at Berkeley, Harvard University, and Stanford University.

The DSP offers underrepresented students research projects in their field of study with faculty mentors. Student scholars receive academic, social, and financial support while becoming integrated into the intellectual climate of the university (Webb and Cortez). Their participation in the discovery and creation of new knowledge at K-State distinguishes DSP students among the student-body (k-state.edu). Scholars enroll in an introductory research seminar for each semester of their first year. Additionally, all Scholars attend monthly meetings consisting of team-building, lectures, presentations, and community service (k-state.edu). Research is available in any field of study that K-State offers.

The DSP succeeds so well because it facilitates effective working relationships between students by enhancing their academic and leadership potential and pairing them with faculty who have strong desires to nurture undergraduate research excellence (Webb and Cortez). When coupled with a dedicated staff whose considerable expertise is grounded in years of varied experience working with ethnically, racially, and economically underrepresented and underserved students, the program thrives (k-state.edu). Because of this synergistic relationship and strong support of the institution's mission of sponsoring undergraduate research opportunities in 2014, K-State founded its Office of Undergraduate Research & Creative Achievement with the DSP at its core. Anita Cortez was promoted to the position of director with a charge to bring benefits similar to those available to DSP to as many undergraduates as possible.

The DSP has as its primary mission to foster a supportive environment and nurture students in an effort to create a positive outcome culminating in a four-year graduation. The points listed below are extracted directly from the K-State DSP website that can be found at the following address: http://www.k-state.edu/scholars/about/index.html:

- to increase the number of intellectually curious students of color and first generation college students who choose K-State;

- to improve retention of such underrepresented students by matching students with faculty mentors for the purpose of providing early opportunities for scholarly research;
- to guide more of such underrepresented students toward graduate or professional school;
- to provide a more diverse community of workers for the twenty-first century.

In addition, there are a number of goals associated with successful membership and completion of the DSP. The most relevant ones, drawn from the DSP website, are these:

- Identify, recruit, motivate, and enable more underrepresented students to obtain a Bachelor's degree from K-State.
- Increase K-State faculty involvement and understanding of the needs and richness of diverse perspectives that underrepresented students bring to the university environment;
- Improve academic success and create opportunity for underrepresented students at K-State;
- Foster development of a community of student researchers by providing educational enrichment activities and ways for students to interact, network, socialize and collaborate with each other and with the larger academic community;
- Establish a "pathway of progress" to provide opportunities for underrepresented students to pursue diverse academic interests and to enter graduate programs, professional schools, or to find placement in their professional fields upon graduation;
- Share with other institutions of higher learning what is learned.

As with most programs serving individuals from varied backgrounds, there is a need to set specific expectations that must be adhered to by all students. All DSP students are made aware of these expectations and the consequences for not maintaining them. Each student is reviewed via first-year seminar observations, periodic faculty reports, and individual meetings with program staff. Students who are found in violation are placed on a remediation program that requires weekly check-ins where overall well-being is assessed (Webb and Cortez). Students who continue to have problems may be suspended or removed from the program—this occurs only in extreme cases and only after the DSP staff has exhausted the options available. In most cases, students will withdraw from the program acknowledging that DSP has made strong efforts to retain them. In reality, the expectations of DSP scholars are not difficult, but they are at the cornerstone of the program. They are as follows:

- Work on the research project six to ten hours weekly and meet with the research mentor regularly;
- Attend monthly group meetings;
- Participate in annual poster symposium;
- Uphold DSP's high standards of academics and integrity.

Furthermore, the DSP research seminar is required for all first-year scholars. Its primary goal is to provide students with the tools that they will need for their personal and academic life. Students are taught essential research skills, methods of communication such as writing and speaking, and presentation styles that include the use of software such as PowerPoint and Prezi. By using both library and online research tools, students are taught how to access, annotate, analyze, and summarize research and data findings. They are also shown and encouraged to use the appropriate style manuals of their selected academic disciplines (e.g., the *MLA Handbook*). In conjunction with this, students are taught how to write research abstracts for their projects. The abstract writing process is an iterative one where the abstract is reviewed and rewritten a number of times before the final product is decided upon. This process takes place over two semesters to support intellectual development. Scholars are also exposed to issues involving research ethics, the institutional review process for both humans and animal research, and plagiarism. Finally, students are encouraged to use critical thinking and "wicked" problem-solving and to engage in intellectual discourse about their work with the seminar preceptor, other students, and their research mentors (Klausman, this volume). This group may include some graduate students working along with them on the project as well as their faculty mentor. The overall aim is to introduce students to the idea of the learning community as a place where they can continue to grow and contribute to throughout their lives (Webb and Cortez).

Beyond these prescriptive elements, the essential question that comes to mind then is, exactly how does DSP mentor student success? We accomplish this through a variety of strategies:

- We value the student by considering the multiple spheres of the students' lives. The DSP uses the multiple dimension identity model as a means of connecting the students directly to the academy (Jones and McEwen; Abes, Jones, and McEwen). These models examine the role race, social class, gender, religion, and sexual orientation—termed self-perception by the authors—play in forming the student's idea about how they fit the institution's mission. These elements are addressed through the student's own filters for generating meaning along with a firm view of the contextual influences such as peers, family, sociopolitical condition, social norms, and stereotypes. These are discussed and addressed for each student in a variety of exercises, discussions, and individual meetings with the seminar and program directors. The idea is to create a place where students are comfortable and can learn how to respond to the aforementioned issues as they navigate through the institution.

- Students are given multiple opportunities to meet and engage in organized activities, such as the "food for thought" meeting. At this pot-luck event, students meet all the other students in the DSP for a meal and shared discussion on a topic such as how to maintain a study schedule. We typically invite guests from the community at large, along with some academics, to present an idea for discussion. We find that by having the students share a meal together, it brings them closer and more willing to be open about things in their lives. It may appear to be a simple event, but it is a very powerful and meaningful one for the students, program staff, and seminar director.
- One critical and touching moment that helps to acclimate the DSP students into the university community by reaffirming both the university and DSP missions, is our induction ceremony. This occurs during the third week of the first semester. Each first-year student is exposed to a short series of fun activities where they are forced to interact with other advanced DSP students. They must reveal who they are, what they are interested in studying, and disclose something that they would like others to know—nothing too personal or revealing. The event ends with the students hearing the DSP principles read by the seminar director, and then each student is called to the front of the room and is "pinned." They are told the meaning and significance of the pin and that they must wear their pins to each DSP event or whenever they are representing the DSP. The second- and third-year students at the event are wearing their pins. The event reaffirms to the students the importance of their group membership and exposes them to the potential for success.

- The DSP capstone experience is the symposium that is held every spring. It is a research forum where students present their yearlong scholarly endeavors (Kinkead, this volume). Moreover, it is a celebration of the academic success of the students. Awards are given to students for their efforts, perseverance, contributions, academics, and overall representation of DSP ideals. The event is well attended by senior administrators, the president and provost, a number of vice presidents, deans, department heads, and community leaders. Families and friends are encouraged to attend and students are delighted to share their results. The event is opened to the entire community and the attendance continues to be robust and beyond expectations. The symposium brings together all the elements, including the hard work that was discussed and examined by the students. First-year students spend the next seminar session processing their feelings and jubilation over the way the event unfolded. They often report a new understanding of why they needed the seminar and how they can see their intellectual and personal growth.
- For faculty, a key dimension of student success involves the amount of contact students have with the university both prior to their arrival and immediately upon entering. This time has to be with the faculty, staff, other students, and the general community. We have found that the more contact, the better the student success. Contact does not have to be formal. It just needs to be consistent and open.

Confronting Institutional Barriers to Support Student Viability

Despite these efforts, one of the most difficult obstacles to overcome is getting faculty to see non-majority students as intellectually viable. We define student viability as the ability to successfully begin and complete projects required in college and university coursework at a level deemed competent and appropriate. We contend that, in many schools, there is an unspoken perception of underrepresented students as unqualified to do college level work. Here are some of the common denominators. These are based on comments made to us by faculty as well as some that appear in scholarly publications:

- The perception of student incapacity can be couched in vague statements about the student's preparation or lack thereof from their high-school or community college (Tinto, Webb).
- There are also those who use a historical perspective as evidence of faculty reluctance or hesitation to work with the non-majority students (Nora and Caberera, Tinto). This attitude does not go unnoticed by the students who often react in one of two ways; they may shut down, or persist only to find their efforts are not well-received (Tracey and Seedleck).
- Faculty and staff may perform *microaggressions* (Sue et al.) that further alienate students. A *microaggression* is defined as "brief and commonplace daily verbal, behavioral, or environmental indignities, whether intentional or unintentional, that communicate hostile, derogatory, or negative racial slights and insults toward people of color" (271). The definition that we use has been expanded to include gender, sexual orientation, age, and socioeconomic status consistent with Sue. Of course, faculty may not be aware that they are using them. This creates more problems because they cannot stop doing what they do not recognize.
- While it may be possible for students to foster relationships with their peers and even some faculty, establishing a sense of community has proven to be much more problematic. This is especially true in a small community where it is difficult to meet new people and where outsiders often do not feel as welcomed. According to the most recent census data, Manhattan, KS is a community of 56,089. The racial/ethnic breakdown is Whites (80.8 percent), Blacks (5.7 percent), Hispanics (5.4 percent), and Asians (5.2 percent). Some of the numbers of people of color can be influenced by the presence of Fort Riley, an Army post located approximately six miles to the west of Manhattan. There are many soldiers and their families who are part of the Manhattan community (US Census).
- The perception of who is welcomed and who is not is the one factor that students of color report as being problematic. On numerous occasions students have reported difficulty with finding housing, securing a sense of belonging within their faith communities, and certainly feeling uncomfortable with the dominant university culture that may not be particularly connected to their own cultural backgrounds. For example, one student reported that his landlord would not come out to fix their heat because "you mexi-

cans know how to stay warm." In another instance, students have been told that apartments were not available, but then had their white roommates check and the apartment became available. Although these things are in violation of the law, students are often reluctant to engage this process, in part because the treatment they have received by law enforcement has been problematic. Another comment was: "the police came to our party and told us the music was too loud, but right down the street we could hear their party noise that went on well after we turned ours down and the police never came to their house." The most disturbing story involves a graduate teaching assistant. A student said, in full earshot of others that she did not have to do what this "nigger" said; she was graduating. The incident was reported to the graduate instructor by the other students who were upset by this event. The student was questioned but denied that she said such a thing. Left with only hearsay, no action was taken. To this day, the graduate student, now a senior administrator at another institution, recalls the hurt that hearing such a thing can do. There are more stories, but these address the issue faced by students, faculty, and staff of color in some environments.

- A residual effect is isolation, which is not necessarily a problem in itself as long as students feel a connection to the institution. However, when the university offers lip service to students instead of real support, it exacerbates students' feelings of isolation and reifies the idea that they are not being welcomed or validated.
- While much of the success that we have had with students come from having enlightened faculty, the pool is relatively small and we rely on this faculty group of fewer than twenty who are pressed into service repeatedly. This can result in faculty burnout. Even among those with the best intentions, fatigue can and does set in. Once this occurs, it becomes difficult to retain those faculty members as mentors.
- Community issues, which the institution cannot control, can also undermine student well-being and success. Recently, some students of color were being questioned by the police and merchants for additional identification in order to enter some of the public drinking establishments near the institution. The reason offered by merchants was that they wished to curb the presence of gangs and gang violence. Some of the students were accused of using gang

signs when, in fact, they were using greeting symbols from their respective fraternities. The problem escalated to the point where the local police had to be re-educated about addressing issues with students of color.

To this list, we wish to add another, protracted example—what we call *invisibility in plain sight*. This has to do with institutional discourse. Certainly, there is a great deal of effort to support and advertise the DSP. The director is involved in many activities focused on students. In addition, the activities, events, awards, and programs are well advertised and receive public support from university entities. The school newspaper often highlights that a student was a member of the DSP when there was a scholarly event or award program. However, very few of these articles included photos, especially those that explicitly show the students. There is a website for the DSP that contains extensive visual records of the students and their activities. Yet, despite the numerous accolades and success achieved by this program, there is no effort on the part of the university's development office aimed at raising funds for this program. In fifteen years there has been mention that it would be done, but during the first author's tenure it never occurred. The recent fund-raising campaign did not include DSP. Rather it was placed within the context of a general undergraduate research program, something that came about as a priority only after DSP had been accomplishing this task for fifteen years without their financial support.

Numerous publications from the development office are replete with photos of K-State students involved in research and scholarly activities, yet none of these show any students of color. On the one hand, one of the recruitment brochures for a program for first-generation students and students of color did not include one photo of current or previously enrolled students. Instead, they used stock pictures of models of color posed as students. Conversely, current university brochures directed at majority students use current or recently graduated students, not models. When photos of students of color are used, they are generally shown in casual and carefree roles and not the scholarly settings in which majority students are depicted. Such institutional texts raise important questions:

- What messages do these send to the current and potential students of color?
- What messages do these send to the faculty? To the community? To the families of the students?

Clearly, such promotional materials suggest a certain perspective about how underrepresented students are perceived. This reflects the subtle, yet pervasive nature of the hidden ideals of what students should be like in an academic setting. Exclusions, whether deliberate or unintended, send the same message: you do not belong here. As this chapter's next section shows, this potent *microaggression* and marginalization (inclusive of social history and cultural messages) can also be experienced by faculty.

Faculty Marginalization in the Academy

In 1992, Farrell published "The Role of the Hidden Agenda in Student Retention Problems." It described how the hidden agenda of having only a few select students of color in higher educational institutions influences the overall success of those students. At that time, he suggested the traditional academy exhibited discomfort with increasing the number of students of color on campus, and that anxiety generated policies and apocryphal myths that would most certainly reduce the number of students and faculty of color in higher education. He raised the question, how was scholarship to be defined in the new academy? He favored using Boyer's earlier and later thinking that scholarship should be more inclusive. Webb, like Boyer, called on the academy to challenge itself to find and value alternative methods of scholarship to complement research publications, prestige scores, and funded grants as the most important measures in academy membership.

The reasoning presented by the author resonated with faculty who participate in undergraduate research programs. Faculty involved in student success programs are often unable to complete some other scholarly tasks due to taking on time- and energy-intensive research mentoring activities. Faculty who choose this pathway typically are not adequately rewarded, or even respected for the work they do in mentoring first-generation and underrepresented students. Those who do mentor underrepresented students often sacrifice more than their prestige. They often have their careers socially retarded. Some of the outcomes can be: being slower to achieve promotion, if at all, and having to explain their work to colleagues who have no interest in assisting this student population. Personal experience has taught us that this is the case. For example, in an evaluation meeting with one of his previous directors, Farrell was told, "that work that you do with THOSE students is because YOU want to, and it WON'T do anything for your career, it is not that important." It is this type of thinking that can serve as a retardant to one's career, not from the work, but from the unenlightened response from the academic gatekeepers. As long as that director remained in place, Farrell received average evaluations despite teaching uncompensated overloads each semester and winning outstanding undergraduate teaching awards and a host of other awards and research grants culminating with the presidential award for outstanding service to underrepresented students. It should be noted that both authors won this award in different years, largely due to their constant work efforts with first-generation students and students of color.

When student mentoring (which in this case directly supports the university's mission of providing research opportunities for groups typically left out of the academic view) is devalued or paid cursory attention by those in power at these research institutions, there are no incentives, other than altruistic ones, for doing the work. The question for campus leaders then becomes: what strategies can we devise to override this culture of institutional disrespect? Although we have described numerous barriers to student success in traditional academic settings, we still advocate that students continue to enroll in these institutions and work toward their personal goals. We have constructed a series of recommendations that we believe could benefit the academy, faculty, students, staff, and community. They are:

- Develop a broader sense and range of how research is defined and fits within a research university's mission.
- Add value to the faculty portfolio for promotion and tenure based on the work with students directly meeting the university's mission of offering enhanced undergraduate experiences.
- Celebrate the accomplishments of faculty who participate in the research mission.
- Reward faculty with incentives, including meaningful monetary rewards and release time for supporting the university's mission.
- Open the opportunity for conducting research to faculty in fields whose research paradigms or methodologies do not always align with the general conceptualization of what research means to the academy.
- Cultivate the faculty and have them serve as ambassadors to others, especially administrators, who often have less direct contact with students and measure things on the basis of outcomes.

- Create a program that can ameliorate the discomfort experienced by underrepresented students (Janangelo, this volume).
- Directly involve students in the primary business of the academy, which is research (Kinkead, this volume).
- Secure financial and moral support from campus leaders.
- Provide training to faculty about how to address issues of microaggressions.
- Develop more community-based research activities and projects (DelliCarpini, this volume).
- Garner support from alumni interested in enhancing the academic reputation of the university.
- Encourage student and faculty participation by having regular meetings with upper administration to flesh out issues and problems.
- Develop a community liaison for research so that the public can become better connected with the students and faculty.
- Honor faculty from across all of the academic fields, just from the traditional STEM areas that seems to be more commonplace (DeRouen, this volume).

The most crucial element needed to ensure that an institution's mission will be accomplished is to have serious buy-in from senior administrators. The very existence of DSP has depended upon this concept since its inception. The first funding for the program came directly from the office of the provost, Jim Coffman. He sponsored the program and touted its merits at each and every opportunity available, even linking it to outside funders who have provided additional funds to the DSP. His strong commitment and the continuous support received from the office of the provost led his successors, M. Duane Nellis and April Mason, to make sure that the DSP became a part of the fabric of K-State. Other champions for DSP include the Dean of Student Life, Pat Bosco, who also continues to support the program and its goals. We believe that without senior leadership, programs aimed at fulfilling any mission of the university, especially as it pertains to first-generation students and students of color, will experience problems. In short, senior administrators have to be convinced, willing to take risks, and willing to stand in support of programs that clearly articulate the institution's mission.

Conclusion: Enlightened Leadership

The one element that we know will guarantee the success of any program is to have leadership that is aware of issues and that have a future orientation. It is not possible to plan if there is no vision on the part of the leaders. In addition, there needs to be a certain willingness to take risks and fail. In essence, we borrow the idea from bench scientists who know that, without experimentation and a number of failures, it is not possible to perfect the formula for success that is needed.

Administrators must be willing to "offend" some traditional academics. They must also be willing to fund student-success-related projects, even when there is limited funding. The recent recession had an impact on all academic programs. However, because of the proven success of the DSP, our senior administrators enhanced rather than reduced the funding for the DSP during those difficult times. This willingness to keep a future vision and to support the program during lean times demonstrated the level of commitment that we had become accustomed to for the DSP.

It is also critical that *program leaders* (staff and faculty members) know what their long-term payoff will be for directing the program. In the case of the DSP, it is measured by the success of the students, the prestige the program brings, and the strong and faithful alumni that the program is producing. Of course, having a larger pool from which to select faculty mentors would make the prospect of working with students much more appealing. Program leaders also need time for renewal, assistance in obtaining external funding, and to have a succession plan. We know of this experience firsthand. Farrell left K-State in January 2014, and because we had not created a succession plan, a great deal of work was shifted onto Anita. However, because Farrell had always maintained excellent records of his previous communications with Anita, they were able to restructure and provide assistance to the new seminar preceptor. Of course, the years of experience and all the skills developed along the way could not be left with the new instructor. Anita, with the help of a new faculty member, was able to fill the gap. As of now, there is no succession plan for Anita. This is a problem. It is incumbent upon the senior administration to begin thinking about how the program would proceed once its historians are gone, and with them the important elements of how to make the program work in a specific institutional context. This issue, coupled with the task that faces the administration of how to incorporate the necessary paradigm shift that must occur in order to continue to grow the program, has to be considered. Moreover, the work of persuading faculty and staff who remain skeptical of, and voice recalcitrance at, expanding the academy is a never ending issue for academics.

The final, and certainly most important element of the DSP, is its *students*. The question of how to keep students motivated and engaged remains constant. There is no doubt that the idea of conducting college-level research is appealing, but there has to be more than that to sustain student interest in the long term. Helping students translate the university experience into other aspects of their lives is the challenge. It is one of the most important things that we do in the DSP. We know that no amount of lecturing or research experience can be considered beneficial without having something to tie it back into the lives of students and their families. In the case of the DSP, helping students develop a goal and devise strategies to reach it is crucial. The belief that you are an integral part of the community and that your presence is welcomed and needed helps foster the type of synergy that leads to programmatic and individual growth, two things consistent with the institution's mission of providing a meaningful experience whereby students become lifelong contributing members to and of the academy. While we believe that we have been successful at achieving this in the DSP, we know we must go further. The issue facing us all (administrators, program directors, and students) is making sure that our mission incorporates the current and future needs and goals of our ever-expanding society.

Works Cited

Abes, Elisa S., Susan R. Jones, and Marylu K. McEwen. "Reconceptualizing the Model of Multiple Dimensions of Identity: The Role of Meaning Making Capacity in the Construction of Multiple Identies." *Journal of College Student Development* 48.3 (2007): 1–22. Print.

Boyer, Ernest L. *Scholarship Reconsidered: Priorities of the Professoriate*. Princeton, NJ: Carnegie Foundation for the Advancement of Teaching, 1990. Print.

"Developing Scholars." *Kansas State University*. Kansas State University. N.d. Web. 4 June 2014.

Husser, William, J. and Tabitha M. Bailey. *Projections of Education Statistics to 2021 40th Edition (NCES 3013-008). US Department of Education, National Center for Education Statistics*. Washington, DC: US GPO, 2013. Print.

Jones, Susan. R., and Marylu K. McEwen. "A Conceptual Model of Multiple Dimensions of Identity." *Journal of College Student Development* 41.4 (2000): 405–14. Print.

Nora, Amaury and Alberto Cabrera. "The Role of Perception of Prejudice and Discrimination in the Adjustment of Minority Students to College." *Journal of Higher Education* 67.2 (1996): 119–48. Print.

Quickfacts. United States Census Bureau. US Department of Commerce, 2014. Web. 14 June. 2014.

Sue, Derald W., et al. "Racial Microaggressions in Everyday Life: Implications for Clinical Practice." *The American Psychologist* 62.4 (2007): 271–86. Print.

Tinto, Vincent. *Leaving College: Rethinking the Causes and Cures of Student Attrition.* Chicago, IL: U of Chicago P. 1987. Print.

Tracey, Terence, J. and William E. Sedlacek. "Prediction of College Graduation Using Noncognitive Variables by Race." *Measurement and Evaluation in Counseling and Development* 19.4 (1987): 177–84. Print.

VanDerWerk, Martin and Grant Sabatier. *The College of 2020: Students.* Washington, DC: Chronicle Research Services, 2014. Web. 6 June 2014.

Webb, Farrell, J. "The Role of the Hidden Agenda in Student Retention Problems." *Strategies for Retaining Minority Students in Higher Education.* Eds. Clinita A. Ford & Marvel L. Lang. Springfield, IL: Charles C Thomas Publishers, 1992. 201–17. Print.

Webb, Farrell, J., and Anita M. Cortez. "Developing Scholars: Targeting Excellence Using the Axiom of Achievement." *Broadening Participation in Undergraduate Research: Fostering Excellence and Enhancing the Impact.* Eds. Mary K. Boyd and Jodi L. Weseman. Mahawah. NJ: Erlbaum, 2009. 257–68. Print.

PART II: DESIGNING AND DISCERNING

5 Out of the Ivory Tower and into the Brand: How the New Two-Year College Mission Shapes the Faculty-Manager

Jeffrey Klausman

> *For in this labor which he undertakes to reconstruct for another, he rediscovers the fundamental alienation that made him construct it like another, and which has always destined it to be taken from him by another.*
>
> —Jacques Lacan

THE BIG PICTURE

When I hear the term *academe* or *the academy*, my mind conjures images of ivy-covered stone walls, broad expanses of grassy quads, crenellated towers, and dons in flowing robes. Or if I borrow from the movies, I might envision passionate—or dissipated—professors (take your pick) expounding unto rapt—or rebellious—youths (take your pick) while out the window an autumn sun burnishes an ancient oak. What I don't envision are slabs of poured-concrete walls baking in an urban setting, asphalt lots with rows and rows of aging cars simmering in the summer heat, or harried instructors rushing through hallways from class to class to class, stacks of papers under their arms. The latter may be every bit as much a stereotype—and in fact, I would argue that it is—but it's a stereotype of a two-year college, and it's likely not in anyone's imaginings of what "the academy" may mean. Yet for those of us who work in the two-year college (and felt most acutely by those with adjunct status at such institutions), the disconnect between the remembered promise of "joining the academy" and the daily mix of delight and dread the two-year college line offers is felt as a kind of longing, of loss, that might teach us something about the changing nature of the two-year college mission and the shifting roles and necessities of the two-year college professoriate. For it's my contention that the two-year college mission has become leaner, harsher, and more corporate than ever, and the need for a faculty who can shepherd that mission will become even more acute while the dividing line between those who can adjust and those who can't (or won't) will be more clearly drawn.

There are roughly 1,600 two-year colleges in the United States ("About Community Colleges") and I can't pretend to speak for all of them or even some. Each is different though, doubtless, they share a great deal even as many are shedding the "community" from their names as they begin to offer four-year degrees.[1] So I want to look closely at my own college as an example, though I can imagine that what makes my school unique—its emphasis on transfer degrees and its lack of more applied technical programs such as welding or diesel mechanics—might render the example less than wholly apt. Still, I think the changes it's undergoing—emblematic of which is its modest branding efforts—are indicative of the much broader trends at two-year colleges across the country, pushed by such initiatives as "Achieving the Dream" and "Complete College America."

What this means is that the new mission of the two-year college is at odds with both what English faculty have been trained in and what they thought they were signing up for. Though I completed my doctoral work nearly two decades ago, tales from current graduate students suggest that not much has changed in the graduate-school universe. If anything, with a shrinking elite (tenure-track faculty lines at prestigious schools), there seems to be an even greater pressure felt within graduate programs to train students for, and place students in, such elite positions. For example, in response to a query I posted on WPA-L in March 2014, I received 13 responses, and not one respondent indicated that a career in a two-year college was encouraged in their graduate programs; none indicated any graduate-school preparation; and most suggested that a desire to work at a two-year college was actively discouraged or even seen as shameful. "My university's mission is to place PhD students into solid and reputable English/writing and rhetoric departments on tenure tracks. That is the mantra, and barely a week goes by that it isn't mentioned," writes one respondent, a current PhD student at a major research university. Another then-PhD student concurs:

> In my doctoral program, I have never received any encouragement to consider a two-year college career. It is never even on the map in discussions of the kinds of "nontraditional" careers we might pursue in an ever-shrinking job market, and there is no coursework or training or information sessions available about what it means to teach in these settings. At the university I attend, I think faculty are primarily invested in working with students who will go on to make an impact in the discipline through their research, and I don't think community colleges are viewed as places where graduate students can go on to make that kind of impact. (Anonymous)

The graduate school system is like an engine that once running can't quite stop but diesels along: programs in composition and rhetoric, and in English studies in general, churn out graduates who are unprepared for positions at half of the colleges in the United States, that is, two-year colleges, while the number of tenure-track jobs at four-year colleges and universities dwindle (see "Report"). To say that such programs have a responsibility to offer viable training may be too much—there's still some who wish to argue that the transformative education one gains in a graduate program is an end to itself[2]—but it's not too much to say that students who figure out the missions and thus the needs of the two-year college, perhaps even in spite of her/his program's best efforts, will have a leg up on the competition. And it's not too much to say that hiring committees, deans, college vice-presidents and college presidents won't care a hoot about a student's transformative experience if that transformation doesn't translate to the college's mission, which is defined more and more in economic terms (Malenczyk and Rosenberg, this volume).

So what is the two-year college mission and where does it come from? Histories of two-year colleges tell different stories—and this is not the place to go into them. But in the past, two-year colleges were seen as holding grounds for students who were not quite ready for the prime time of universities. These "junior colleges" were designed to provide terminal education, not transfer, though students' desires reshaped the missions of junior colleges toward access to all of higher education (see Frye). So while these junior colleges were purportedly a training ground to keep undesirables out of higher education and prepare them for the workforce, they failed. On the other hand, the modern community college movement, whose beginning is often located in the liberal 1960s, purportedly was meant to democratize education, much like the GI Bill after World War II: by providing cheap and ready access to higher education for the masses, social and economic stratification could be eroded. There's some argument now that a half-century of this effort has failed and, in fact, has leant itself to an even greater stratification. Ann Larson, citing Peter Sacks, an education researcher, notes in *Inside Higher Ed* that "the chance that a low-income child will earn a bachelor's degree is no higher today than it was in 1970, a grave contradiction in the meritocratic narrative of the education gospel." She adds, "This is a position much at odds with the official designation of two-year colleges as democratic ports of entry to the middle class" (also see Simmons).

It's not my place to take a stand in such a debate. Besides, I think the argument is irrelevant; democratization is no longer the aim if it ever was. Contemporary two-year colleges (and here I'm including all colleges that have roots as a two-year college and continue to maintain the open-admissions policies that mark such colleges) have now a new mission, whether that is articulated in mission statements or not, whether that is openly acknowledged by administration or not, and whether faculty know anything about it or not. And that mission is to serve a neoliberal vision of an economic order in which ideas like democracy and transformation and enrichment have no value because they have no meaning as part of the language (Kroll; Rose and Dustin; Davies). Here is what Dan Lundquist, vice president for marketing and enrollment management at the Sage Colleges in New York, writes in the *Chronicle of Higher Education*:

> The future of higher education is important—and unknown—and it will be significantly affected by environmental factors beyond the control of academe. But it can be significantly influenced by leadership from within academe . . . on the local level, active, experience-guided, and *market-sensitive* tactics can yield positive results and make institutions stronger with no sacrifice of integrity or dignity. (Emphasis added)

I don't want to make too much of the "market-sensitive" tactics Lundquist mentions, though he goes on to say that the liberal arts suffer "a lack of awareness, understanding, and appreciation in the market," where *the market* is the final arbiter. From here, it's not too far a leap to a comment Arne Duncan, then Secretary of Education, offered:

> We need more graduates with high-quality degrees and 21st-century knowledge and skills—not more graduates with meaningless paper credentials. And today, several states, like Colorado, West Virginia, and Kentucky, are doing a better job than others of making progress toward their portion of the 2020 goal, of having America regain its place as the *best-educated workforce* in the world. ("Remarks," emphasis added)

In fact, "education" has no meaning if it is not a synonym or direct pre-requisite for "job/career training"[3] that builds the workforce. In contrast to the generic "mission" of two-year colleges, which the American Association of Community Colleges presents as "to provide education for individuals, many of whom are adults, in its service region" ("About Community"), the new two-year college mission is oriented not to individuals but to "success" in neoliberal terms: job placement and direct transfer, both in service of the "21st-century knowledge economy" and America's "competitiveness," as Education Secretary Arne Duncan's recent remarks make clear ("Linchpin," "Remarks").[4] Achieving the Dream, the highly influential "non-governmental reform movement," funded in part by the Gates and Lumina Foundations, is based on this belief:

> Community colleges remain the nation's gateways to good jobs for millions of students who dream of a better tomorrow . . . Those without an education will be unable to compete in a national landscape that more than ever before demands high-level job skills. ("About Us.")

While one might argue that this new vision ultimately serves the individual because it serves her/him economically, note that the individual, so to speak, is no longer defined in classical, romantic, or even democratic terms but is but a piece in an economic game whose benefit can only be measured in economic terms. In short, the "individual" is defined economically. The value of this is that it can be justified and explained to a state legislature's budget committee; more importantly, it can be sold to corporate and foundation heads; anything else cannot.

How This Looks on the Ground

The number one complaint I've heard among two-year college faculty is workload. Most full-time faculty teach a 5-5 load. Even with lower caps for writing courses than for lecture-based courses, that's a lot of papers to read, a lot of classes to teach, and a lot of students to manage. On top of that, there's the nagging sense that one should maintain currency in the field—it's tough to let training in one's specialty, gained through rugged years in a competitive PhD program, go to seed, though in fact that's what many two-year college faculty with doctorates do. Add to the teaching load committee work and departmental responsibilities and we can see why research by two-year college faculty is under-represented in the discipline: Who has time or energy for research and publication, especially when such research and publication not only is unrewarded but often arouses the enmity of one's colleagues?[5]

Against that daily grind, most faculty, when they look up, see a college that is changing before their very eyes. It's not too much of a stretch to say that every two-year college in America is, has, or soon will be revising their developmental-writing program under pressure from exterior forces, either explicit ("Achieving the Dream," state legislative mandates) or implicit (cultural awareness of completion rates and other data from programs at other schools). And the days when "academic freedom" meant one could design and teach one's classes as an island unto oneself, if not past already, are certainly under pressure to be so, as "success" is measured more via "big data" and "data analytics" and less by student evaluations. For example, my college is an Achieving the Dream college and as part of that we have adopted "evidence-based" reform where "evidence" is defined empirically (see "About Us," Achieving the Dream). And with writing being radically redefined by ever-changing technologies and success being measured in terms of job or transfer readiness comes mounting pressure to redesign writing courses to tap into that energy, usually at the expense of a traditional humanities-based writing course, to say nothing of a belletristic writing course. The humanities, literature—for the most part, these are irrelevant.[6]

So when a faculty member with a 5-5 load looks up, she sees a college moving in a direction she could not have anticipated when she studied Foucault or Flannery O'Conner or Feminist rhetoric or whatever formed the core of her graduate program. And she may feel some dismay and either resign herself to irrelevancy (however doggedly she may fight for her courses in literary or film studies) or immerse herself in persistence rates and learning theory and placement measures and become what some call, not without some disdain, "the new faculty-manager."[7] There is no third option. And since "irrelevancy" is not on anyone's list of preferred qualifications for new hires, and thus not an option for joining the full-time cadre, it would make sense to understand what is relevant—to wit, an example.

Currently, at my institution, Whatcom Community College (mid-sized, with 4,500 FTE, 8,000 headcount ["About the President"], and roughly a 75 percent to 25 percent split between transfer to prof-tech, though I still think of it as "little"—perhaps I am lost in the past as Simmons hints at), we are re-inventing just about everything. We are implementing multiple-measures of placement with (I hope) a goal of vastly expanded directed self-placement for our writing courses. We're piloting and revising a new accelerated-learning model to mainstream into first-year composition the majority of our students who place into our developmental writing courses. We're overhauling the curriculum of our first-year composition course with emphases on writing in new media, information literacy, technical or professional writing, and analytical writing—in short, writing that our students have to do in their other courses right now and with the acknowledgment that composition soon if not now must move beyond the tyranny of the metaphor of "the paper."[8] We're also re-envisioning our second composition courses, required of transfer-degree-seeking students, so that they more closely align with junior-level writing requirements at our neighboring university. We're trying to integrate coherent study- and reading-skills into all of our classes to meet the needs of the less-prepared students we are now admitting directly into first-year writing (having adjusted our placement process to push more students into FYC thereby reducing the misassignment rates even at the expense of lowering the overall success rates—more data analysis). And we may be developing a technical-writing certificate that we can "sell" to local employers—more "job readiness." This is just in English—the same or more is going on across our campus, especially in math.

Social planning theory offers the term "wicked problems" to indicate those that are difficult or impossible to solve because of "incomplete, contradictory, and changing requirements," and/or are the off-shoots of other, intractable problems ("Wicked"). Most of the long list of reforms I laid out above fall into this category: I don't think we'll ever finish revising our developmental writing program or finish the "new curriculum" for English 101; we'll make some headway toward completion but then other issues will arise: we'll gather new data that suggests a different way of seeing the problem, or we'll realize that our strategy actually addresses a problem that doesn't really exist but is part of some other problem. Or, just as likely, some other agenda, funded by some other outside source (think "venture philanthropy," see Parry et al.), will command our attention. What will remain the same for the foreseeable future is the new college mission.

Our College's New Mission

Against this "culture of reform," which is the polite term for it, is another set of reforms. The college is "looking outward," toward the state legislature, toward the business community, and toward the international economy. Our college president holds a doctorate in community college leadership ("About the President")—our first president to have such a degree—and she has done and continues to do a marvelous job of leading the college into 21st-century economic and political waters. As a former officer of the American Association of Community Colleges (AACC), she has her pulse on national trends and spends a great deal of her time monitoring events in our state and national capitals and at our various state boards. She leaves the running of the educational side of the college mostly to her vice president, who also manages the new administrative structure she has put in place—vice presidents, deans, division chairs, chairs—as she oversees the college's foundation, which accounts for more and more of the college's funding, and the business and marketing offices, which account for the college's public image. That public image is vitally important and, I believe, represents one prong of a two-pronged approach to growing and shaping the college, what might be called the college's new mission.

As part of that public-image development, my college has a marketing campaign built on the message "I am Whatcom" (see Figure 1), which has now progressed to the second stage focusing on "I chose Whatcom." Here, "Whatcom" is synonymous with my college's name, Whatcom Community College. (Whatcom is also the name of our county as well as the name of our oldest middle school—but we've appropriated the term.) The marketing director explained that the campaign came from the realization, in talking with people throughout the community, that nearly everyone in our service district had some connection with the college: they have attended classes themselves for credit or through community education, had children or relatives attend classes, have worked or known somebody who has worked at the college, or otherwise is invested in the college's interest (Vermillion).

Figure 1. "I Am Whatcom." Photograph by Jeffrey Klausman

Placards went up on public busses proclaiming "I am Whatcom" and featured people from the college and the community with different stories to tell, each focusing on some aspect of the college's success—academics, diversity, training, life-change. Those invited to participate in the campaign, to have their pictures and stories included as part of the campaign—and those who were not—might make for interesting study, but the image itself is what matters.

Figure 1 presents one such "I Am Whatcom" bus placard. The caption reads, "Whatcom has quietly become a national player in cybersecurity education," a nod to our computer-information systems program which regularly fields a team in national cybersecurity competitions and places well against such heavyweights as the University of Washington. Quoted is Mark Knittel, owner of a local technical services company and advisor to the Computer Information Systems program. The college, the campaign suggests, is "us" already, embedded deep in the community.

Thus there is no need to sell the college *to* the community; the college *is* the community.

This can be seen as ironic since the college's future is less and less local and more and more national, even international. The Achieving the Dream grant from the Gates Foundation and the Lumina Foundation drives our developmental-education reform. Our international program brings in big bucks each year.[9] And we answer to our state boards, our commissions, and our accreditors far more than any local agencies. While it could be argued that this is all done on behalf of the community, it's worth noting that the board of trustees, appointed by the governor, is a fair representation of the corporate and professional class in our area—business leaders and lawyers—hardly representative of the larger community. Labor, for example, is not represented and neither is the majority of the general population, the seventy percent or so without college degrees, those who are relatively "uneducated" ("WCC Board"). Consequently, we align our college to national, even international trends and not to local needs except insofar as those local needs happen to coincide economically.

What this means for faculty is that unless a faculty member can speak the language of the corporate trends, he will likely not have much of a hand in shaping how the reforms play out on the ground. And perhaps more to the point, a faculty member who is "not in the know" will not secure reassign time, leadership positions, or the kind of professional development opportunities that may enhance their institutional value. Funding to attend a conference on medieval literature, for example, is probably extremely difficult to come by for most faculty at a two-year college (unless a pool of money has been set aside and is continuously grandfathered in from budget to budget—I suspect that getting new money to do that would be a battle). But in February of 2014, my college sent eleven people, all expenses paid, to a five-day workshop on developmental education reform at Disney's Coronado Springs Resort in Orlando, Florida, literally all the way across the country—courtesy of Achieving the Dream funding. The plenary and concurrent sessions focused on such topics as "state and national policy," "building internal leadership," "systemic institutional improvement," and "strategic partnerships" ("Dream 2014"). Faculty from English who attended saw nothing like what they would see at the MLA, RSA, or CCCC.

Knowing This, Why Do I Feel So Bad?

Implicit in what I've said so far is the understanding that I'm setting up "the academy" as the discourse of the Other, in Jacques Lacan's terms, a sort of background matrix of meaning that can't ever be articulated but functions as a field of force against which one's "implicit longing for recognition" (Lee 59) is experienced as desire. In other words, we hold in our minds an image of wholeness—for example, the romantic notion of "the academy" I mentioned at the outset—towards which we orient ourselves in the often unarticulated hope of being appropriated by that wholeness. However, we never can, of course, because if you remember your Lacan (popular briefly in comp-rhet studies in the 1990s) desire can never be satisfied but is "empty" in that it's a play of signifiers—residue of the discourse. Speech (and action, symbolic as are words) moves towards wholeness but falls short of achieving it. In the passage from "The Function and Field of Speech and Language" I quote as the epigraph to this chapter (Lacan 42), we can see that a "fundamental alienation" is inherent in desire in that the speech one adopts—"academic discourse," for example, which one "must appropriate or be appropriated by," as David Bartholomae reminds us (4)—ultimately belongs to an Other: a language or a discourse system, and no discourse system can grant wholeness. Inherent in such a system, Lacan asserts, is alienation: speech "falls away" from the language that gives it birth even as that speech is cast toward that fullness of language.

An example: No one ever studies in a PhD program the field of "two-year college English faculty" whose contingencies I've laid out above. Except in educational leadership programs, one rarely studies data analytics or multiple-means of placement, though in the stark reality of the new faculty manager, one might retrain in such areas. Instead, one studies composition theory or literary analysis or in some body of literature. However, in the experience of many, these studies offer no guidance whatsoever to the realities they face as a two-year college English professor. The Modern Language Association (MLA) has acknowledged this reality with its emphasis on redesigning traditional graduate studies to prepare those earning a doctorate for careers outside the traditional academic path ("Report").

Yet as the mission of the two-year college is shifting, so is the language of the Other. Whereas originally, the Other might be envisioned as the Ivy League college, from which I am ("always already," in the parlance of the time) alienated as a two-year college faculty member; now the Other is a neoliberal "modern" two-year college driven by success defined in economic terms by empirical data. I am doubly alienated (unless I adopt the language of this new Other, in which case, I only postpone the alienation). This "falling away" from full speech—either in the form of irrelevant speech (constructed "like an other") or empty speech (reconstructed "for another")—leaves a sense of longing, of loss. For many faculty, they feel that this is not what they signed up for, not what they went to graduate school for—and yet this is what is.

What Graduate Schools and Administrators Can, Should, or Shouldn't Do

I hesitate saying that anyone should do anything but that each should explore for one's self the ethics of buying into (or being bought by) the neoliberal system that is defining the mission and thus the nature of the two-year college; until then, one cannot really say what is advisable. I can say that this would constitute an act of faith, insofar as we are talking about "full speech" whose effect is to "reorder past contingencies by conferring on them the sense of necessities to come," as Lacan says (48). That is, by "making sense" of how we have come here, via speech in discourse—the language of the Other, whether "academe" or a newer neoliberal version of that—we create for ourselves (or have created for ourselves) a sense not of reality but of "truth," the sense of "necessities to come," what "must happen" given our individual histories. But here, of course, the "truth" will not set us free but rather situate us within a discourse system.

I can also say that my college is hiring right now, as I write this, and the message from the hiring committee is that we're looking to hire someone who can lead us through these reforms. It's not enough to be a good teacher or even an excellent one—we have enough good and excellent teachers among our adjunct faculty ranks. Excellence in the classroom is a necessary but not sufficient qualification.[10] What is "sufficient" for hiring to a tenure-track position is a clear understanding of what is driving the changing shape of the two-year college mission, what national trends are defining the options for responses to those pressures, and experience and leadership in shaping the reforms. What is "sufficient" is speaking the (neoliberal) language of the Other, of having the capacity to lead reform efforts that promise quantitative evidence of success in economic terms.[10] Anything else is superfluous—nice, perhaps, but in the end, valueless.

Notes

1. Roughly half of the thirty-three community and technical colleges in my state now offer bachelor's degrees, and recently the Seattle Community College District voted to drop the word "community" from the three colleges in its district (Turnbull). This past spring, I've heard that my college is proposing an applied bachelor's degree in a computer-science-related field, according to Division Chair Meeting minutes of March 20, 2014. We'll see if we decide to keep "community" as part of our name or whether we join the wave and jettison that moniker of the past.

2. Richard Bullock writes, "To offer professional degrees that require huge investments in time, money, and effort for 'enrichment,' as I've heard some colleagues from other schools argue, seems disingenuous at best, self-deceiving at worst."

3. It would be easy to link this to competency-based education, which according to some promises to "transform higher education." For instance, here is some of what Lipscomb University measures for in-coming competencies: "active listening, organizing and planning, presentation skills and problem-solving and decision-making" (Fain). It's not hard to see that these competencies are far from a classical notion of education wherein one "reads" subjects, not demonstrates competencies.

4. I have had numerous conversations with two-year college faculty who regularly conduct and publish research and present at conferences; all of them, when asked, have mentioned the resistance they've received at one time or another from their colleagues and administration. In fact, a former TYCA National chair told me personally that she was forbidden by her college president from attending any more out-of-state conferences in spite of an earlier assurance that the college would support her leadership activities.

5. See Marc Bousquet's "Tenured Bosses and Disposable Teachers" for a discussion of how the new "managerial" faculty, "complicit" in a corporate system subsume and misrepresent critical and culture studies as "outdated" and "part of the problem" (59–60)—a foundational position for program and course design generally.

6. Bousquet: "If rhet-comp is the canary in the mine for the academy more generally, what it tells us is that the professorial jobs of the future are for an increasingly managerial faculty" (59).

7. We are not taking Kroll's challenge, to teach "critical discourse"; such an approach would require a tremendous amount of energy to defend and sell across campus and, frankly, would be a battle we'd be unlikely to win, even in my own department. Instead, a course designed around the practicality of writing in the disciplines and professions is an easy sell and not one requiring too much personal sacrifice. That it fits with Complete College America's agenda is only perhaps an uncomfortable coincidence.

8. Kathi Hiyane-Brown, WCC President, writes, "I would underscore that focused growth management in a number of areas continues to be critical as we rely more heavily on them as revenue sources to help fund the College's operating budget—such as Running Start, eLearning, and International Programs."

9. A colleague who is adjunct once asked me why he wouldn't be hired since he's such an excellent teacher and had worked at the college for so long. I said that I couldn't speak about his situation directly, but I could say that there was no reason for the college to hire an excellent adjunct faculty member into a full-time line since it already had that person's services very nearly full time at about half the cost.

10. Perhaps not ironically, as I work on this article, I am also putting together an assessment report on our piloted Accelerated Learning course, which combines developmental with college-level writing; a major part of that report is the statistical analysis of completion and success rates. My dean was especially pleased to see a Pearson correlation between placement test scores in reading and success rates of .532 for the developmental course and .497 for the college-level course, both well above the .05 level (2-tailed) needed to show significance. These data are useful since my college now emphasizes "data-based decision making" and Achieving the Dream is an "evidence-based reform" movement.

Works Cited

"About Community Colleges." *American Association of Community Colleges*. American Association of Community Colleges, n.d. Web. 24 July 2014.

"About the President." *Whatcom Community College*. Whatcom Community College, n.d. Web 22 July 2014.

"About Us." *Achieving the Dream*. Achieving the Dream Inc., n.d. 22 July 2014.

Anonymous 1. "Re: Grad Students and Two-Year College Missions." Message to the author. 1 April 2014. Email.

Bartholomae, David. "Inventing the University." *Journal of Basic Writing* 5.1 (1986): 4–23. Print.

Bousquet, Marc. "Tenured Bosses and Disposable Teachers." *The Minnesota Review* . (2003): 58–60. Print.

Bullock, Richard. "Re: Question re: Non-Tenure Track Positions in Writing Studies." WPA-L. 2 April 2014. Mailing List.

Davies, Bronwyn. "The (Im)possibility of Intellectual Work in Neoliberal Regimes." *Discourse: Studies in the Cultural Politics of Education* 26.1 (March 2005): 1–14. Print.

Division Chairs' Meeting Summary. Whatcom Community College. Kulshan Hall Conference Room 226, Bellingham, WA. 20 March 2014. PDF file.

"Dream 2014: The Achieving the Dream Annual Institute on Student Success." *Achieving the Dream*. Achieving the Dream, Inc, n.d. Web. WA. 20 July 2014.

Duncan, Arne. "The Linchpin: The New Mission of the Community Colleges." US Department of Education. 5 Sept. 2010. Web. 22 July 2014.

—. "Remarks of U.S. Department of Education Secretary Arne Duncan at the TIME Summit on Higher Education." US Department of Education. 18 October 2012. Web. 22 July 2014.

Fain, Paul. "Competencies Come to Campus." *Inside Higher Ed*. Inside Higher Ed, 22 April 2014. Web. 22 July 2014.

Frye, John H. *The Vision of the Public Junior College, 1900–1940: Professional Goals and Popular Aspirations*. Santa Barbara, CA: Praeger Publishing, 30 December 1991. Print.

Hiyane-Brown, Kathi. "2013–14 College Operating Budget, Memo to Board of Trustees." 3 July 2013. PDF file.

Kroll, Keith. "The End of the Community College English Profession." *TETYC* (December 2012): 118–129. Print.

Lacan, Jacques. "Function and Field of Speech and Language in Psychoanalysis." *Écrits: A Selection*. Trans. Alan Sheridan. NY: W.W. Norton, 1977: 30–113. Print.

Larson, Ann. "Higher Education's Big Lie." *Inside Higher Ed*. Inside Higher Ed, 3 June 2006. Web. 22 July 2014.

Lee, Jonathan Scott. *Jacques Lacan*. Amherst: U of Massachusetts P, 1990. Print.

Lundquist, Dan. "When Trying Harder Doesn't Work." *Chronicle of Higher Education*. The Chronicle of Higher Education, Dec. 2012. Web. 22 July 2014.

Parry, Marc, Kelly Field, and Beckie Supiano. "The Gates Effect." *The Chronicle of Higher Education*. The Chronicle of Higher Education, 14 July 2013. Web. 22 July 2014.

"Report of the Task Force on Doctoral Study in Modern Language and Literature 2014." *Modern Language Association*. Modern Language Association of America, 30 May 2014. Web. 22 July 2014.

Rose, Jeff, and Dan Dustin. "The Neoliberal Assault on the Public University: The Case of Recreation, Park, and Leisure Research." *Leisure Sciences* 31 (2009): 397–402. Print.

Turnbull, Lornet. "Three Seattle Colleges Dropping 'Community' From Names This Fall." *The Seattle Times*. The Seattle Times Company, 14 March 2014. Web. 22 July 2014.

Simmons, Trum. "After 40 Years, Has the Grand Experiment Failed?" *Chronicle of Higher Education*. Chronicle of Higher Education, 27 March 2009. Web. 22 July 2014.

Vermillion, Mary. Personal interview. 15 Jan. 2014.

"Wicked Problem." *Wikipedia*. n.d. Web. 22 July 2014.

"WCC Board of Trustees." *Whatcom Community College*. Whatcom Community College, n.d. Web. 22 July 2014.

6 The Pen and the Drone: Manumotive Writing Programs and the Professional Imagination at West Point

Jason Hoppe

At many colleges and universities, institutional missions can still feel somewhat far from the work of individual programs and departments, not to mention any given classroom; at the United States Military Academy (USMA), by contrast, institutional mission is ubiquitous, and almost universally regarded as critical. Curricular initiatives, support services, even individual classes often stand or fall according to the degree they are judged to correspond to West Point's sole charge:

> The United States Military Academy's mission is to educate, train, and inspire the Corps of Cadets so that each graduate is a commissioned leader of character committed to the values of Duty, Honor, Country and prepared for a career of professional excellence and service to the nation as an officer in the United States Army.

Even this one brief sentence suggests what is at stake in its interpretation: a perpetual tug of war between what it means to "educate" and "train," to foster academic pursuits and heed martial imperatives—a struggle which the Academy itself perhaps rather incongruously understands as the diplomatic coexistence of "Athens" and "Sparta" (Betros 123-27, 155-61, 225-38, 301-07). To attain their bachelor's degrees, all cadets complete an extraordinarily comprehensive core curriculum in the arts, sciences, and engineering (twenty-seven courses); yet West Point has always been first and foremost beholden to military needs, and every one of its graduates goes directly into the armed forces. Ergo not simply "service to the nation" but "service to the nation as an officer in the United States Army" (Bugle Notes).[1]

Singular as they might seem, I would argue that the intricacies of its mission actually *diminish* the distance between West Point and other colleges and universities in our day: the longstanding rivalry between Athens and Sparta anticipates similar tensions between academic and commercial interests that have recently made their way to the forefront of other campuses. As deftly chronicled by scholars such as Marc Bousquet (*How the University Works*), Andrew Delbanco (*College: What It Was, Is, and Should Be*), and Benjamin Ginsberg (*The Fall of the Faculty*), the battles these tensions have triggered at civilian institutions seem increasingly lopsided. In fact, tellingly dystopian versions of the predicament higher education faces are becoming all the more prevalent: they herald a demise in which the school essentially conforms to corporatized discourses and values, to market-driven demands and managerial whims; on this account, research and pedagogy risk compromise beyond repair, being crushed under the weight of the bottom-line and other outside interests. No more universities, as the art historian Max Haiven and others allege, just "edu-factories."

Whatever their accuracy, images of "edu-factories" perfectly illustrate the alarm and cynicism that trends in higher education today evoke not only in many scholars and teachers but also in countless students, administrators, and alumni (Klausman, Malenczyk and Rosenberg, this volume). To some readers, few things will conjure the dystopian world of the "edu-factory" quite like a military academy (Fleming). And West Point is not without its problems: here too there are legitimate fears that the drone—shorthand for the specters of corporatization, mechanization, and slapdash technologization that trouble higher education today—threatens to displace hard-won and humane ways of learning and teaching.[2] One could surely ask, in the classic adage to which my title alludes—is the pen really mightier than the sword or, as it rather ought to be put in our day, the drone? At West Point, of all places?

Successively exploring the nature of a couple major writing initiatives we have enacted, the institutional complexities they negotiate, and more briefly, the wider implications of our experience, this chapter grapples directly with these questions. The answers it offers may well prove surprising; by and large they are encouraging. As the founding Director of our Writing Fellows Program and the Writing Center it now supports, I have asked our cadets to cultivate a "professional imagination." At first glance, this term likely seems less oxymoronic today than it has in many decades, given the ubiquity of popular literature on nurturing creativity in business, science, and industry as well as prominent internet archives like Big Think. At West Point, the term foregrounds how the writing initiatives we have designed aim to synthesize ostensibly opposed interests and perspectives in a holistic course of intellectual development—not only the academic and military but also the pedagogical and managerial as well as the humanistic and vocational or, indeed, the imaginative and professional. What makes the syntheses this chapter depicts unusual is that they take place on resolutely scholarly grounds: the story I have to tell is one in which the sustained, variegated, imaginative study of writing—in the grand, imperiled tradition of the liberal arts college with which West Point is allied—pushes back against more narrowly instrumental and nearsighted curricular alternatives (Alberts; Baker, Baldwin, and Makker). Finding a career in our case means first finding oneself holistically as a writer and communicator, identities not exclusive to any one profession but essential to all.

By privileging intellectual development as professional advancement, the initiatives I describe seek to supervene the drone by appropriating its supposed strengths—chief among them the efficient production of more precise vocational competencies—within a markedly academic environment. In short, the pen as a sort of innovative throwback. The idea is that by patiently working toward less familiar, more varied understandings of critical thinking and writing, West Pointers will better comprehend and appreciate the diverse ways of knowing and communicating they are likely to meet with in the intersecting careers they pursue, in the army and beyond.[3] Moreover, this multiperspectival study will better prepare them for those careers, over the long run, than would overhasty specialized instruction as undergraduates. It is in this sense, at last, that the pens our Writing Fellows take up are "manumotive": slower, broader, hand-powered engines of student progress nonetheless more expansive and potentially more effective than the drones that would supplant them.[4] Yet, at the same time, this figure—the manumotive—serves as a constant reminder that we must consciously labor to preserve this practice amid conditions that sometimes threaten it, that we must stand up for the learning process, for imaginative inquiry, and for the careful craft they demand.

Values and Operations

At its most basic level, this chapter discusses West Point's belated establishment of a rather conventional academic operation, a student-led Writing Center, within the elastic framework of an enterprise that is quite unconventional, notwithstanding its prosaic name—the Writing Fellows Program. Originally based in the Department of English and Philosophy (2012-2016), this program enables select students majoring across the disciplines at USMA not only to empower their fellow writers across the corps of cadets—primarily by offering individual consultations at the Writing Center—but also to build a scholarly community by virtue of the progressive and cohesive course of study they undertake in academic argument, the shape of writing within their own major fields, college pedagogy, professional communication, personal narrative, and public rhetorics.[5] This communal study—the benefits of which of course ultimately circle back to the consultations and workshops conducted at the Writing Center—is supported by experienced civilian and military faculty with whom Writing Fellows formally engage in individual mentorships and other forms of serious scholarly collaboration, including making presentations at academic conferences, drafting essays for peer-reviewed journals and other publications, and holding discussions with other writers at peer institutions and myriad professional venues.

Growing each of these initiatives—the larger Writing Fellows Program (established in August 2012) and the Writing Center it facilitates (opened in September 2013)—has depended upon disciplined execution of our own strategic plan. Step by step, this still-evolving plan ties the expansion of these endeavors to the increasing engagement of other members of the USMA community, including faculty across academic departments, librarians, the registrar, and other offices devoted to student learning at the Academy. The plan is an imposing one in its fundamentals alone: developing wholly new academic courses, securing an array of faculty mentors, recruiting and retaining elite Fellows, coordinating their peer-to-peer training with existing academic services, designing multiple research agendas to assess the initial results of their work and our own, and effectively communicating our own mission to everyone from first-year cadets to top administrators. All of these efforts have involved immense labor, yet executed in tandem they have also made it possible for us to gain firm footing for these projects in short order, increasing exponentially the number of "stakeholders" invested in their success (DelliCarpini, Hansen this volume).

But in the beginning, August 2012, things seemed considerably less grand. There were limited resources and less time: I only arrived at the Academy earlier that summer, hired to teach three to four classes per semester and direct what would become the Writing Fellows Program and Writing Center.[6] I immediately began to work closely with three colleagues thoroughly versed in the ways of West Point: my department head (Colonel Scott Krawczyk), a senior professor charged with guiding my progress (Colonel John Nelson), and another senior professor coordinating the first-semester composition course, EN101, required of all cadets (Lieutenant Colonel Peter Molin). Together, we did our best to simply lay the groundwork for growth, pinpointing core values and setting into motion what operations we could to realize them. Our emphasis fell jointly on research, teaching, and mentoring, all matters congruent with the Academy's storied focus on leader development. We designed an abbreviated practicum to pilot the program and persuaded six third-year cadets who had excelled in writing-intensive courses to give it a shot. Though inevitably less robust than the full-on gateway seminar that would be planned a year later—notably, with more time—the periodic meetings this practicum required nonetheless acquainted our inaugural Writing Fellows with several different approaches to academic argument, a smattering of landmark essays and recent debates in composition studies, and basic principles of peer consulting. In the lattermost area, our efforts were buttressed by the Fellows' prior completion of a more general peer-to-peer training course already in place on campus, run by USMA's Center for Enhanced Performance (a generalized student support service) and certified by the College Reading and Language Association.

Armed with this knowledge and advice they received from individual faculty mentors, the Fellows carried out their primary missions of teaching and mentoring small populations of first-year students ("plebes" in the West Point parlance) in designated sections of EN101 that were taught, in turn, by their own mentors. The restricted scope of our operations was born of necessity, but it also had the significant advantage of allowing us to assess more completely the results of the individual tutoring sessions and occasional class workshops Fellows would lead. By the end of the semester, we had modest evidence of diminished failure rates among the fifty or so plebes with whom Fellows worked relative to the thousand cadets in other EN101 sections who were not eligible for our pilot program—doubly significant in that most of the eligible students had been identified as "at-risk" writers on the basis of admissions information. Combining this evidence with numerous anecdotal accounts of the Fellows' helpfulness, we relayed news of our fledgling successes to the Dean of the Academy (Brigadier General Timothy Trainor), who expressly recognized our efforts at the conclusion of the fall term—a crucial step in legitimating them. Yet equally important for our momentum was the continuing "buy-in" of the cadets we had named Writing Fellows and brought together as a group despite their very different backgrounds, majors, and interests. Given their supreme commitment, like that of their school, to leader development, we needed to present these cadets with greater opportunities for the spring: our solution was to circle back to research and, indeed, the professional imagination, by urging the Fellows to return to the brief reflective and analytical essays they had authored for the practicum and expansively rework this writing for an academic conference.[7]

Perhaps the driving factor of this decision was a set of conditions unique to service academies: cadets may not receive any additional wage for their work beyond the regular stipend they collect on account of their military commitment. Unlike other colleges and universities, then, where students can be paid for the tutoring they do, we reward our cadets solely with academic credit. By policy, cadets who formally consult with their peers under the auspices of our Writing Fellows Program (and now the Writing Center) must be enrolled in one of our multipurpose academic courses, which hold them accountable for the quality of their work while also reinforcing the synthesis at the heart of our initiatives: high performance—a high grade in these courses—demands that Fellows not simply acquit professional duties but imaginatively explore their nuances. Thus even ostensibly run-of-the-mill peer consulting sessions, for instance, often involve further reflection and further written work. In the case of our second semester, though, this academic imperative took shape not as a for-credit course (which we could not procure in time, much less staff) but rather as the professional opportunity represented in a scholarly conference held nearby at the University of Connecticut. The panel that I and four of the inaugural Fellows organized explored how the pervasive hierarchies and strident senses of individualism at USMA pose unique challenges to many of the ideals so frequently, and understandably, valorized in composition studies, indeed in the very title of the conference—"Collaboration and Conversation." At bottom, the semester-long effort this endeavor required—the conception and drafting of the panel proposal, more reading in foundational scholarship, intensive revision of the papers themselves, and ultimately participation in the conference—underscored the main tenets of our program: patient, multiperspectival study in which students and faculty together conduct research that makes sense of their learning and teaching, contributes originally to high-level scholarly conversations, and above all enhances the resources on hand to all cadets for their development as writers.

During the following academic year, 2013-14, we embarked upon major operational expansion of the program in keeping with these tenets; most significantly, we established the Writing Center, linking with the library and an office of information technology to secure semi-permanent physical and digital homes for the peer-to-peer consultations that inaugural Writing Fellows had to schedule and execute individually.[8] Despite the inevitable restrictions in our services that were necessitated by our limited resources and personnel—constraining the numbers of appointments we could offer, when we could offer them, and to whom we could offer them—the Writing Fellows met with great success. In its initial semester, with an active staff of fifteen (including eleven new Fellows) and with consultations available only to the thousand or so plebes enrolled in EN101, the Writing Center conducted 317 sessions; impressively, forty-five percent of all clients visited more than once, and ninety-nine percent indicated they would recommend the Writing Center to others. To support and standardize our budding operations, though, we also had to remedy other shortcomings of the preceding year. We dedicated ourselves to developing a more vigorous academic experience for the Writing Fellows, beginning with the three-credit hour gateway seminar I led ("Writing Process and Pedagogy"), but also continuing on in the spring with a follow-on one-credit course and conference opportunity as well as in the early summer with a two-week extra-curricular seminar ("Writing Today"). Along with the stability augured in a regular Writing Center, this more comprehensive, carefully sequenced course of study was meant both to sustain scholarly and professional growth in our Writing Fellows and, just as importantly, to cultivate greater intellectual community among them (Efthymiou and Fitzgerald, this volume).

While not every Writing Fellow participated in every aspect of the program (an impossibility given their crammed schedules and teeming responsibilities), the range and interconnectedness of the opportunities we designed was meant to serve multiple purposes and speak to multiple audiences—to make the case for the coherence and power of our initiatives to the Writing Fellows themselves as well as to other members of the institution. For instance, like the practicum it supplanted, "Writing Process and Pedagogy" stood out for its multifacetedness: seminar-style examinations of contemporary scholarship in college composition and pedagogy, individual mentorships with faculty experienced in the teaching of college writing, and active peer consultations with fellow cadets in the Writing Center. The culminating scholarly production of this seminar sprang from each of these activities: Writing Fellows collectively authored a pamphlet titled "Tips for the TEE" that sought to prepare plebes to excel on their much-dreaded "term-end examinations" (TEEs). The twenty-page text opened with engaging personal essays in which Writing Fellows reflected on their own TEE experiences and continued with pithy primers on planning for timed writing events and completing them successfully—knowing suggestions on how to pace oneself and condense the distinct stages of the writing process to suit this peculiar writing situation. Distributed to the thousand students then enrolled in EN101, circulated among faculty in other departments and academic support services, and kept prominently on file in the Writing Center, this publication served a host of objectives: Writing Fellows sharpened what they had learned about writing over the semester and meaningfully reworked it for a concrete pedagogical purpose; plebes walked away with a handbook that outlined, crucially in their own idiom, tactics for producing good writing under pressure, a resource they could draw on in any number of stressful writing situations to come; and other faculty not yet involved in our initiatives gained a greater awareness of what the Writing Fellows Program might mean for their own classrooms.

Subsequent to this project, four of the new Writing Fellows chose (like their predecessors) to fashion a panel relevant to yet another spring academic conference. Again connecting their own experiences to landmark scholarship in the field, their papers dealt with how students variously struggle to find their authorial voices: one cadet endorsed constructive forms of feedback to erode the confusion and debilitating self-criticism first-year college writers often experience, another cadet combated the negative effects of cadets' obsession over their grades by illuminating ways to demystify faculty assessment and link it to students' own compositional processes, and two more cadets advocated for a revisionary understanding of the importance of oral debate in organizing student writing and investigated (in the context of the prior year's iteration of EN101) the implications of assigning struggling or basic writers into "mainstream" composition courses or distinct "at-risk" sections. As a group, these papers interrogated specific institutional concerns only in the context of wider research agendas; they came to courses of action only through sustained intellection, thereby marking their authors as students genuinely and prudently engaged in their own educations, exemplary leaders in the mold of the West Point mission.

Yet probably the most compelling innovation of the Writing Fellows Program's second year—possibly the best example of what the "professional imagination" can be—emerged in the form of "Writing Today," a transformational academic course that I co-directed with another departmental colleague, Major Paul de León (and in subsequent years with Lieutenant Colonel Sean Cleveland). In distinction to the painstakingly "gradual" gains of our gateway seminar, "Writing Today" can be characterized as "transformational" by virtue of its greater concentration (it spanned just two weeks) and its even greater synthesis of diverse prerogatives. After first taking part in structured dialogues about their own writing and their most pressing concerns for the development of writing skills at USMA, six cadets set out with us to Washington DC to complete a tripartite study: discussing contemporary ideas about academic writing and pedagogy with other scholars (at Georgetown, Johns Hopkins, the Naval Academy, and the Council of Graduate Schools); surveying the significance of writing in various professions, often concerned with political or military matters (we have met with congressional representatives, senior staff in the White House, several NPR and Voice of America journalists, Smithsonian curators, and assorted members of the security community, including Pentagon speechwriters and high-ranking intelligence analysts); and, ultimately, exploring the cathartic value of personal narrative to soldiers with the Veterans Writing Project. In working their way through these diverse experiences—sometimes congruous, sometimes not—cadets wrestled firsthand with principles of effective writing in a wide range of rhetorical situations: in four successive days, for instance, they weighed—and occasionally wrote out for themselves—the different meanings concision, clarity, and writer bias take on in journalistic broadcasts, college essays, talking points and analytic reports for National Security Council meetings, daily briefs for the President, and public speeches for the Army's Chief of Staff. Again, to emphasize: the distinctive contribution of this course lies not in its depth but rather its paradoxical combination of compression and breadth. If it cannot (on account of its brevity) enable cadets to master more complex ways of knowing and writing, the many intersecting perspectives that "Writing Today" brings into focus nevertheless nurture in its participants the profound curiosity at the root of all imaginative and, indeed, all professional endeavors. Simply exposing cadets to these worlds—not prematurely immersing them—differently whets their appetites for further study while also engendering in them respectful appreciation for paths they themselves might not take but that they will almost certainly encounter in their careers as conscientious officers and citizens.

"Writing Today" is probably the most eminently marketable representation there is of the worth of the Writing Fellows Program, and for an institution famously concerned with leader development and vocational readiness, it is perhaps the most fitting. Probing "the role of writing at West Point, how military leaders can communicate effectively in today's complex and rapidly changing environments, and the uses writing will have in the Army and worlds of tomorrow," as we put it in our promotional flyer, is a fairly enthralling undertaking at a military academy. And yet, in its execution, in all the advance researching, sharp questioning, and serious writing participants were asked to undertake, "Writing Today" harkens just as strongly to the value of the predominantly academic approach we have emphasized in building the Writing Fellows Program and Writing Center as a whole—and the value of that approach to our institution. But of course communicating and sustaining that value is another story. In practice, it has meant very carefully aligning our program with stated institutional priorities as well as calibrating it to meet the particular challenges that in some way impact every academic enterprise at the Academy, especially new ones (DeRouen, this volume).

Priorities and Challenges

On one level, the unique institutional priorities at West Point are crystal clear, succinctly articulated in the mission statement with which this chapter began. Yet that one grand sentence is of course only the tip of the institutional mission iceberg, only the most visible of the myriad related expressions that, nested within one another, shape programming at the Academy, just as at other colleges and universities. In addition to the omnipresent mission priorities that influence West Point from the outside—most prominently the needs of the "Big Army"—there are many more specific guidelines issued within its walls according to the strict hierarchies of the place: from the Superintendent (a lieutenant general akin to a university president) on down to the Commandant and Dean (brigadier generals who oversee military and academic domains, respectively) and then to standing committees, department heads, and so on.

From the perspective of program development, the pure density of this structure is at once dauntingly byzantine and yet surprisingly admissive of deft maneuvering. Program development is, in a nutshell, initially a matter of smart rhetoric. This is not to be cynical: to initiate—indeed even now to sustain—the Writing Fellows Program and Writing Center we had to figure out where and how our rationales for them were in fact already laid out for us in the foundations of our institution. Practically speaking, we were not so much *adding* something new to the Academy as *fulfilling* its own existing objectives. In this regard, the most relevant statements of institutional mission, for us, were not the most grand; instead, we have drawn what we need from two more detailed texts, the "West Point Leader Development System" (WPLDS) and "Academic Program Goals" (APG). Here, for instance, are three of the most pertinent student learning outcomes specified in the WPLDS, along with brief excerpts from the fuller explications of their meaning:

> *Develop, lead, and inspire.* Graduates develop, lead, and inspire people and facilitate these abilities in others . . . They train, motivate, and influence others to achieve common goals, critical tasks, and organizational objectives with purpose and commitment, while treating them with dignity and respect.
>
> *Think critically and creatively.* Graduates explore issues, ideas, and events in-depth as well as apply standard practices, innovative thinking, prudent risk-taking, and mental agility . . . They engage both well-defined and ambiguous situations using methodical and reflective thinking as well as rapid analysis . . . They are open-minded and employ their knowledge and skills to make meaningful connections and distinctions across different experiences, concepts, perspectives, and cultures. When appropriate, graduates transform ideas or solutions into entirely new forms by diverging from conventional ways of thinking or reimagining established ideas, ways of thinking, or solutions.
>
> *Communicate and interact effectively.* Graduates communicate clearly, candidly, and confidently in diverse settings using suitable means. They project professionalism and maintain proper bearing. They employ active listening and critical reading to

ensure understanding and demonstrate effective interpersonal and negotiation skills. Graduates convey clear and concise information using oral, written and non-verbal means and employ appropriate technology to accomplish the mission and enhance professional relationships . . . ("West Point Leader Development System Outcomes")

These passages represent only a small selection of the institutional prose that guides leader development at West Point. Yet they should make plain to almost any reader how closely the writing programs I have described align with the USMA mission. And, to be frank, drawing such obvious connections is just what we have done in pressing forward with our initiatives: in correspondence, meeting presentations and proposals, manuals of policies and procedures, and indeed our own mission statements, we have forcefully articulated our precepts and goals—quite authentically—in language which mirrors that already ratified by our institution.

Yet such robust articulations of institutional priorities also hint at the foremost challenges to programming at West Point, particularly to ambitious ventures like ours. In short, the density of institutional mission at USMA can also be understood as compensation for the definite gaps it experiences in that other IM—*institutional memory*. These gaps result from the persistent upheaval of West Point's most vital personnel, faculty as well as administrators. In part, the upheaval stems from "Big Army" policies: almost all servicemen and women, including the far majority of those officers who teach at USMA, regularly rotate assignments so as to accrue varieties of experiences that prepare them for promotion. The constant flux these rotations produce is all the more pronounced at West Point, however, given its distinctive faculty model—what the institution refers to as its "blend of excellence." This model results in a faculty body comprised of civilian doctoral faculty (about twenty percent) and active duty military officers (nearly eighty percent), around a third of whom hold terminal degrees and nearly three-quarters of whom only teach at West Point for two- or three-year terms before returning to other military duties ("USMA Faculty Manual" 11-13).[9] This deliberate structural flux, further intensified by assorted movements or mandatory retirements of senior military faculty and administrators as well as by the number of civilian faculty who also hold temporary appointments, means that each USMA class of cadets will over the course of their four years at the Academy witness an *approximately seventy-five percent turn-*

over in the faculty who teach and mentor them. This astounding fact of life at the Academy obviously places enormous stress on its teaching and programming—not to mention efforts to sustain anything new.

Such institutional turnover, moreover, is really only a more specific instantiation of the larger challenge of *time*. The short-term appointments of most West Point faculty mean that significant time is spent on either end of the stint just getting up to speed with unfamiliar conventions and duties or getting ready for the next job, whether academic or military. In between, faculty rocket back and forth among the five domains USMA uses to assess their performance—scholarship, teaching, service, and faculty and cadet development. Such a busied atmosphere has sternly tested—and will continue to test—the mission of the Writing Fellows Program. It badly exaggerates, for instance, the challenges that Writing Centers everywhere face in effectively communicating their most basic principles—that tutors are not editors or proofreaders or teaching assistants but rather more akin to consultants, that they do not "fix" specific papers so much as focus on them to get at more general points about effective writing and the writing process, and so forth. To head off misunderstandings, we have sought to meet these communicative challenges iteratively and variously, in websites, handouts, posters, meetings, and even campus news articles. But there has also been another such challenge that hits even closer to home—in the individual faculty mentoring that comprises an integral part of our Writing Fellows' experience. To control the increasing diffusion of these partnerships with our growing numbers—in the gateway seminar every Writing Fellow gets an individual faculty mentor, and in our third year (2014-15) we moved to more than two dozen new Fellows—we have had to be even more exact about what mentorship means: we now stipulate, in one succinct page, set numbers of individual meetings and classroom visits as well as the kinds of discussion they ought to generate. If such expression seems part and parcel of the "Big Army" approach—quantify everything—it is nonetheless shrewdly so: articulating these standards precisely has helped us to secure greater compliance with the letter of the program and often the spirit, as we persuade mentor and mentee alike of its mutual benefits; regardless, the precision better positions us to gauge the performance of our mentors and plan future assignments accordingly.

But the issue of time is still most acute on the ground floor, where it affects the cadets themselves: the challenge of "cadet time" at USMA has been around for generations now and it has only gotten worse in the last decade (Betros 64, 152-55). In essence, West Point cadets are relentlessly buffeted by competing concerns—military, academic, social, and personal—and nearly all of these concerns, even social and personal ones, somehow necessitate obedience to the "chain of command." Most cadets enroll in five or more academic courses and anywhere from two to four physical and military training courses per semester, in addition to discharging countless other orders and obligations on a daily basis. Given these extraordinarily crowded and micromanaged schedules, it's no wonder that a recent longitudinal study found that cadets get, on average, right at *five hours of sleep per night* during the academic year, roughly two fewer hours than do peers in related studies (Miller, Shattuck, and Matsangas 1629). Cadet time, then, is surely the scarcest resource at the Academy. Any new program that wants a piece of it must therefore find ways to cut through the noise and make itself understood, amid all the drain and distraction of other legitimately compelling programs, as essential. This challenge has affected every dimension of our communications and operations: not only does it constrain how often cadets use the Writing Center, or whether they are even aware of its existence, but, more fundamentally, it shapes how many Writing Fellows we are able to recruit and, equally importantly, how many we are able to retain subsequent to their enrollment in our gateway seminar.

In environments as taxing and rich in opportunity as West Point, the allures of academic credit and professional experience, even distinctive branding (in the iconography we've begun to invent so as to identify our services and our Fellows), only go so far. The challenge of time cannot be met simply with overtly formal measures and material incentives. Instead, I would argue, it must be addressed by community building—by the forging of genuine personal connections out of shared aspirations and the varied exertions they entail, whether in the week-in, week-out efforts of the seminar room and Writing Center or in the rush of concentrated experiences like "Writing Today." This is the way, as a program, we have taken and the way we are headed still: winding toward the "professional imagination" not merely as an educational concept but as a social act and force for community.

Prospects and Perspectives

Easier said than done, one might demur: building communities is hard, often uneven work. Some of the challenges the Writing Fellows Program faces in the attempt are more trying than others; some, like the institutional turnover and time I have highlighted, can feel intractable—to the extent that they threaten the ideal at the seat of our efforts, our belief that the Academy can and must cultivate slower, broader engines of student progress. In our era there seems to be no abandoning "engines," and the figure of the manumotive reminds us of their risks: the danger is that the balance we seek tilts more toward mechanical efficiency than real community, steamrolling the patient craft and meaningful intellectual dialogues we strive to combine. It's the indefatigable notion, in old army speak, that the "next man up" will suck it up and do the job—no matter how well and no matter what it takes. No matter, say, how many hours of sleep a cadet gets or how many responsibilities a faculty mentor carries. Thus the possibility for alienation or cynicism, the chance that we edge further from community and closer to the edu-factory—that the pen comes to look, and perform, more like a drone.

It is from this vantage that the cultural critic Jonathan Crary's piercing meditations on our "non-stop life-world" are especially instructive:

> ... many institutions in the developed world have been running 24/7 for decades now. It is only recently that the elaboration, the modeling of one's personal and social identity, has been reorganized to conform to the uninterrupted operation of markets, information networks, and other systems. A 24/7 environment has the semblance of a social world, but it is actually a non-social model of machinic performance and a suspension of living that does not disclose the human cost required to sustain its effectiveness. (8-9)

In short, the "24/7 environment" erodes vital differences between the human and the machine, what is essential versus what is disposable. At the core of Crary's polemic is the idea that sleep is the ever more harried yet so far ineradicable representative of such distinctions, and the final bulwark against their collapse. Notably, Crary places the military at the vanguard of the cultural tides he deplores; of course sleep is also under duress at West Point. From one crude angle, absorbing initiatives like the Writing Fellows Program and Writing Center only intensify this duress, regardless of how much they might intend the reverse—to restore, for instance, the qualities that researchers have singled out as endangered in cadets, including "decisions that involve creative solutions, dynamic replanning, managing competing demands, and complex communication" (Miller, Shattuck, and Matsangas 1629). In this tangled reality, even the well-intentioned community building we have pursued hazards something less sanguine: it demands of all its participants—cadets as well as faculty—not just professional but also much affective labor, as we consolidate our actions into perpetually more consummate behaviors, identities, and indeed, forms of community. Promoting the "professional imagination," from this perspective, calls to mind the latent perniciousness that Miya Tokumitsu, anticipating Crary, locates in Do What You Love (DWYL) mantras, which on her critique both enable and obscure exploitation, nudging us to forget that "emotionally satisfying work is still work."

What, then, is to be done? The question of our prospects given these difficult perspectives is a hard one. There is no perfect solution to the dilemmas of time and labor that, here as elsewhere in higher education, have burdened the writing initiatives we have brought forward as well as the intellectual community we have sought to grow around them. What we have done in the Writing Fellows Program, though, is continue to bear out the effectiveness of our endeavors and deliberately hinge their expansion on the procurement of greater resources: making more classes and subjects eligible for consultations at the Writing Center, for instance, has led us to require more faculty mentors engaged from multiple departments and to talk more seriously about writing across the curriculum. In fact, over the past eighteen months, the success of these initiatives and the vision of the Dean and department heads who have supported them has fueled the design of a cross-curricular writing program—set to begin initial operations in the fall of 2016—that promises to transform the culture of writing education across the Academy. The success of the Writing Center, meanwhile, has recently led to its endowment by Mr. William D. Mounger (Class of 1948), for whom it is now named. Such steps are crucial to ensuring the long-term viability and growth of these programs—and the people at their core. The communities we build, then, must be carefully and confidently planned, and they are no less communities for that, for their requirements being defended every step of the way in a zero-sum, institutional world. This work is not easy—balancing teaching, mentoring, assessment, scholarship, and, above all, negotiation and argument—but then again, it's work.

The bottom line, though, is that it is work in an age when the "bureaucratization of the imaginative," as Kenneth Burke put it many decades ago, is at warp speed (225-29). Though Burke is better remembered today, at least in composition circles, for his evocative characterization of intellectual work as parlor discussion, his earlier thought remains just as relevant. In one common way of speaking now, "getting perspective" effectively means "getting with the program," that is, accepting emerging realities as inevitable by resigning oneself to the notion that they are not, as it were, "that big of a deal in the grand scheme of things." Except that they are: the developments that Crary or Tokumitsu (or Burke, many years ago) aim to critique are just that—a big deal, the grand scheme of things. This chapter, accordingly, has spoken about perspective and our prospects in an opposite way—of counterintuitive action and collective empowerment. The multiperspectival study that Cadet Writing Fellows carry out means something more like "questioning the program": they take multiple, critical views of writing and teaching in the world, moving far beyond the appearances and techniques that immediately present themselves—qualities essential to officers who must navigate increasingly ambiguous situations, unfamiliar cultures, and complex problems (Barnes and Samet). It is in this regard that the perspectives they take ultimately recall the "perspective by incongruity" Burke himself proposed to combat the surging mechanization and bureaucratization of his day. For Burke, the deliberate rational work of weighing multiple, often incongruous perspectives, imbues prevailing social realities and customs with fresh interpretative possibilities (308-14). For him, as for us, the end goal is to shake up blinkered and conventional ways of seeing, living, and working—to reckon with our worlds, institutional and otherwise, as more imaginative professionals.

NOTES

The views I express here are my own and do not reflect official policies or positions of the Department of the Army, Department of Defense, or United States Government. In addition to the countless administrators, colleagues, and cadets who have contributed vitally to the growth of the USMA Writing Fellows Program and Writing Center, I thank Joe Janangelo for his keen, patient feedback on this piece and especially Chelsea Adewunmi for her insightful and inspiring conversation on the same.

1. While the USMA mission statement has in some fashion always referred to the specific outcome of officership, the nature of this reference in relation to other concerns has changed significantly over time. For instance, while the present statement (2005-) represents civic "service" exclusively in terms of military "career," its predecessor (1998–2005) understood these as entities as

distinctive and quasi-equivalent: "professional growth throughout a career as an officer in the United States Army; and a lifetime of selfless service to the nation." The history of USMA mission statements can be traced in the *Bugle Notes* pocketbooks long distributed to all cadets.

2. Exchanging "drone" for "sword" is at once historically appropriate and, for my purposes here, more conceptually accurate. In so adapting the term, I do not intend to trivialize either the actual devastation that automated weapons have wrought in recent years or the thoughtfulness and integrity of those individuals who serve honorably in a military that has systematically escalated their usage.

3. Although all West Point graduates are commissioned as second lieutenants, they receive assignments across the army's sixteen main branches and must work effectively not only within but across these branches. This is not even to touch upon the range of careers they engage after concluding their military service, which these days a quarter or more West Pointers are wont to do as soon as their initial terms of service (five years) required of them are up. Tim Kane has argued influentially that the problems the army in particular has experienced in retaining its young officers stem, in part, from a dearth of incentives for creative thinking and innovation.

4. Relevant to my intentional preservation of the ostensibly outmoded "pen" in the symbolic dyad that governs this chapter are recent neuroscientific studies that illustrate the benefits of writing by hand for children and students (James and Engelhardt; Mueller and Oppenheimer). Moreover, fast-developing haptic technologies hold the potential to reinvigorate older paradigms of learning whose supposed "outdatedness" may soon prove a thing of the past.

5. Cadets are invited to join the Writing Fellows Program chiefly on the basis of their success in writing-intensive courses; with an eye toward assembling as diverse a group as possible, we also consider their academic majors and companies (the residential groups into which they are divided, each numbering around one-hundred and twenty students). Unlike in traditional Writing Fellows programs, on the model of what Tori Haring-Smith created at Brown University, Cadet Writing Fellows are not presently embedded exclusively within specific courses.

6. In point of fact, I only defended my dissertation in American literature later that winter; the case of my hiring at USMA as an ABD, in part on the basis of my directorship of the Writing Center at Johns Hopkins (2008–2012), therefore testifies all the more strongly to the importance of fostering professional development and leadership opportunities for doctoral students.

7. For thorough accounting of the roles research may and does fill in Writing Centers, see Babcock and Thonus, *Researching the Writing Center*. The resolutely academic nature of our initiatives in general, and our specific embedding of the Writing Center within the Writing Fellows Program, aligns with Muriel Harris's emphasis of the scholarly value of Writing Centers and their

centrality to university missions ("Preparing to Sit at the Head Table") as well as with other recent advancements of these principles, for instance as recounted by Matthew Schultz ("Recalibrating an Established Writing Center").

8. Vital to this radical expansion was Lieutenant Colonel Sean Cleveland, who took up the advisory role that Colonel Nelson had filled in the program's first year on account of the latter's deployment to Afghanistan (itself a telling example of the extraordinary organizational flux described later in this chapter).

9. The majority of West Point faculty are highly-motivated mid-career officers in their thirties; in the view of the Academy, they combine significant military leadership experiences with cutting edge educations attained in the completion of master's degrees (or in some cases doctoral degrees) immediately before their arrival at USMA. The term "blend of excellence" dates from the early 1990s, when Congress pushed West Point to begin employing civilian faculty; for additional details on its meaning at the Academy today, see "Faculty Manual," 10–14.

Works Cited

Alberts, Hana R. "America's Best College: How West Point Beats the Ivy League." *Forbes*, 24 Aug. 2009. 84–86. Print.

Babcock, Rebecca Day and Terese Thonus. *Researching the Writing Center: Towards an Evidence-Based Practice*. NY: Peter Lang, 2012. Print.

Baker, Vicki L, Roger G. Baldwin and Sumedha Makker. "Where Are They Now?" *Liberal Education* 98.3 (Summer 2012): 48–53. Print.

Barnes, Julian E. "Gen. Dempsey Finds Military Lessons in Literature and a Zombie Attack." *The Wall Street Journal* 1 April 2014. Web. 14 August 2014.

Betros, Lance. *Carved from Granite: West Point Since 1902*. College Station: Texas A&M UP, 2012. Print.

Bousquet, Marc. *How the University Works: Higher Education and the Low-Wage Nation*. NY: New York UP, 2008. Print.

Burke, Kenneth. *Attitudes Toward History*. 3rd ed. Berkeley: U of California P, 1984. Print.

Crary, Jonathan. *24/7: Late Capitalism and the Ends of Sleep*. New York: Verso, 2013. Print.

Delbanco, Andrew. *College: What It Was, Is, and Should Be*. Princeton: Princeton UP, 2012. Print.

Ginsberg, Benjamin. *The Fall of the Faculty: The Rise of the All-Administrative University and Why It Matters*. NY: Oxford UP, 2011. Print.

Haiven, Max. "The Ivory Cage and the Ghosts of Academe: Labor and Struggle in the Edu-Factory." *Truth-out.org*. Truthout, 30 April 2014, Web. 4 August 2014.

Harris, Muriel. "Preparing to Sit at the Head Table: Maintaining Writing Center Viability in the Twenty-First Century." *The Writing Center Journal* 20.2 (2000): 13–22. Print.
James, Karin H. and Laura Engelhardt. "The Effects of Handwriting Experience on Functional Brain Development in Pre-Literate Children." *Trends in Neuroscience and Education* 1.1 (Dec. 2012): 32–42. Print.
Kane, Timothy. "An Army of None: Why the Pentagon is Failing to Keep Its Best and Brightest." *Foreign Policy*. The Foreign Policy Group 10 Jan. 2013. Web. 17 July 2014.
—. "Why Our Best Officers Are Leaving." *The Atlantic*. The Atlantic Monthly Group, 4 Jan. 2011. Web. 4 July 2014.
Miller, Nita Lewis, Lawrence G. Shattuck, and Panagiotis Matsangas. "Longitudinal Study of Sleep Patterns of United States Military Academy Cadets." *Sleep* 33.12 (2010): 1623–1631. Print.
Mueller, Pam A. and Daniel M. Oppenheimer. "The Pen is Mightier Than the Keyboard: Advantages of Longhand Over Laptop Note Taking." *Psychological Science* 25 (June 2014): 1158–68. Print.
Samet, Elizabeth. *Soldier's Heart: Reading Literature Through Peace and War at West Point*. NY: Farrar, Strauss, and Giroux, 2007. Print.
Schultz, Matthew. "Recalibrating an Established Writing Center: From Supplementary Service to Academic Discipline." *The Writing Lab Newsletter* 37.9–10 (May/June 2013): 1–5. Print.
"The New West Point Leader (WPLDS) Development System Outcomes." West Point, NY: 16 Jan. 2014. PDF file.
Tokumitsu, Miya. "In the Name of Love." *Jacobin* 13. Baskar Sunkara, n.d. Web. 4 July 2014.
"United States Military Academy Faculty Manual: A Blend of Excellence." West Point, NY: Dec. 2005. PDF file.
United States Military Academy. *Bugle Notes: The Handbook of the Corps*. West Point, NY: United States Military Academy, 1924. Print.

7 The BYU English Department's Future Scholars Program: Planning for a Faculty to Match the Institutional Mission

Kristine Hansen

"Consider the lilies of the field," which neither toil nor spin, and "the fowls of the air," which do not sow, reap, or gather into barns, said Jesus as he taught his disciples to trust in their heavenly father for their daily needs (Matthew 6:26-28). "Take therefore no thought for the morrow," he concluded, implying they need only have faith (Matthew 6:34). Yet, in another place, Jesus asked, "Which of you, intending to build a tower, sitteth not down first and counteth the cost, whether he have sufficient to finish it? Lest haply after he hath laid the foundation, and is not able to finish it, all that behold him begin to mock him" (Luke 14:28). This second teaching obviously stresses the importance of prior planning and might seem to contradict the first. At Brigham Young University (BYU), which is owned and operated by the Church of Jesus Christ of Latter-day Saints (also called the LDS Church or Mormon Church), professors in the English Department try to reconcile the paradox by trusting that the Lord will provide while trying also to be good stewards of the mandate and the resources given us by the church to advance the university's mission. This chapter will describe one effort to prepare future scholars in the discipline of English, some of whom might eventually return to take faculty positions in the department. Before describing this program, however, I summarize for readers the university's mission and aims, as well as its unique expectations for faculty. Next, I situate some facts about the university in a comparative, historical, and contemporary context to help the reader understand the unique challenges BYU faces as it prepares for the future. By describing how well BYU is currently doing in achieving its mission, I will show how a strong future faculty is the key to its continued success. Finally, I will describe the English Department's Future Scholars Program to show how English faculty are learning to "count the cost" and helping to provide for excellent future professors who can build on the foundation already laid.

BYU's Mission, Aims, and Honor Code

BYU adopted its institutional mission statement in 1981. Perhaps what makes this mission statement unique is the degree to which it aligns with the theology and mission of the affiliated church. It boldly declares, "All students at BYU should be taught the truths of the gospel of Jesus Christ. Any education is inadequate which does not emphasize that His is the only name given under heaven whereby mankind can be saved." The mission statement clearly depicts the university as an integral part of the church, established to "assist individuals in their quest for perfection and eternal life" by providing "a period of intensive learning in a stimulating setting where a commitment to excellence is expected and the full realization of human potential is pursued" (*Mission and Aims*). Perhaps also unique is the degree to which university administrators and faculty are expected to take the mission to heart and enact its tenets.

To support the mission statement, the university published in 1996 the much longer *Aims of a BYU Education*, which describes in some detail how students' education at this institution should be "(1) spiritually strengthening, (2) intellectually enlarging, and (3) character building, leading to (4) lifelong learning and service" (*Mission and Aims*). Faculty are strongly encouraged to plan courses and other learning activities with these aims in mind. To help new faculty get accustomed to their roles at BYU, the Faculty Center holds a seminar for new faculty every other week in the fall. Each new faculty member is assigned to choose an established faculty member as a mentor by winter, and the Faculty Center then trains the mentor in ways to help the new professor. Each May, the Faculty Center gives new faculty two weeks of intensive training, in which the mission and aims are emphasized. Finally, in an eighteen-month Faculty Development Series, each new faculty member chooses goals to focus on in teaching, research, and citizenship. For more established faculty, the Faculty Center also disseminates reports and teaching suggestions via its website to ensure that faculty don't lose sight of the aims. The 1967 words of Spencer W. Kimball, then President of the LDS Church, are often repeated to today's faculty. Kimball instructed professors that it was not expected "that all of the faculty should be categorically teaching religion constantly in their classes," but they should always strive to keep their "subject matter bathed in the light and color of the restored gospel" (qtd in Welch and Norton 54). Course and teacher evaluations ask students to rate their professors each semester on their ability to blend the lights of faith and reason in their courses. Professors who get high marks for courses that are both intellectually enlarging and spiritually strengthening are currently being interviewed by Faculty Center personnel to learn what happens in their classes.

In addition to the principles stated in the Mission and Aims documents, the university has long had a rather detailed honor code that includes behavioral and dress and grooming standards to be observed by both the students and the faculty. (About two percent of students in 2014 and two to five percent of the faculty at any given time are non-LDS, but they also agree to meet the same standards with a few allowances made to honor different religious backgrounds.) To be admitted to the university, students must agree to abide by the honor code and must be endorsed by their local ecclesiastical leader (called a bishop) as believers in the church's doctrines and in compliance with the church's moral teachings. To be hired at BYU, prospective faculty must also be endorsed by their bishop (or, if they are not LDS, by their local clergyman) as faithful members of the church, willing to comply with the honor code and contribute to the university mission. Prospective faculty must also complete an interview with one of the church's General Authorities (top-level leaders of the church). Then, to maintain continuing status at the university, both students and faculty have to be periodically endorsed by their bishops as in compliance with all expectations. As a result of these requirements, students and faculty who are less than fully committed to the teachings and behavioral standards of the sponsoring church are not likely to feel comfortable on the campus or even to desire to be there. Those who are willing to meet the standards for selection and continuance at Brigham Young University find great unity of purpose in a community of like-minded students and teachers as well as excellent support for their efforts to create the kind of university the LDS Church wants.

BYU's Profile in a Secularized Academic Landscape

It is rather unusual for a university in the twenty-first century to set standards of dress and grooming, let alone of personal behavior and religious belief and practice for students, faculty, and staff. But it is not at all unprecedented. As Marsden's *Soul of the American University* has shown, most institutions of higher education in America began as Protestant colleges, established primarily for training ministers, then expanding their curricula to include other interests and professions.[1] Marsden states, "As late as 1870 the vast majority of these colleges were remarkably evangelical. Most of them had clergymen-presidents who taught courses defending Biblicist Christianity and who encouraged periodic campus revivals" (4). Faculty and students at these colleges were expected to comply with strict rules about moral behavior and to exhibit their faith by their walk and talk, for example by enrolling in theology courses and attending services at the campus chapel on a regular basis. But by the late 1920s, most of these colleges had become secularized, as influential college presidents increasingly began to believe, as Harvard's Charles Eliot said, "A university cannot be built upon a sect" (qtd in Marsden 192). As the new president of Princeton in 1902, Woodrow Wilson declared that Princeton was "a Presbyterian college only because the Presbyterians of New Jersey were wise and progressive enough to found it." Wilson eliminated required Bible classes, later making them elective; he retained mandatory attendance at daily chapel, but halved the length of chapel services from twenty minutes to ten and allowed many unexcused absences (Axtell 330). As more American scholars agreed with the position that inquiry, particularly scientific inquiry, could thrive only if colleges were free from the burden of religious dogma and domineering ecclesiastical oversight, formerly Protestant colleges weakened ties to the churches that had founded them. One strong incentive for colleges to cut their denominational apron strings came from Andrew Carnegie, who in 1905 founded the Carnegie Foundation for the Advancement of Teaching and offered to match funds for retiring professors from colleges declaring themselves nonsectarian (Nasaw 671-72).

Drawing on the work of Marsden and Burtchaell, organizational behavior scholars Alan Wilkins and David Whetten identify four structural factors that contributed heavily to the secularization of higher education from 1870 to 1930: (1) the creation of nonsectarian moral values for education that did not require "allegiance to a particular religious tradition," values such as "free inquiry, democracy, [and] service to humankind";

(2) increased hiring of faculty for their academic expertise and ability to teach specialized subjects without regard for professors' commitment to any denomination or even to general Christian values; (3) changes in the funding of colleges (which had never received a great deal from their sponsoring churches anyway) to greater reliance on student tuition, private industry, foundations, and governments, the last of which often required colleges "to give up hiring preferences and specific religious requirements" as a matter of separating church and state; and (4) changes in boards of trustees to include fewer clergy and more alumni and leaders in business and other fields (Wilkins and Whetten 8-9).

About the same time that formerly denominational colleges were starting to secularize, BYU started to become more strongly identified with its sponsoring church. When it was established in 1875, BYU was called the Brigham Young Academy. Its founder, Brigham Young, LDS Church leader and governor of the Utah Territory, charged the academy's first principal, Karl G. Maeser, "not to teach even the alphabet or the multiplication tables without the Spirit of God" (Young qtd in Maeser 79). Nevertheless, the new academy was not then thought of as a flagship school for the church or even the predecessor of such (Wilkins and Whetten 12). It was renamed Brigham Young University in 1903, more than a quarter century after its founding. And not until 1918 did the LDS Church make a strong financial commitment to supporting it. Then in the 1930s and 1940s—when the secularization of most formerly Protestant colleges was complete—the church began to clarify and increase the extent to which it desired the university to align its mission with that of the church. In consequence, the four structural features that Wilkins and Whetten identified as responsible for secularization were reversed at BYU: (1) the church asserted its centrality by requiring students to take religion courses; (2) it required faculty to be (with few exceptions) members of the sponsoring church; (3) it increased its contribution to funding the university; and (4) its governing board became one hundred percent church leaders (13-14). As a result of this trajectory, BYU became almost—though not entirely—an anomaly in American higher education.

Today BYU is one of only nine US institutions of higher education that are both religiously affiliated and ranked in the Carnegie classification of universities as "very high" or "high" in research (Wilkins and Whetten 11).[2] These nine universities have managed to keep a religious identity despite pressures to secularize in the quest to become leading research institutions. Yet Wilkins and Whetten claim that BYU is "more closely tied to its affiliated church and more intentionally religious than any of the remaining religious universities" (5) because of its more overtly religious mission statement and goals, more demanding curricular requirements in religion, more selective faculty hiring, higher level of church funding, and a board of trustees composed solely of church leaders. It's not my purpose here to summarize their entire argument, only to note they provide persuasive evidence that BYU at this point in its history has not only bucked the century-long trend of secularization in American higher education but has, in large measure, succeeded in creating what it set out to make in the mid-1900s: a university whose students and faculty demonstrate academic excellence without compromising strong commitment to the religious values and principles of the sponsoring church.

BYU's Dual-Hybrid Mission

The church has set BYU on a course to become what Wilkins and Whetten call a "dual hybrid university," one that tries to reconcile seemingly incompatible "scripts" (21-22). There are two pairs of such scripts. One script is that for a "real university" as this has been defined in our day, largely by secular institutions; the corresponding script is that for developing strong faith and moral character as defined by the LDS Church. Yet another script was put in place when the LDS Church made a stronger financial commitment to BYU and simultaneously decreed that it would largely be an undergraduate teaching institution. Wilkins and Whetten suggest the church chose this focus because it could "influence more students at what could be argued is a relatively more vulnerable life stage than would be the case for graduate students" (27). (Doctoral programs are present at BYU, but they are few, mainly in STEM fields, and any new ones proposed must support the mission of undergraduate education.) This script from BYU's Board of Trustees dictates a primary focus on excellent teaching of thirty thousand undergraduates without high numbers of graduate students to teach lower division courses, as happens at other large research universities. However, the undergraduate teaching script is paired with a second one for producing peer-reviewed research at levels significant in both quantity and quality. These two pairs of scripts create constant challenges and tensions, particularly for faculty, as they try to be productive scholars but also excellent teachers to relatively high numbers of students, and as they balance respect for the academy's values and standards for creating knowledge with the church's call to be faithful to revealed truths. Despite the difficulty, so far the indicators of success are positive.

There is much evidence that BYU has created a university that attracts and graduates students whose intellectual strengths are matched by their spiritual development. Today more students apply for admission to BYU than there is room to accommodate because the LDS Church's membership rolls keep growing and because the Board of Trustees in 1976 capped enrollment at 30,000. Thus, the competition among students for admission ensures that each new entering class is academically a little stronger than the one that entered the previous year. Over the years, the admission standards have steadily risen to the point that in 2013 (when 49 percent of 11,603 applicants were admitted), incoming students had an average ACT score of 28.3 (about the 91st percentile), and an average high school GPA of 3.8 (Y Facts). Wilkins and Whetten claim that "the top 1,500 students in the BYU freshman class, about the size of the entire freshman class at Harvard or Stanford, look equal on paper to students at those universities in terms of intellectual ability" (31). BYU is among the top ten institutions in the nation receiving AP scores. In 2013, AP scores were reported to BYU from 4,096 high school students, who took an average of 4.5 AP tests (College Board). In 2013-14, *US News and World Report* ranked BYU first in the "most popular university" category, i.e., first in the number of accepted students who actually enroll; its retention rate of new freshmen in 2012-13 was 89 percent (Y Facts).

Not only are the students academically strong, they are also committed to LDS values and teachings, as evidenced by measures that may not be immediately understood by those outside the faith. At the time they enroll, 96 percent of new students have completed four years of studying church doctrine and history in daily courses, often held at 5:00 or 6:00 a.m. before the students start their day at high school. Eighty-four percent of new students have also completed personal development programs to demonstrate their commitment to Christian service and moral living (Wilkins and Whetten 31-33). At BYU, they take 14 credits (seven 2-credit courses) in religion—effectively a minor—in addition to all other courses required for their major, for general education, and for other minors they may choose to take. In 2013, 86 percent of the men and 13 percent of the women (53 percent of all students) had taken time away from school to serve at their own expense as full-time missionaries for the LDS Church, for periods lasting from 18 to 24 months (Y Facts).[3] Largely due to this missionary service, approximately 70 percent of graduating students are proficient in another language (Wilkins and Whetten 33). It's clear that the students are themselves "hybrids"—young people who are committed equally to high academic achievement and to their faith.[4]

Given this profile of the student body, also clear is the need for a faculty equal to the task of mentoring bright, motivated, and faithful students. What is the evidence that BYU is succeeding in maintaining a faculty to carry out its dual hybrid mission? As of 2012, BYU had 1,267 full-time faculty, about 90 percent of whom were tenured or on the tenure track (Y Facts); probably about 90 to 95 percent held terminal degrees.[5] Wilkins and Whetten show that since 1972, both the quantity and quality of faculty research at the university have increased. The number of publications from 1972 to 2012 increased more than five-fold, and the influence of BYU professors' research, as measured by citations during the same period, also rose dramatically (32). As someone who has been on the BYU faculty for 27 years, I can say that research expectations for faculty and departments keep rising and that recruiting and hiring exceptional new faculty are considered key to future improvement. However, teaching is likewise very important, and new faculty are hired for their promise in both teaching and research. Teaching and research are typically valued equally in deliberations about faculty raises, retention, and promotion. A professor whose research met expectations but whose teaching didn't could very well be terminated at third-year or sixth-year review.

While professors have been reaching new highs in research and publication, they have also created strong programs to prepare undergraduates for careers and graduate school. Several academic programs now have enviable national rankings.[6] Perhaps the best overall evidence that the faculty is offering excellent undergraduate education is that from 1995-2006, BYU ranked in the top ten nationally in the number of its undergraduates who went on to earn doctorates, and since 2007 it has ranked in the top five (Y Facts). Perhaps one key reason for this statistic is that faculty have in recent years been given strong incentives to include undergraduates, as much as possible, in their own research and to mentor students in original research and scholarship. To support this, the university's Office of Research and Creative Activities awards more than one million dollars to faculty mentors and roughly five-hundred thousand dollars each year to more than three hundred undergraduates who submit meritorious research proposals. Undergraduates may assist faculty with creative work and scholarship, work in labs, and co-author papers with faculty members. Such work often results in student performances, presentations at conferences, publications in academic journals, and even awards for research in competitions with graduate students from other institutions (Y Facts).

Challenges for Faculty Hiring

All of the above has been a long prelude to the points I make next: Despite all the indicators of success, there is nevertheless a constant concern (though nothing approaching despair) about the ability of faculty to sustain the march onward and upward. That concern comes from the fact that the available pools to hire new faculty from are, to put it bluntly, often shallow or even dry. This is not to say that we don't get excellent applicants, just that they are not always the kind we're fishing for. Where most universities might get five hundred responses to a job ad, we might get five, so we don't have the luxury of drawing candidates each year from any field of our choosing. This scarcity of potential faculty to meet particular needs is partly due to the distinctive mission and aims of the university and its honor code and ecclesiastical endorsements, all of which make it significantly more likely that only active members of the LDS faith will desire to teach at BYU. Moreover, in its job ads BYU expresses a preference for hiring qualified "members in good standing of the affiliated church" (such a preference is entirely legal for a private university). In contrast, several other religious research universities do not discriminate on the basis of religion and even express a desire to hire more diverse faculty. Although BYU does hire non-LDS professors occasionally, a department has to make a strong case to the university administration for doing so, and the administration, in turn, has to make a strong case to the Board of Trustees.[7] If no qualified LDS candidates are available for the fields needed, and no non-LDS applicants are approved, departments must either make do with temporary appointees or part-time faculty or do without.

Interestingly, the board's preference for LDS faculty is supported by a high percentage of the BYU faculty. In a 2002 survey conducted by Lyon, Beaty, and Mixon, 82 percent of BYU faculty said they would rather go shorthanded for a time in order to wait for an LDS candidate to hire. In contrast, only 55 percent of faculty at Baylor, 38 percent at Notre Dame, and 28 percent at Boston College would prefer to wait to hire a faculty candidate belonging to their affiliated church. Availability of LDS faculty is not the only concern; professors' desire to support the university mission is also a factor. A 2005 study conducted by Lyon, Beaty, Parker, and Mencken found that BYU professors were more than twice as likely as professors at five other religious universities (Baylor, Boston College, Georgetown, Notre Dame, and Samford) to agree that Christian perspectives should be integrated with secular learning. Faculty responding to the survey were asked to indicate whether they agreed or disagreed that Christian perspectives should be included in core curriculum courses about God (e.g., philosophy courses), the nature of the universe (e.g., physics), society (e.g., sociology), and human beings (e.g., biology and psychology), or anywhere else in various disciplines as opportunities arose. The fact that BYU faculty much more strongly agreed with systematically integrating faith and learning is not surprising since, as explained above, such integration is precisely what BYU's mission is about.

THE FUTURE SCHOLARS PROGRAM

While the BYU board, administrators, and current faculty know what they want in new professors, it isn't easy to find established scholars or newly minted PhDs whose academic qualifications and level of commitment to the LDS Church are equally strong. This is one of the reasons that, in 2005, the English Department started what is now called the Future Scholars Program (FSP). We realized that, in effect, we will have to keep doing what we have been doing more or less already, and that is to cultivate future professors—at least some, if not most of them—from among the ranks of our students. Currently there are 54 full-time tenured or tenure-track professors in the English Department, and 88 percent of them earned either a bachelor's or a master's degree (or both) at BYU. The question we're answering with FSP is whether we can be more strategic about preparing qualified undergraduates for graduate school.

FSP was the brain child of two professors, John Talbot and Nick Mason, who as advisors to the BYU chapter of Sigma Tau Delta (an honor society for English majors) realized that they were often dealing with students who wanted a vocation in English and whose talents and qualifications should have been good enough to get them into the best graduate programs, but the students' acceptance rates were below expectations. Talbot and Mason thought what was needed was an intensive course in mentoring such students about the details of preparing strong applications for graduate school and the realities of a professional career in English. Talbot formed an organization to help students understand the differences between undergraduate and graduate education and how the latter provides training for a professional life. Mason's contribution was to formalize this approach in a one-credit course and find a way to identify the students who should be enrolled. He encouraged faculty members to approach promising students in their junior year and encourage them to apply for FSP. The goal of the course was to identify PhD-bound students early enough in their undergraduate career that there would still be time to help them prepare strong applications for the best graduate schools and to give them some careful instruction about what they could expect if they were accepted. When other responsibilities drew Mason away from FSP, he co-taught the course for one year with Matt Wickman, who assumed responsibility for it in 2007. Wickman has co-taught the course twice with Brian Roberts but has mostly taught it alone. However, he invites guest lecturers frequently to discuss such things as choosing a graduate school that is a good fit, choosing a mentor, and planning and preparing a strong *curriculum vitae*. The guest lecturers are usually young professors whose experience in graduate school is relatively recent, so that students don't hear only about Wickman's experiences in graduate school fourteen years ago.

Now that Wickman has taken the course through seven iterations, he has found that the best way to recruit students for FSP is to email all English majors letting them know about the course, what it does, and how to apply for admission. He sends a second email to all English faculty asking them to nominate outstanding sophomore or junior students for the program. Wickman then approaches the nominated students to invite them to seriously consider joining FSP. He stresses to them the importance of preparing for graduate school when it is just barely on the students' radar screen. To be considered, the students must fill out an application form listing courses taken, courses currently enrolled in, and the names of three persons who can speak to the student's potential for success in graduate school. Students attach two things to this form: (1) a one- or two-paragraph description of why they would like to participate in FSP and of what they have done thus far to prepare for graduate work, and (2) an unofficial transcript of all courses taken at BYU or other universities and grades earned. Wickman and another faculty member separately look over all applications and recommend admission or denial. If one recommends admission and the other doesn't, the student is admitted. All students who want to join FSP are also interviewed by Wickman, who says he doesn't want merely to sequester "elite" students, but also to nourish and protect the hopes of late bloomers or others who may not qualify outright for high-ranking PhD programs. Some, he believes, may be able to take "the long way round" into the profession by applying first to a less competitive MA program and developing themselves more slowly to qualify for a strong PhD program.

After seven years, the curriculum of FSP is somewhat fixed but still fluid. First, the course helps students understand that English is a discipline with many fields, and students need to choose a field to specialize in. Students learn how institutions of higher education are classified, what Research 1 institutions are, and which institutions are in the top tier and which in the second tier for various fields in the discipline. The course helps students understand what their life would be like if they became professors at various kinds of institutions—what kind of salaries they could expect, what kinds of teaching loads they might have at different institutions, the research expectations, and the research and travel support they might expect. It asks students to consider what kind of institution they might want to teach at and what sort of graduate school experience would best prepare them for their desired career. With this sort of background in place, students can then think more clearly about programs they would want to apply to. An assignment related to this part of the course requires students to research graduate programs they might apply for to learn about admission criteria, size of each entering class, costs, and so on. Students then create a narrow list of targeted programs. They are taught to think about selecting a school that is a good fit for them personally, a place where they will find a graduate mentor and be helped to succeed in their program.

The curriculum also includes very practical, hands-on work. Students are taught how to prepare for the GRE and how to prepare a *curriculum vitae*, a letter of intent, and a writing sample. The letter of intent is given particular stress. Students write drafts of their letter of intent and get feedback from Wickman. They learn the writing sample must be much more than a good seminar paper, and that they will either have to significantly revise an existing paper or start over on something new. Because an excellent writing sample takes so long to prepare and because students really need more time to mature in the discipline before writing something that will be impressive, they don't complete the writing sample in the FSP course. But they do prepare a prospectus for their writing sample and get feedback on it from Prof. Wickman. (A second one-hour course they can enroll in later gives them the opportunity to focus more completely on the writing sample; Wickman also generously volunteers to help students with the writing sample at any time.) Students come to understand that their letter of intent and writing sample will be read as their "pitch" to the chosen school. They learn that professors at their chosen graduate school want to find promising young people to mentor and to help develop into peers. A final assignment in FSP is to examine three to four journals in the student's field of interest to understand the kind and level of research they will have to produce as a scholar in the field.

In addition to the above, the course discusses larger issues such as the state of the humanities in higher education at the present time. Wickman is an excellent professor for the course in this respect because in 2012 he was appointed Director of the Humanities Center in the BYU College of Humanities, an assignment that requires him to read constantly and broadly about higher education and to host or attend the presentations of up to four or five guest lecturers in various humanities disciplines each week. Many of these guests are invited to speak to the continuing relevance of the humanities in education and public life. Because he remains abreast of developments in higher education, Wickman levels with students about the present discouraging state of the job market, but he also encourages optimism about what the humanities have to contribute to society in general and higher education in particular. He does not discourage students from following the path toward a career in academia, if they really want it.

Wickman also spends time discussing quite frankly how students with strong LDS beliefs might have those beliefs challenged in a secular graduate school, which may be indifferent or occasionally even hostile to religion. He encourages students to imagine how the LDS-defined personal and social roles they currently inhabit may be thoughtfully defined and articulated as the students encounter others whose ideas about roles and behavior are very different. To take one simple example, LDS graduate students, who observe a religious health code that prohibits alcohol, will have to plan what to say and do when they are invited by fellow graduate students to go out for a beer or when they are invited to professors' homes and offered alcoholic beverages. Wickman and other professors speak to students about their personal experiences integrating faith and study and about the ways they learned to maintain and explain LDS beliefs in the face of challenge. Ultimately, it will be up to each student to negotiate graduate school from a position of religious faith or not, as they choose. But FSP helps students understand how other schools will likely be rather different from BYU, and it gives them strategies for maintaining their balance as both believers in revealed religion and scholars who understand academic assumptions and values and can use the academy's secular methods of inquiry.

So far, Wickman reports between sixty and eighty students have completed FSP at the rate of about eight to twelve students per year. Of those, the great majority have decided that a PhD and career in academia is not for them. On average, only two to four students each year have chosen that route, for a total of fifteen to twenty. A high number of those have been accepted at outstanding schools such as Berkeley, Chicago, Duke, Michigan, Princeton, Stanford, and UCLA—and have been offered excellent financial support. The success of FSP in the English Department has been significant enough that in 2013-14 an FSP course was developed for the other departments in the BYU College of Humanities (foreign languages, linguistics, and philosophy). To prepare for this, Wickman showed the English FSP syllabus to faculty in the other departments, who thought the general course topics would transfer to their fields but that specifics would vary by department. Wickman taught the initial course of seven students, and to ensure that the specifics would be covered, he brought in guests from around the college every week and had the students identify and meet with prospective mentors in their individual departments or fields. Wickman will likely teach the college version of FSP two more times before handing it off to other faculty. Of course, it's far too soon to say much about the success of this second program, but the fact that the idea is spreading speaks to the need other departments feel to prepare future faculty.

Wickman keeps track of where the alumni of FSP have gone, and he tries to stay in touch via occasional emails. He has learned that some FSP students have decided that they won't try to get academic teaching jobs after completing the PhD, and others have decided that they won't seek such a job at BYU. However, a few are now getting close to wrapping up PhD work, and they are very much interested in job prospects at their alma mater. In addition to tracking FSP students' progress in graduate school, the department also informally tracks other former undergraduate students who either didn't hear about FSP or didn't choose to participate in it but have gone on to graduate school. Such students have always turned up in our hiring pools, and we expect that within a year or two, we will begin to see applications from them as well from former FSP students. When that happens, there is, of course, no guarantee that we will hire any of them—quality will always be paramount in any decisions—or hire them immediately, since department needs will always have to be balanced against candidates' areas of specialization. But at least with FSP we will have increased the odds that there will be a few more "fish" in our hiring pool and perhaps more who meet the particular needs we have in a given year.

The Future Scholars Program has so far seemed successful enough that changes to it from year to year have been minor. However, there is concern about whether it is reaching all the students it was intended for. Perhaps not all the faculty are aware or invested enough in it to "sell" it to the kinds of students who should be encouraged to enroll. Perhaps also it is not yet pitched at the right level for the students who do enroll, not well designed enough to empower the ones who have the aptitude and disposition for graduate study while helping students who lack those qualities to think about other career options. Before much longer, there probably should be a careful study, involving surveys and interviews, of those who have gone through FSP to determine its strengths and weaknesses more empirically. The ratio of those who have enrolled in FSP to those who have gone on to graduate school is about four to one, a figure that may seem discouragingly low. But besides preparing possible future faculty, a main goal of FSP is, in Wickman's words, "to give all the course's students, irrespective of their future career choices, a better sense of the life of humanities departments within universities." To send FSP students out into the world with a better sense of how higher education operates, of how humanities disciplines figure in this picture, and of how their own education has helped them think about their strengths and goals is not an insignificant outcome, even if those students never become professors.

Whatever the future might bring, at present both professors and students in BYU's English Department see FSP as an indication that we are "counting the cost" and trying to determine whether we will have sufficient resources to finish building the tower that our predecessors laid the foundation for. I think the chances are much better than even that the Future Scholars Program will, over the long run, prove to be a boon to the department as we seek to build the kind of faculty we need to achieve the university's lofty mission and aims (Klausman, this volume). In the next few years, we will see whether there are alumni of FSP in our hiring pool. In the meantime, we can do more to assess how well FSP is working and then fine-tune it and any other instructional programs we offer students to make them equal to the best students in the country in English studies. We can certainly mentor students in FSP (or outside it) to prepare them to succeed in graduate programs at the best universities. But we also need to realize that we can't "take thought for the morrow" in every way. In the end, programs can only do so much to realize institutional missions. In the end, missions are realized because of individual desires and commitment. The students we teach in FSP will themselves ultimately be responsible for how well they do in graduate school and also for how strongly they continue to adhere to the LDS faith. Perhaps the best thing we professors can do is model for our students that it is possible to be both a scholar and a believer, someone who prepares as well as possible through planning and hard work but who also demonstrates faith in God and in the religious teachings we have accepted. The example of faith we set for students may be the best evidence and the best incentive for them to believe that the mission of BYU is both possible and worth pursuing.

Notes

1. While the emphasis here is on Protestant colleges, it should be noted that the Roman Catholic Church also sponsors colleges in the US, but most of them were founded much later. Catholic University of America was founded as the nation's only pontifical university in 1889, for example, and various orders established other colleges around the same time to protect Catholic youth from the growing secular ideology in higher education. Midway through the twentieth century there were many institutions with strong Catholic identities. However, Burtchaell argues that Catholic universities are now going through the same secularization process that Protestant ones did about 100 years ago (Janangelo, this volume).

2. The others are Baylor University, affiliated with the Baptist Church, and seven universities affiliated with the Roman Catholic Church or one of its orders: Boston College, Catholic University of America, Fordham, Georgetown, Loyola of Chicago, Notre Dame, and St. Louis University (Wilkins and Whetten 15).

3. The total percentage of returned missionaries is likely to rise significantly, since in 2012 the LDS Church lowered the minimum age for missionary service to eighteen for young men and nineteen for young women. The number of young people applying to serve jumped nearly five hundred percent after the age change.

4. Lest it seem that the LDS Church is interested in providing higher education only for the academic elite of its younger generation, I note that the church also strongly supports two other institutions of higher education—BYU-Idaho, with about 22,000 students, and BYU-Hawaii, with about 2,500 students, mainly from Asia and the Pacific Islands. Both institutions have relatively low academic admissions standards but the same high expectations that BYU has for personal behavior and religious discipline. The faculty at both schools have rather high teaching loads with little or no expectation to do research. There are no extramural athletic programs at either school so that all resources are focused solely on education. In addition, the LDS Church sponsors an extensive network of Institutes of Religion near 2500 university campuses across the United States. These are places where LDS students can go to take religion courses, worship, and socialize with other members of the faith while working on their college studies.

5. It's difficult to get a stable figure to represent the percentage of faculty with terminal degrees, since the faculty is always changing. However, the percentage is likely always trending upward. BYU's student body grew rapidly in the 1960s and early 1970s, and since faculty hiring had to keep pace, many new faculty with only master's degrees were given full-time continuing appointments. When the size of the student body was capped in 1976, many of these older professors were still on the faculty. For example, in 1984, of full-time professors tenured or on the tenure track in the English Department, only 69% percent had terminal degrees. By 1994, this figure rose to 83% as older faculty retired and were replaced by new hires with terminal degrees. By 2004, the figure was 95%, and in 2014 it is 100%.

6. For example, BYU's accounting program is ranked first in the nation by *Business Week*; its public relations program is ranked fifth by *PR Week*; its entrepreneurship program is ranked eighth by *Entrepreneur*; its MBA program, seventeenth by *Forbes*; and the *Wall Street Journal* reports BYU graduates are ranked eleventh by recruiters (Y Facts).

7. In any given year, probably less than five percent of the entire campus faculty is non-LDS. Some non-LDS professors stay only a short time, while others have had long, happy, and distinguished careers at BYU, with several of them serving in important administrative roles and winning the university's highest awards for teaching and scholarship.

Works Cited

AP in Higher Education. *2013 Summary of AP Scores Reported to Brigham Young University*. New York: College Board. Message to the author. 13 June 2014. Email.

Axtell, James. *The Making of Princeton University: From Woodrow Wilson to the Present*. Princeton: Princeton UP, 2006. Print.

Burtchaell, James T. *The Dying of the Light: The Disengagement of Colleges and Universities from Their Christian Churches*. Grand Rapids, MI: Eerdmans Publishing, 1998. Print.

Kimball, Spencer W. "Education for Eternity." *Educating Zion*. Ed. John W. Welch and Don Norton. Provo: BYU Studies, 1996. 43–63. Print.

Lyon, Larry, Michael Beaty, and Stephanie Mixon. "Making Sense of a 'Religious' University: Faculty Adaptations and Opinions at Brigham Young, Baylor, Notre Dame, and Boston College." *Review of Religious Research* 43.4 (2002): 326–48. Print.

Lyon, Larry, Michael Beaty, James Parker, and Carson Mencken. "Faculty Attitudes on Integrating Faith and Learning at a Religious College: A Research Note." *Sociology of Religion* 66.1 (2005): 61–69. Print.

Maeser, Reinhard. *Karl G. Maeser: A Biography*. Provo: BYU Press, 1928. Print.

Marsden, George M. *The Soul of the American University*. Oxford: Oxford UP, 1994. Print.

Mission and Aims of Brigham Young University. Brigham Young University. Brigham Young University, n.d. Web. 19 June 2014.

Nasaw, David. *Andrew Carnegie*. NY: Penguin, 2007. Print.

Wilkins, Alan L., and David A. Whetten. "BYU and Religious Universities in a Secular Academic World." *BYU Studies Quarterly* 51.3 (2012): 5–52. Print.

"Y Facts." *Brigham Young University*. Brigham Young University, n.d. Web. 19 June 2014.

8 Designing and Delivering General Education Curriculum at a Small Liberal Arts College

Anita M. DeRouen

Aligning curricular reform with a campus's mission and overarching strategies is complicated; the reform effort alone demands a tremendous outlay of resources, foremost being social and administrative capital. This chapter explores the relationship between institutional mission and curriculum development. In it, I relate how my colleagues and I called upon our school's recently adopted strategic plan to create and sustain general education reform and delivery.

The chapter will proceed in four parts. I'll begin with institutional context, mission, and the strategic plan, ending with a brief discussion of previous general education reform efforts. Next, I'll discuss the development of the curriculum in relationship to the strategic plan, with a focus on two key areas: the academic program itself and the campus commitment to developing student leaders in local and global contexts. Finally, I'll discuss our accomplishments and challenges (Behm, Hoppe, this volume). Throughout the narrative of this campus experience, I've tried to highlight the salient learning points that I've gleaned through the curriculum development process. I hope that faculty and other campus leaders facing their own curricular reform process in a variety of contexts will find these reflections helpful.

INSTITUTIONAL CONTEXT AND MISSION

Millsaps College is a selective, small liberal arts college located in Jackson, Mississippi with an undergraduate student population of approximately 900 students and a faculty/student ratio of 9:1. Founded in 1891 by members of the Methodist Church and named for former Confederate officer, Major Reuben Millsaps, the school has a long-standing commitment to educating Mississippi's young men and women. In addition to its programs in traditional liberal arts areas of study, Millsaps is the home of the Else School of Management, an AACSB accredited management program with international recognition for excellence.

The school's vision and mission statements presented below clearly articulate its institutional character:

Mission

Millsaps College is dedicated to academic excellence, open inquiry and free expression, the exploration of faith to inform vocation, and the innovative shaping of the social, economic, and cultural progress of our region.

Vision

Building on its motto, *Ad Excellentiam*, its strong heritage of social justice, freedom of thought, and reflection on life's most important questions, and its central location in the capital city of Mississippi, Millsaps engages students in a transformative learning and leadership experience that results in personal and intellectual growth, commitment to good citizenship in our global society, and a desire to succeed and make a difference in every community they touch.

These two statements, refined over the years, hit upon what I see as key elements of the Millsaps character:

- Academic Excellence
- Social Justice
- Liberal Values
- Engagement in the local community/context, as well as global community
- Personal responsibility and impact

As we embarked upon the complicated process of curriculum redesign, we found ourselves first drawn to the College's Mission and Vision statements and then connecting to the newly developed strategic plan.

Learning Point #1: Mission and Vision statements—or any statement of institutional identity—can provide valuable focal points for curriculum development.

These statements were instrumental in developing and adopting the College's current strategic plan, Across the Street and Around the Globe. As soon as the plan was revealed, these words were embraced by the College community, the first really resonant articulation of the College's identity that I'd experienced in the several years I'd been on the campus. Millsaps faculty and students are everywhere; we have research and teaching facilities in various locations in Latin America, long-standing research projects and connections in Africa and Europe, and a growing number of programs in Asia. We have long-standing partnerships in our local community, our faculty and students bringing the classroom into the city of Jackson as we work with our neighbors to improve education, healthcare, and small business opportunities. Adopted in 2012, the plan focuses on six strategic goals, three of which seemed most connected to the development of a new general education curriculum: *Ad Excellentiam*, which focuses on the campus's commitment to academic excellence; Local and Global Experience and Influence, which focuses on our established and growing engagements in local and global contexts; and Ethical Heritage and Church Relations, which focuses on our continuing mission to develop students capable of engaging in the important work of social justice.

Learning Point #2: Timing counts.

The plan's release couldn't have come at a better time. In the fall of 2011, a ten-member committee was formed to revise the current general education curriculum, commonly referred to as "the core." Since I'd set foot on the campus three years prior as Assistant Professor of English and Director of Writing & Teaching, I'd been exposed to whisperings and committee conversations about the general education curriculum's problems. Faculty members across the curriculum were teaching a troubled-but-respected, supported-but-burdensome first semester writing seminar. Our two track humanities core was seen as having a Rolls Royce (Heritage) and a Yugo (Topics) option. There was a perceived imbalance among the divisional contributions to the curriculum, with business school faculty contributing a handful of teachers and courses, a science faculty getting to double count introductory disciplinary courses, and a humanities faculty developing interdisciplinary courses. We also had unassessible learning outcomes in the form of lofty Liberal Arts Abilities (Malenczyk and Rosenberg, this volume). There were more, of course, but these were the issues that seemed to provide constant tension when the conversation turned to the core. There was a desire for change and improvement, but without some strong guidance, it was difficult to get any purchase on a new plan or direction. The strategic plan—along with the mission and vision statements—came along at just the moment they were needed.

Learning Point #3: It's easy to make change quickly, but that change needs to be deployed with careful consideration. Don't squander the energy behind reform with hasty changes; understand the desire for/stomach for change and determine the desired scope.

The committee gathered around a small table in the library of the sociology/anthropology department. Depending on how you sliced it, we were a pretty lopsided group: three members of the English faculty, no lab scientists, one mathematician, one modern language faculty member, one philosopher, one computer scientist, one anthropologist, one business faculty member, and the Dean of the College. The committee worked quickly. Within six weeks, we had "developed" a curriculum revision to present to the faculty for a vote; in retrospect, the rapidity of the proposal development belied the committee's conversation and the campus's preparedness for change.

That the committee failed should have been no surprise; at the time, the understanding was that the faculty, deeply immersed in strategic planning, program review, and the reaccreditation processes, was eager and hungry for a real change, for an entire review and revision of the current system. There was an underlying sense that piecemeal and bolted-on changes wouldn't do; they couldn't address the fundamental problems of coherence/clarity, perceived inequity, and faculty preparation. I don't think we even put the proposed curriculum up to the faculty for an official vote; initial responses from various quarters indicated resistance to adoption and opposition to change that didn't address the issues. By mid-November, the committee's work was done, and it closed with a two-page report outlining the issues and recommendations coming out of its conversations.

In light of this, the then-new dean of the college decided to give the faculty what it appeared to want: a carefully constructed committee representing key aspects of the academic and college program charged with building a new curriculum from whole cloth. A team of five (of which

I was a member) was sent to an AAC&U conference in New Orleans in February 2012 to gather information about current conversations in curriculum reform and assessment, and in the fall of 2012 a new committee was constituted to develop a new core. I'll save you the anticipation: the curriculum was developed and supported by faculty vote in the Spring of 2014. Implementation began in Summer 2014, with the new curriculum scheduled to launch Fall 2015.

Developing the Academic Program

The new committee, referred to as the core review, worked on the new curriculum from July 2012 until we submitted a final version to the faculty for vote in February 2014. Those first months were rough. We met in a narrow seminar room in the social sciences building for about an hour once a week. We had the right mix of people around the table—faculty and staff selected because of a particular role that they play in the academic and student life programs along with elected representatives from the College's three divisions to round out the academic picture. I was there in my role—Director of Writing and Teaching—and I appreciated having that hat to help focus my participation. As the sole untenured faculty member on the committee, I needed the mantle of my role at the College to undergird my participation.

Learning Point #4: Know where you are and where you're headed; clear direction is key for any committee's success.

Our dean wisely began with the committee charge, a document we batted around for a couple of weeks until we felt we had a good sense of what our mission was. We constructed a timeline for the committee's work, everyone around the table slowly understanding that this was not a one-term committee appointment, but one that would extend over years. We elected a chair. We started the hard work of figuring out how we, as a committee, would do our work. Since the strategic plan would not be officially revealed until October 2012, the committee worked with the elements that we had—the mission statement, the vision statement, and the committee charge. These, along with our understanding of the timeline we were working under, helped us to begin shaping the foundations of the new curriculum even in the absence of the strategic plan. Both the understanding of the lengthened timeline and the use of key statements about our college's character were necessary elements to the committee's ultimate success.

Learning Point #5: In moving your institution forward, know where you are and where you've been; honor the past but don't be beholden to it. Identify and grapple with sacred cows.

Of course, the previous curriculum also loomed large; a key failing of the previous committee's work was the lack of desire to "put everything on the table." Certain elements of the current core were seen as sacrosanct: the popular Heritage course, a multidisciplinary arts and humanities survey spanning a full academic year and taking up one half of a first-year student's available course slots; the first-year seminar, commonly referred to as core 1, a writing course situated in a variety of topical and disciplinary contexts; the element of "choice," most commonly held up by humanities faculty to support the two track system of delivery of the humanities core (Heritage vs. Topics). These sacred cows had their less savory elements. Core 1, the cornerstone of the college's successful and long-standing Writing Across the Curriculum (WAC) program, was difficult to staff effectively, with each division and department responsible for sorting out how it would fulfill its requirements to send teachers into the course. Some departments relied upon the same staff members annually to teach the course, while others used rotation systems to ensure that everyone got a term (or did their time). Ensuring course consistency and quality was difficult, if not impossible, and lack of course "ownership" by any one department or division in the College made it even more difficult to foster enthusiasm among the faculty for teaching the course. These elements—and a host of other interconnected ones—had pushed us to wanting a redesign for our general education curriculum in the first place, and we had to find a way to break the grip of the past (Janangelo, this volume).

Learning Point #6: Begin by focusing on the fundamental elements of student learning. Resist the urge to deal with structural concerns first and, instead, decide what you want students to learn.

The mission and vision statements proved particularly helpful in those first months. While we didn't adhere to them—or, in later moments, to the letter of the strategic plan—they were important touchstones as we tried to determine our initial student learning outcomes. What, we asked, can the Millsaps graduate do? What does the graduate know?

We quickly understood that doing and knowing were going to develop different parts of the new curriculum, and since general and universal learning outcomes were the first order of business, we ruminated on the domain of doing first with the mission and vision statements in the backs of our minds and conversations.

Swirling around this discussion of outcomes, though, were the constant pull of disciplinarity, the various idiosyncrasies of the course schedule, and concerns about staffing. In the early months, we worked to constantly remind ourselves and one another that we were embarking on a long process with many parts and stops along the way. It was hard, I think, for us to put ourselves into a creative mindset; we met during the work week, entering that narrow room for a mere hour among the many others spent teaching students, meeting with colleagues, researching projects, assessing student work, and a host of other responsibilities. It took time to get us transitioned from the world outside of that room to the creative activity that needed to take place in it.

Learning Point #7: Use the available inputs, but don't feel beholden to them.

We also drew on the work of an earlier committee tasked with outcomes identification during the strategic planning process. That committee had recommended three college-wide learning outcomes: communication, critical thinking, and collaborative skills, and these were readily seen as key goals for student learning with some concern, particularly from faculty in Arts and Humanities Division, about the ubiquity of collaborative skills. Still, the current committee felt it necessary to generate its own outcomes to ensure that we were fulfilling an important but unwritten part of the mandate: to start with a clean slate and take everything off the table.

Learning Point #8: Make sure the group is willing to cast a critical eye on all aspects of the previous and proposed curriculum. If the group needs to begin with a "clean slate," make sure the slate is actually clean.

I don't think the importance of this sort of approach and consensus can be overstated: if an initiative is to succeed at curriculum reform, it must be willing to inspect all assumptions and to examine as many angles as possible (Behm, this volume). Stories about reform efforts over the previous decades were legion; it was clear to everyone that from its initial launch, there were problems with the core curriculum that stemmed primarily from its signature elements, but there was little consensus on how to go about fixing what was clearly broken. The committee's commitment—to the process and, most importantly, to each other—to consciously work against replicating the old model was key to achieving success.

In the end, we utilized a backward design model to determine learning outcomes. We generated lists of activities; those list items were grouped between meetings, revealing consensus on the three previously suggested outcomes and one other: problem-solving and creative practice, the eventual name that we gave to a collective desire to ensure that our graduates "know how to fail." These outcomes were presented to faculty over two months' time, allowing for robust discussion before a successful faculty vote at the end of the fall 2012 term. Next came the part of the process everyone seemed most anxious about completing and most reluctant to really dive into: determining what disciplinary areas would constitute the new core.

Learning Point #9: Anticipate friction, tension, and resistance around any efforts to reform general education curricula.

There is a natural resistance to and tension surrounding attempts at general education reform. General education curricula are stable spaces for departments and disciplines; if your department offers a course that fulfills a requirement, you are guaranteed some modicum of stability. If your department provides multiple courses, you're bulletproof. While we felt tremendous support from colleagues to undertake this work, the campus context was one of great underlying tensions (Klausman, this volume). The college parted ways with both its previous president and academic dean in summer 2009; the current president began his tenure at the college in Fall 2010, with the new academic dean starting in the summer of 2011. With a new president and dean came a renewed sense of purpose and a lot of institutional soul-searching. A comprehensive review of the academic program resulted in program and staff shifts and reductions, a strategic planning process revealed and articulated fundamental messages about the college's mission and character, and a visit from our accrediting body (SACSCOC) highlighted the need for measurable learning outcomes. All of this work and change, of course, happened within a three-year window, a massive upheaval for any institution, but even more so for a small liberal arts college with a faculty of fewer than one hundred.

The conversation about what students should know, then, took place while faculty were recovering from the loss of dear colleagues and the loss or reduction of under-performing disciplinary areas. A certain amount of turf protection was to be expected, and the committee had to work hard to put those desires aside; we also, though, had to periodically remember that we were a political body, with a successful faculty vote on our proposed curriculum a necessary outcome. We met in December 2012, right as the term was ending, and attempted to get consensus on the issue of knowledge domains.

For some, the meeting was too short; some members were ready to begin the winter break while others were eager to dig into the task and take advantage of the relative freedom of the space between ending and starting classes. We met over lunch, each committee member receiving one of two curriculum development texts to read over the break to go along with their catered meal.[1] We used Post-It pads to create large lists of knowledge domains that we then hung on the wall to examine for points of agreement and dissent. Then the hour or so was up, and those that needed to leave, left. The remaining group, though, continued the discussion on the walk back to our offices. Five of us ended up in a meeting room with a whiteboard where we spent another hour hammering out a model for a new curriculum based in both the learning outcomes and the lunchtime dialogue.

Our draft plan was ambitions, but when I look back on that initial curriculum design, I'm struck by how many of its principles made it into the final curriculum adopted by faculty in April 2014. The key elements—breadth of curricular exposure, a focus on interdisciplinarity, introduction and development of core skills/outcomes, engagement with the community—these were all present, as was a healthy balance of designated courses and proficiency requirements.

Learning Point #10: Constantly monitor the group's work process, keeping what works and changing what doesn't.

Over the course of the following term, the committee developed and considered a number of alternate models, and with each of these, we had to negotiate the usual aforementioned roadblocks for curricular development: sacred cows, departmental and program histories, "the way we've always done things," and competing hierarchies of disciplinary importance, among others. At times the tasks felt overwhelming; we continued to rely on work methods that were successful, checking our initial "wish lists" for student learning and knowledge domains, and breaking into small work groups to imagine new models. We also made necessary changes. We identified a new meeting time, place, and length, finding that we were more productive—and less stressed—with a weekly two-hour work session. The longer meeting time gave everyone a few minutes on the front end to shake off the baggage of the day. We also had a better space. A new seminar room—still somewhat narrow and tucked away within the suite of offices assigned to the Sociology/Anthropology departments, but still a vast improvement overall—provided ample workspace and campus isolation. The core curriculum provided snacks and beverages, a small but effective addition to our regimen that helped to create a sense of community within the committee, the importance of which cannot be over-stressed. These changes were crucial to the committee's work and provided the closest thing we could get to a working retreat in the middle of an always-busy week.

While we were making progress, though, we needed to truly immerse ourselves in the work of redesign to break through the final hurdle. The dean's office provided the perfect opportunity: attendance for five committee members at AAC&U's 2013 Institution on General Education and Assessment in Vermont.[2] Committee representatives traveled to the conference with a draft curriculum model and emerged with both a new design and rollout plan and recognition of a key missing element: incorporation of a piece clearly tied to the strategic plan.

GETTING "ACROSS THE STREET AND AROUND THE GLOBE"

Learning Point #11: Consult with experts when you can.
Learning Point #12: Draw on institutional strengths.

One of the pluses of attending a gathering like the one in Vermont when you're engaging in curriculum reform is the ready access to experts; while that time may be limited to a brief conversation over coffee or a short discussion section during a break in the schedule, such feedback and insight can quickly reveal shortcomings and strengths. A brief meeting with Ashley Finley, whose expertise in assessment with the VALUE rubrics was helpful, demonstrated a huge hole in our plan: the absence of our school's long-term and signature commitment to community-engaged learning. We'd considered it early in the planning, of course, particularly in the wake of the strategic plan's announcement, but that conversation strand was lost as we deliberated over how much space in the new curriculum would go to various disciplinary units on the campus. The conversation with Ashley Finley was a much needed wake-up call, although we didn't fully realize the necessity of her suggestion until we were revising the curriculum after an initial presentation to the faculty.

Learning Point #13: Your curriculum isn't just a collection of classes; it's a collection of lived experiences.

An educational institution offers more than a series of classes; it offers an experience, and the Millsaps experience has been wrapped in a mantle of engagement for quite some time. The character of our institution is one of service based in justice and calling across the whole education; where possible, we encourage students to bring what they've learned in one area into another and to find connections among disparate disciplinary areas and the practical arenas they enter. Each institution must understand this aspect of its mission if the mission is to be achieved; for Millsaps, the key phrase is found at the end of the college's mission statement: "the innovative shaping of the social, economic, and cultural progress of our region." Institutional mission statements generally include such lofty language; finding an appropriate way to incorporate that language into the lived experiences of the students is a challenge. In the end, we developed a co-curricular requirement that ensures all graduates participate in the college's rich opportunities for engaged learning.

Lessons for the Individual: One Committee Member's Story

One repeated element of our conversation around the learning outcomes and the idea of community engagement was the necessity of faculty modeling the various processes and skills involved to students. In that spirit, I offer the following anecdote from the experience to demonstrate how curriculum developers can ease the frictions between program/disciplinary needs and expectations and curricular innovation. In this example, I relate the various challenges and thought processes I experienced related to the curriculum's design to support communication skills development.

As we began the work of identifying the key knowledge domains to be experienced, our conversation was sometimes stymied by our history, the spectre of the previous core hanging over any attempts to break out of disciplinarity, one of the stronger recommendations of the previous committee. While we had begun this phase of the work by repeating our previous process—generating lists to achieve a sense of the various domains we might consider—we quickly began drafting curricular options, creating course-shaped boxes (that generally already existed) and moving them around on four-year calendars. We were tinkering with the old core again instead of creating something new, and I found my walks back to my office increasingly frustrating (Behm, this volume).

Learning Point #14: Learn to recognize the briar patch.

We were entrenched. It became clear that all things were not on the table, that while we were relatively comfortable with tossing out the actual math class requirement in favor of a quantitative reasoning proficiency, for example, the will to sacrifice long-standing signature courses was simply not there. I had my own dog in the hunt; while my program did not "own" it, I had served as director of the freshman/transfer writing course, Core 1, for several years, and I felt, in that role, in my role as Director of Writing and Teaching and as the sole representative of the rhetoric and composition community on my campus, that I must advocate for the maintenance of the required first-year writing course. While I was willing to put it on the table, I did so with my fingers crossed behind my back.

Learning Point #15: Know your role—on the committee and in the institution—and understand its limits in spheres.

I could only play that part for so long. As the conversations progressed, it became clear that my colleagues were seriously considering dispersing the composition course across other elements of the curriculum. To me, this option was untenable; the stand-alone course is as valuable as any disciplinary introduction, and I was greatly concerned that despite their best intentions, my faculty colleagues would be less likely to focus their attention to writing in intentional and explicit ways if that instruction had to happen in a context that was primarily focused on delivering other disciplinary content. The arguments against my position seemed insurmountable at times: faculty dissatisfaction with teaching the course, a feeling of ill-preparedness to teach the course from various disciplinary quarters, the long-standing research projects undertaken by the Heritage classes as a model for embedded writing instruction. It was at this point that I felt my lack of tenure most strongly; the people at the table might be part of the decision down the road to grant me tenure, and while I had done a pretty good job protecting myself so far, I could see that this might be the sort of hill I'd have to be willing to die on, that arguing the case for the standalone course might cause me to expend more social and professional capital than could be healthy for a young faculty member.

Learning Point #16: Know what's not negotiable.

I turned to the work of colleagues off campus. Jill Gladstein and Dara Rossman Regaignon's work in *Writing Program Administration at Small Liberal Arts Colleges* armed me with the data that I needed to appeal to my campus colleagues; the vast majority of colleges of our type offer some form of explicitly focused writing course in the first year, information that was not lost on my colleagues. I was able to demonstrate how our current system relied on a combination of explicit and embedded requirements to prepare the whole writer. A key moment of group realization came when a colleague in mathematics likened the first semester writing course to an introductory course in a particular discipline; she instinctively understood the function of the College Algebra course, for example, in preparing students for work in mathematics but also in a variety of other disciplines. Opening that window helped shift the conversation away from the diffusion of initial writing instruction to other courses entirely; the committee was now ready to consider how to continue offering explicit instruction in communication skills while making room for other additions to the curriculum.

Learning Point #17: . . . .but don't be afraid to negotiate the things that are.

Having secured a place at the table for the writing course, I turned my attention to a practical and very real problem: delivery. Kathleen Blake Yancey's edited volume, *Delivering College Composition: The Fifth Canon*, explores the issue of how we deliver these courses in a variety of contexts, from the large university to the small college, from the classroom structure to the curricular content. Exploration of these various sites and contexts for writing instruction helped me to see a fundamental problem with our current configuration. Years before, when the core 1 course was initially conceived, WAC was a new approach for the faculty; over the years, the approach had become so firmly embedded in our campus's academic culture that nearly all courses utilized some combination of high- and low-stakes writing and communication assignments to both engage student learning and demonstrate student knowledge. A 2010 census of assignments in class syllabi revealed that 88 percent of classes included high-stakes, low-stakes, or both types of assignments; the remaining 12 percent of courses without writing assignments were primarily specialized music and voice lessons and some theatre performance courses. There are no college-wide requirements for writing assignments beyond the initial core courses; clearly, our culture values writing as a tool for learning and communicating. The faculty was on board overall. The question, then, was how to get them behind this first step?

Our initial proposal included a first-term communication seminar, similar in concept and staffing model to the course that we'd been teaching for about twenty years. There wasn't much argument about it per se; rather, the conversation turned on the issue of staffing three distinctly different seminars in the first year, with faculty most vocally concerned about the perceived lack of rigor in the proposed problem-solving course. As the committee struggled to find an appropriate solution to the seminar problem as we revised the core, the communications seminar seemed, once again, to be on the block, not because of a lack of value but because of its physical placement in the curriculum. The fall term was too heavy; committee members and many faculty felt that the problem-solving seminar was a more appealing and appropriate course for the first term. The solution to the humanities core problem—the creation of a spring-term, two-course seminar to be required for all students—felt like too much material too quickly. The committee began to toy with the idea of folding the communications seminar into the new humanities core and spreading that course over two terms.

I was back in the same space, but the terms had changed in the interim. The business faculty, who were once part of the teaching corps for the Core 1 course, were now responsible for their own designated course in the new curriculum; the science faculty were looking at increased activity in a new STEM requirement and the new problem-solving seminar. While both groups were strongly supportive of communication in their disciplinary contexts, they were historically less enthusiastic about teaching the introductory course, and the changes to the curriculum afforded them a certain amount of possible leverage for opting out. Other committee members who had varying levels of familiarity with the course expressed both their dissatisfaction with the perceived "lock step" nature of the current course and their concern that any new seminar would have the same problems.

Learning Point #18: Listen to what is said and what isn't.

That conversation was like lancing a boil. I came to understand that the work that I had done to support faculty who were less prepared and less confident to teach the course—creating sample syllabi and schedules, requiring the course-wide use of a common rhetoric text and handbook—was perceived by more experienced faculty as top-down mandate to change their methods. The meeting was tense and difficult for me; I listened, I explained, and I tried to maintain an assertive but compassionate perspective. I looked at the curriculum on the board, then at the member of the business faculty who was seated directly beneath the spot where a communications seminar might reside. As I explained that the sample schedules were developed to aid faculty who were less confident, she smiled and nodded, pointing to herself and saying "like me." That one connection—and affirmation—showed me the solution.

Learning Point #19: Reallocate resources strategically. Don't be afraid to shift the culture. Learn to pivot. Do this all with an eye toward the ultimate goal/purpose.

What if, I suggested, we staff the communications seminar with humanities faculty only, thereby giving "ownership" of the course to one division (thus generating some focused support for its teaching)? This signaled a seismic shift in culture; the WAC nature of the faculty for that course had historically been one of its strong suits. Pivoting away from that commitment was a risk, but given the strong contextual support for WAC on the campus, it was a pivot that I felt we could make, particularly if the message accompanying the shift was couched in the language of disciplinarity—that this course was but the first focused encounter with writing, that we as a faculty have been and continue to be committed to developing student communication skills across all of the disciplines we reach. What, after all, is the purpose of creating campus-wide learning outcomes if they are not meant to inform and infuse the entire curriculum?

Learning Point #20: One relatively small concession can reframe the entire discussion and open new avenues for development.

There was more discussion, including a decision to place the communications seminar in the second term with the understanding that first-year students would engage in developmentally appropriate writing tasks in both the fall problem-solving seminars and the first half of the humanities seminar. That decision allowed us to start thinking about the first-year experience as a coherent whole, with students developing skills and exploring key knowledge domains that would undergird their entire undergraduate experience. In this way, the willingness to rethink the necessity of older delivery systems in light of current conditions proved valuable for more than just "saving" the course; it also made possible the advancement of our design beyond a simple set of sequential courses to a curriculum where each part depended on the others.

Concluding Thoughts

Learning Point #21: Celebrate accomplishments.
Our accomplishments were significant. Within the space of two years, we had developed and approved a new general education curriculum that both aligned with the college's strategic goals and answered the need for students better equipped to deal with the rapidly changing world and workforce they face. We did so with overwhelming faculty support; in the final vote, over eighty percent of the faculty approved the new general education program. There is a great deal of energy on campus as we move into the implementation phase, with faculty eager to accept assignments to design new courses and generate new avenues for student and curricular engagement with the surrounding community.

Learning Point #22: Anticipate challenges and encourage robust community dialogue to address and solve them.
There are also challenges. Committees working on developing new courses, for example, are experiencing some of the same rough beginnings that our committee faced. While we seeded each course development committee with at least one member of the core revision group, those committees have to enter a strange discourse space where they are expected to pick up the work of one group and begin their own; to do so requires a tremendous amount of work on the front end to clarify intentions and expectations, align vocabulary and concepts, and iron out possible disagreements with the curriculum as proposed.

Another challenge will be working out what "counts" for various proficiencies and co-curricular expectations. For example, a new universal foreign language requirement will likely tax our existing placement testing methods, and we are already seeing lively conversations about what languages count, with faculty arguing for the inclusion of non-traditional languages like American Sign Language and computer languages as possible ways of fulfilling the requirement. As groups work toward resolving these issues, I have no doubt that they will experience some of the same challenges faced by the course development groups as well as some of their own.

Since the student learning outcomes will be assessed throughout the students' engagement of the academic program, the transition from the first year through the fourth will be another area of challenge. Faculty opted to dispense with a middle assessment at the start of the junior/third year, but the retention of the assessment point at graduation will necessitate attention to the learning outcomes in the majors themselves. Our campus already has a robust and required senior seminar program and comprehensive examination in each major area of study; helping disciplinary faculty align these with the outcomes will require lots of close work with programs utilizing various means of curriculum organization.

Perhaps the greatest challenge, though, will be in developing and maintaining a sense of curricular coherence throughout the campus community. The activity of branding the curriculum—naming the various unique components and developing the language that will represent it to the campus community and prospective and incoming students—will prove instrumental in fostering a sense of unity for the curriculum (DelliCarpini, Kinkead this volume). The thoughtful continuation of the curriculum into the major fields of study is another part of achieving this coherence. By demonstrating the connection between the curriculum, the campus mission and vision, and the strategic plan, we hope to enable a successful achievement of this coherence in the campus culture's understanding. The final learning point is that, whether the reform effort is large or small, college-wide or isolated to one program or course, there are a number of factors to consider on the road to the completed project, and the specific institutional context will invariably exert pressures on the process. As I've discussed here, though, it's possible to harness aspects of the culture that prove helpful and find ways around those that impede progress through diligence, dialogue, and an openness to change.

Notes

1. *Designing and Assessing Courses and Curricula: A Practical Guide* (Diamond, R., 3rd Ed. Jossey-Bass: 2008); *Shaping the College Curriculum: Academic Plans in Context* (Lattuca and Stark, Jossey-Bass: 2009)

2. This group of five had some overlap with the previous group that attended the New Orleans conference. The author, the dean of the college, and the core curriculum director attended both AAC&U events.

Works Cited

Diamond, Robert M., *Designing and Assessing Courses and Curricula: A Practical Guide*. 3rd Ed. San Francisco, CA: Jossey-Bass, 2008. Print.

Gladstein, Jill M. and Dara Rossman Regaignon. *Writing Program Administration at Small Liberal Arts Colleges*. Anderson, SC: Parlor Press, 2012. Print.

Lattuca, Lisa R. and Joan S. Stark. *Shaping the College Curriculum: Academic Plans in Context*. San Francisco, CA: Jossey-Bass, 2009. Print.

"Strategic Plan: Across the Street and Around the Globe." *Millsaps College*. Millsaps College, n.d. Web. 24 July 2014.

Yancey, Kathleen Blake. "Delivering College Composition: A Vocabulary for Discussion," *Delivering College Composition: The Fifth Canon*. Ed. Kathleen Blake Yancey. Portsmouth, NH: Heinemann, 2006. 1–16. Print.

PART III: RELATING, REFLECTING, AND RESISTING

9 When Fantasy Themes Collide: Implementing a Public Liberal Arts Mission in Changing Times

Rita Malenczyk and Lauren Rosenberg

In this chapter, we explore what it means to administer a writing program within a public liberal arts institution. Unlike WPAs in private liberal arts colleges, we—the coordinator of First-Year Composition (Lauren) and Writing Program director (Rita)—have to respond to the needs and backgrounds of a state university population, as well as to pressures from the larger state community college and university system of which our institution is a part. Particularly, as WPAs in a public comprehensive institution, we are susceptible to shifts in the mission of our university as they are dictated by our legislature. The pressures we experience take the form of directives to standardize placement; to align our curricula with the Common Core State Standards; and to focus on developing "the next generation of workers," among others. In other words, in our system, the specter of efficiency is always present, in apparent contradiction to the values of the liberal arts implied by our institution's current vision statement.

In what follows, then, we describe those sites of apparent contradiction and discuss how we navigate them. As places of conflicted identity, public liberal arts institutions are ripe for the construction of what Ernest Bormann called rhetorical visions, which a range of audiences is expected to accept and to take part in. However, when those rhetorical visions collide—or time out—WPAs can find themselves in a bind: if part of our jobs is to develop programs that align with institutional mission and vision (see, for example, Vander Lei and Pugh), with which mission and vision do we align our programs? And what do we do when a mission or vision conflicts with our personal values and the values of our discipline? Ultimately, we advocate for what we value as teachers and WPAs: access and the right to a quality education. Based on a Deweyan vision of education as a right (one that state governments have a duty to maintain), we look at the conflicts of mission and vision that we face, mindful too of how our students are positioned by these colliding interests and agendas. This chapter looks into the binds and pulls that affect us in our complicated roles as administrative faculty. We consider institutional and political pressures in relation to the changes in institutional mission that accompany changing leadership, how these sometimes opposing rhetorical visions operate, and what we might do to maintain the integrity of our programs while also looking ahead.

Mission and the Problem of Identity

Located roughly one and a half hours south of Boston, two hours northeast of New York City, and ten minutes down the road from the main campus of the University of Connecticut, Eastern Connecticut State University is currently designated Connecticut's public liberal arts institution. Prior to this designation, Eastern's identity (and that of the other three Connecticut State Universities, Central, Western, and Southern)—was similar to that of many other state colleges and universities throughout the country: a former normal school that became a regional comprehensive.[1] And like other such schools, it was, in the public mind, the place where you went if you didn't have the test scores, grades, or money to go elsewhere. In Beverly Donofrio's *Riding in Cars with Boys*, a 1992 memoir set in Wallingford, Connecticut, Donofrio describes a conflict with her mother over whether she'd attend Central, Southern, or the University of Connecticut; her parents prefer Central or Southern because it's cheaper, but Donofrio counters with "UCONN's . . . harder to get into, but it's a better school." This perception of the Connecticut State Universities (CSUs) as second-rate was, as one might expect, pervasive in reality as well as in literature. When Rita first got to Eastern she would do an ice-breaking exercise in FYC that she'd done as a graduate teaching assistant at New York University: on the first day of class, have students interview each other and compose an introduction that included the answer to the question "Why did you come to Eastern?" When almost all the introductions included the phrase "Because I didn't get into UCONN," she cut that question out of the list. This attitude toward regional comprehensives is, of course, pervasive throughout the country, where the flagship research university is typically the more desirable when contrasted with schools in the "other" system.

Recognizing public perception as a problem in attracting motivated, high-achieving students who would be drawn to a liberal-arts education, Eastern's administration began a new public-relations campaign. A strategic plan was implemented that included as one point to make Eastern "a university of first choice," with revamped brochures that showcased students doing things traditionally associated with a private liberal arts education: sculpting, performing plays, reading, listening attentively in class. Admissions standards were also raised somewhat, with higher SAT scores and stronger high school records being required for entrance. This campaign has, if anecdotal evidence is any indication, increased Eastern's desirability in the minds of prospective students.

However, like the first-year student who leaves home a well-scrubbed honors student and returns for Thanksgiving having discovered all sorts of places to put body piercings, institutions that try to reinvent themselves always carry the burden of their history. Eastern's identity is split in a way that of private colleges is not: said identity resides in part with Eastern's new mission but also in part with its history and continued identity as a regional state university, where value and practicality coincide. Eastern's motto, "A Liberal Education. Practically Applied," as well as a new internship program called Liberal Arts Work!, reflect the very real anxiety of what remains Eastern's and similar institutions' primary clientele. The working- and middle-class parents whose children attend Eastern, many of whom did not go to college, worry that a liberal education will lead to unemployment and that more vocation-oriented majors, such as Business or Computer Science, are safer paths for their children to take; they pass this anxiety about the marketability of traditional liberal-arts majors (English, History) down to those who become our students (Klausman, this volume).

Anxiety surrounding marketability is not the only factor at stake. Our first generation students sometimes tell us (publicly in class discussions or more privately in our offices) about the tensions they experience with family members who imply that their attitude has changed since they went to college: now they must surely believe they are "better" than their relatives and friends who did not go to college. While clearly an expression of anxiety over class ascension, our students' experiences with this kind of tension are disturbing and real. They worry, as writers such as Richard Rodriguez and Victor Villaneuva have clearly documented, about becoming distanced from family when they assimilate the discourse of the university. The truth is that they *do* change from the influence of their liberal arts education in ways that our society promotes. Parents worry that their children's increased cultural capital will translate into rejection of them; these concerns for both generations remind us how powerful the emotional aspect of college attendance can be and just how important it is to take their worries seriously.

Yet Eastern is committed—admirably, in our view—to continuing to serve a clientele of first generation, working- and middle-class students, a commitment reflected in its existing vision statement: "Advancing its position as a model for social responsibility, environmental stewardship, and *educational access*, the University will be recognized as a resource that is responsive to the needs of the region and the state" (emphasis added). When the astrophysicist Neil DeGrasse Tyson gave Eastern's commencement address a few years ago, he opened by commenting on the fact that over half of our students are first-generation (Stacom et al.); the cheer that filled the auditorium in response demonstrated the students' recognition of, and pride in, their roots and their accomplishments, a demonstration that surely was not lost on the members of the administration seated on the stage.

What was also probably not lost, however, is that maintaining a commitment to a large first-generation population—in other words, to access—requires ignoring (to some extent) measures of educational quality and institutional desirability generally accepted by the public. For example, SUNY-Geneseo—another public liberal-arts college on which Eastern sought to model itself in the early days of its self-reinvention—trumpets the mean combined SAT Critical Reading and Math scores of its admitted students in its viewbook, presumably to assure prospective students that they will not be sitting in classes with people not as smart as they.[2]

Complicating matters even further is Eastern's place within a larger system. While the Connecticut State University system had been separated from the community college system since its beginnings, the two were merged in 2011, due to Governor Dannel Malloy's desire for the system to operate more efficiently. Malloy's perception was that CSU and community college students were taking too long to finish their degrees, a national issue well-documented in *The Chronicle of Higher Education* and *Inside Higher Ed* (see, for instance, *The Chronicle*'s "College Completion" site, and Fain, "Getting More Complete" and "Forks in the

Road"). Malloy argued that the state economy was suffering as a result, and that much of this delay was caused by the separation of the CSUs and community colleges into two different systems despite the high rate at which students transfer between them. Malloy's view initiated the change in public higher education that we grapple with now: "We need to make it a lot easier, particularly for people who are under pressure because they're working, they're raising children, make it easier for them to earn their degrees. And we need to get a lot of the bureaucracy out of the way and to flatten the management of these systems" (Malloy, qtd. in Lambeck). As a result of the merger and Malloy's expressed desire for efficiency, a governor-appointed Board of Regents (BOR) replaced the CSU schools' individual system offices and boards of trustees. More recently, there has been discussion from the current president of the BOR about standardizing courses, exporting courses from one college to another by video, and not duplicating programs at different campuses. It seems that in his view, the newly merged system creates one campus, in which the primary concern is efficiency of delivery, not uniqueness of any one school's mission (DelliCarpini, this volume).[3] While we recognize the importance of providing college access to a range of students, not just those of traditional age, this view nevertheless ignores benefits that may accrue to students of all backgrounds and ages from a sense of connection to a place, a sense of support from a faculty to whom they have physical access, and the opportunity to conduct their own research projects with close mentoring and advising.

Fantasy Theme Analysis

We see this very complicated scenario, in which mission statements, goals, ideals, and perceptions collide, as a conflict of rhetorical visions. In "Fantasy and Rhetorical Vision: The Rhetorical Criticism of Social Reality," Ernest Bormann describes how fantasy may become reality for a particular group or groups. Bormann's work draws on that of psychologist Robert Bales, who studied "the dynamic process of group fantasizing" (396) and claimed that

> The culture of the interacting group stimulates in each of its members a feeling that he has entered a new realm of reality—a world of heroes, villains, saints, and enemies—a drama, a work of art . . . In such moments, . . . one is transported to a world which seems somehow even more real than the everyday world . . . One's

> feelings fuse with the symbols and images which carry the feeling in communication and sustain it over time. One is psychologically taken into a psychodramatic fantasy world, in which others in the group are also involved. (Bales, qtd. in Bormann 398)

From Bales's study, Bormann theorized that not only did moments of fantasizing to create reality happen in small groups (a process he called "chaining out a fantasy theme") but also "in larger groups hearing a public speech:"

> A rhetorical vision is constructed from fantasy themes that chain out in face-to-face interacting groups, in speaker-audience transactions, in viewers of television broadcasts, in listeners to radio programs, and in all the diverse settings for public and intimate communication in a given society. Once such a rhetorical vision emerges it contains dramatis personae and typical plot lines that can be alluded to in all communication contexts and spark a response reminiscent of the original emotional chain. (398)

As an example of rhetorical vision in action, Bormann cites the American Puritan colonists of the seventeenth century, who through the speeches of their ministers came to see themselves as participants in part of a larger drama, that of the struggle of God's chosen people. The fantasy theme of the Puritans as soldiers "conquering new territories for God" (402), was repeated over and over to "spark a response" in the listener: "The relationship between a rhetorical vision and a specific fantasy theme within a message explains why so much 'persuasive' communication simply repeats what the audience already knows" (398). Bormann notes that despite the squalor and drudgery of their everyday lives, the Puritans, due largely to the preaching of their leaders,

> led an internal fantasy life of mighty grandeur and complexity. They participated in a rhetorical vision that saw the migration to the New World as a holy exodus of God's chosen people. The Biblical drama that supported their vision was that of the journey of the Jews from Egypt into Canaan. John Cotton's sermon delivered when Winthrop's company was leaving for Massachusetts was on the text, "Moreover I will appoint a place for my people Israell[sic], and I will plant them, that they may dwell in a place of their own, and move no more" (402).

Education is, of course, a prime site for the playing-out of rhetorical visions at both the national and local level, and the Puritan vision is not absent from this scenario. As Linda Adler-Kassner has claimed, following Sacvan Bercovitch, the jeremiad—a form of Puritan rhetoric in which the audience was reminded of its "chosen" status and continually exhorted to build God's kingdom in the New World—remains part of the public discourse surrounding education to this day (38-58). Adler-Kassner notes that

> The Progressive Era version of this jeremiad has served as an enduring frame surrounding stories about the purpose of education in the United States. Through it, education is seen as an essential training ground for preparing students for participation in the democracy. But because of the porous and flexible nature of the progressive pragmatic jeremiad, it supports multiple, conflicting stories about how that purpose should be accomplished. (38)

At the university level—at our university, at any rate—"stories about the purpose of education in the United States" take the form of mission and vision statements that, as Adler-Kassner notes, sometimes conflict in their goals. In what follows, we describe and analyze the two rhetorical visions that have emerged at Eastern, a liberal arts vision and a more business-oriented, vocational one, and discuss how we position ourselves and our administrative work in relation to those competing visions.

THE LIBERAL ARTS VISION

In 2006, when Lauren interviewed for her job at Eastern, the school had just redefined itself in the way we have described, as the liberal arts campus of the Connecticut State University system. While the legislature had given it the "public liberal arts" designation in 1998, the school did not become a member of the Council of Public Liberal Arts Colleges until 2004, and the new mission was still inchoate. As a job candidate, she was prepped by the search chair: when you meet with the academic vice president, the chair said, he will want to know how you define a public liberal arts education.

It went as the search chair promised. As soon as the interview started, the vice president brought up the idea of a public liberal arts education. He referenced an article in *Business Week* about Amherst College president Anthony Marx that called Marx a "campus revolutionary" because of his vision of admitting more lower-income students into the elite college (Symonds). Luckily, Lauren was familiar with Marx's vision, which she had already considered a fantasy of the liberal arts—though a different version, to be sure, from the one the vice president was promoting. Marx, however, was a key "dramatis personae" in what was becoming the rhetorical vision Eastern would promote: the vice president was taking Marx's vision in new directions that he felt would create a *particular* vision for Eastern, with Lauren (at least at this point in her career) aspiring to play a part in this drama.

A couple of years earlier, in a commencement address, Marx had laid out his rhetorical vision by claiming that at Amherst, "Compared with Europe... we have instead chosen to invest in providing the wherewithal for success by means of education. As a society, we are *venture capitalists of the mind* more than custodians of the body" (emphasis added). This is an example of the liberal arts re-inventing itself in changing times, proclaiming to the public via mainstream media (*Business Week*) and to the private sector (graduates and their families) that the institution is committed to reaching out to new populations of students, students from nontraditional backgrounds, "talented" students who must be recruited and funded differently because they are the new "venture capitalists." Marx's vision introduces a metaphor of finance into liberal arts education.

In this speech, Marx also acknowledged that the economic disparity in this country influences which colleges and universities—in other words, which fantasies of the liberal arts—students and their families choose or "chain into" (to use Bormann's phrase): "And of those who do aspire to college, many either do not know of the top colleges or set their sights lower. Prestige that attracts can also intimidate" (Marx). Here's the fantasy expressed in Marx's rhetoric:

> Though we believe we are a society of educational venture capitalists, instead we are still investing far more in blue chips than in start-ups. We should know better. Where this great diverse world's young people are concerned, supporting more of the start-ups, as well as the blue chips, will more than enhance our investment. (Marx)

In other words, it would be a wise investment to admit and support more students from lower-income backgrounds (the "start-ups"). Their presence would "enhance" the contribution of the traditional "blue-chip" student.

During Lauren's interview, Eastern's vice president asked what she thought of the idea of the new venture capitalist, and she came up with a response appropriate for this administrator (who was also an economist). But in our opinion, what he really wanted to know was: how do you envision the idea of importing Marx's vision of the liberal arts to this public institution? The designation, "a liberal education practically applied" was new, and what it meant was yet to be fully articulated. What Lauren understood from his questioning was that it would be the job of new faculty to define the vision.

In the moment of the interview, she answered by inventing a connection, essentially bridging two fantasy themes. She compared Marx's rhetorical vision, which also has a theme of inclusivity, though cast in the language of investment, to what she imagined this state school wanted: to claim the right to the liberal arts and offer it to its students, thus making college seem, well, more like college. The liberal arts as she understood it from her experience as a graduate of a liberal arts college? An ideal that promises expansiveness, abandon, a sort of luxury to suspend time, and permission to explore and play (DeRouen, this volume). Wonder. Freedom of the mind. A sense of possibility. Could anyone, not just the wealthy, participate in this version of the four-year American college? That day in the vice president's office, Lauren argued that certainly, the ideals of the liberal arts could—and should—be available to students at a regional state college just as they are assumed to underpin private elite schools.

Lauren got the job. But she was aware that there was an aspect of the liberal arts ideal that she had neglected to make explicit in her meeting with the vice president (and why would she, in an interview where she had been asked to spin out a fantasy theme?). It was the liberal arts notion of suspended practicality. In true liberal arts colleges, students are given permission to ignore practical concerns for four years and study such wonderful (and impractical) disciplines as art, theatre, poetry, philosophy, and music because, presumably, they are in an enchanted moment, a period of wonder when the mundane can be ignored. Lauren had argued for John Dewey's vision of democratic education in which "all share in useful service and all enjoy a worthy leisure" (256).

There are other fantasies of the liberal arts that come to mind too, all operating and colliding simultaneously. The classical notion of the liberal institution providing the environment for development of a particular man/citizen is played out in *The Education of Henry Adams*, another rhetorical vision. Adams's 1918 autobiography, a self-indulgent but honest examination of his life, considers how the act of living itself is an education, and in this way the author creates a liberal arts ideal. Adams is considered a model of the liberally educated individual who dedicates his life to a study of the world around him. When the author attends college, he has this to say about his own formal education:

> Harvard College, as far as it educated at all, was a mild and liberal school, which sent young men into the world with all they needed to make respectable citizens, and something of what they wanted to make useful ones. Leaders of men it never tried to make. Its ideals were altogether different. The Unitarian clergy had given to the College a character of moderation, balance, judgment, restraint, what the French called *mesure*; excellent traits, which the College attained with singular success, so that its graduates could commonly be recognized by the stamp, but such a type of character rarely lent itself to autobiography. In effect, the school created a type but not a will. Four years of Harvard College, if successful, resulted in an autobiographical blank, a mind on which only a water-mark had been stamped. (50-51)

For Adams, the institution's "stamp" offers little more than social capital; his self-education has greater value. However, in his description of the "mild and liberal" college, Adams identifies features of the liberal arts that he criticizes yet embraces. A liberal arts education teaches qualities of citizenship that include "moderation, balance, judgment, restraint," traits that one will need for a career in, say, diplomacy, government, or the church. It is certainly not a vocational model, but instead a program for creating respectability and excellence. And, of course, it is a model that stays with us, re-spun into more inclusive contemporary versions. Still, it remains a fantasy of training citizens, as Adler-Kassner suggests.

So, then, is it possible to "practically apply" the liberal arts? Can all students pursue their interests with abandon like Adams? Are they entitled to that sense of wonder? To lose and redefine themselves in the ways that a liberal arts vision promises while also "practically applying" what they learn? We see the yoking of the liberal arts with practicality to be a collision of incompatible rhetorical visions. The concept of the liberal arts "practically applied" was, at Eastern, a way to sell its working and ascending middle-class students something previously reserved for the upper classes, the promise of education with leisure time and space for rumination. But Dewey would argue that the kind of education we promise to the working public still does not match what is available to the elite classes:

> The idea still prevails that a truly cultural or liberal education cannot have anything in common, directly at least, with industrial affairs, and that the education which is fit for the masses must be a useful or practical education in a sense which opposes useful and practical to nurture of appreciation and liberation of thought. (257)

Many of our working- and middle-class students are accustomed to operating in the world with the implicit understanding that their decisions must be economically responsible, and therefore worthwhile. They must be able to defend their decision to attend, and maintain their commitment to their decision to study, for the four years when they could have been active in the workforce. The burden is on them to continually measure the value of college versus work. Many of their choices already have been about practical application; one can see how they are interpellated by the "practically applied" tagline. They are the intended consumers of this particular version of the liberal arts fantasy. And this version, geared to this population of practical consumers, is its own rhetorical vision. Bormann asks, "How are the members of a rhetorical community characterized" (401)? One could say that students at Eastern "participate in a rhetorical vision" that envisions the liberal arts as accessible to all; the liberal arts experience as potentially universal to everyone, no matter what one's social class, is in Bormann's terms, a fantasy "chaining out." However, given the conflict between rhetorical visions encapsulated here, this fantasy fails to be a truly enabling one—a rhetorical vision that can help students really achieve what is being promised to them—and is, rather, a bill of goods (Klausman, this volume).

Of course, we are aware that institutional fantasies help both to maintain the reputation of universities and also to promote changes within them. We know that the fervor generated by campus traditions as well as by revised missions are what encourage clientele (parents and students) to "chain into" such fantasies and thereby aid in solidifying the fantasy. People and institutions depend on their fantasies; they also depend on campus leaders to arrive with new rhetorical visions. The public expects to see campus culture spun differently with each change in leadership, whether institutional or legislative. Yet, we question how these changes impact both our students' educational experience and our writing programs. As Vander Lei and Pugh observe, "If students experience institutional mission most significantly in the classroom, then writing faculty experience institutional mission most importantly in the writing program" (112). Changes in institutional mission play out in terms of the values and design of writing programs. Thus, changes in leadership directly affect our actions as WPAs.

THE SPECTER OF EFFICIENCY: REDEFINING THE FANTASY IN CHANGING TIMES

In the eight years since Lauren's job interview, Eastern's rhetorical vision has shifted. The economic downturn, followed by the election of Governor Malloy and his new administration, brought about the merger of the Connecticut State Universities with the community colleges and the appointment of the BOR. Simultaneous with that was the passage of a state law, Public Act 12-40, intended to streamline developmental courses so that (as advocated by such organizations as Complete College America) more students might graduate, the assumption being that efforts to dispense with any programs meant to serve underprepared students will somehow improve education and make it more efficient. We have already noted, too, the BOR president's emphasis on efficiency in how the CSUs deliver curriculum.

We are, then, entering another period of redefinition that disrupts the liberal arts vision entirely. The concept of "a liberal education practically applied" is being replaced by this one, articulated in the following current statement from the BOR:

> As we chart our course for ConnSCU's [Connecticut State Colleges and Universities] future, we are about to embark on a transformational journey that will place our 17 institutions on the path to becoming Connecticut's world-class system of higher education. By uniting our ConnSCU institutions as one interconnected system, bolstering enrollment, strengthening online learning capacity, and better aligning coursework with the state's strongest industry growth sectors, our journey will improve the student experience and better prepare them to compete in the global economy. This transformational plan will create a synergy among our institutions resulting in centralized

services, cost reductions, and efficiencies—and in doing so, ConnSCU will continue to be accessible and affordable to our students, and a major contributor in the development of our state's economic growth, business expansion, and workforce development efforts. (Connecticut Board of Regents)

This particular rhetorical vision is articulated in terms of a fantasy journey: "We" (meaning the BOR who are "charting our course") will "embark on a transformational journey. . . . [O]ur journey will improve the student experience and better prepare them to compete in the global economy." There are a couple of different journeys going on here:the course-charting journey of the BOR—the heroes, with an eye toward "world-class" competition—and that of the students, who are being taken along, and taken in, as the travelers on this journey. The travelers, like the system that produces them, will become transformed by their education (through coursework that aligns with industry) into efficient, industrious, and competitive members of the workforce. This metaphor of a journey essentially re-spins education into a low-cost program of worker preparation. The BOR statement promises that even the coursework will be re-charted to align with their vision.

This vision, of course, essentially replaces the liberal arts fantasy with a vocational fantasy that is stripped down to a bulleted list of pathways—efficient, cost-effective, skills-linked—that will ensure students emerge in four years with a product, a "stamp" (although a vastly different stamp from the one Adams bemoaned), ready for the state's workforce. Unlike the previous vision, this competing one hardly sends a message of liberal thinking, or of any kind of thinking, for that matter. Thought, inquiry, and critique are hardly mentioned in the ConnSCU vision. Instead, "ConnSCU provides a rigorous education preparing students to be strong competitors in the global marketplace and providing a comprehensive talent pool to the state's employers" (Connecticut Board of Regents).

How, then, does this change in rhetorical vision affect us as WPAs? As Vander Lei and Pugh have noted in their advice to WPAs on responding to mission, "As with all things, WPAs should consider not only the rhetorical possibilities but also the limitations of clarity and consensus when working with institutional mission" (115). In other words, how do we respond to these changes of mission in a way that is professionally responsible given the conflicting interests implicit in our complicated roles? Even though we are WPAs with the responsibility of representing our university's rhetorical vision in our programs, we are also faculty with commitments to our students and to our own needs as scholars in rhetoric and composition.

Much depends, however, on whether the BOR can pull off its vision at Eastern and if there are spaces for protest. Faculty will surely object, and already there is some movement toward resistance. But will the state's residents buy this vocational fantasy? Bormann says that people have to willingly participate in a fantasy theme for it to be successful. Then again, maybe people don't have a choice if they want higher education they can afford. This is what they get for their dollars. No more liberal arts. Instead, they become "a comprehensive talent pool to the state's employers" (Connecticut Board of Regents). Then, what happens to the promise of the liberal arts? Does it return to only those who can afford it? Is it taken away? Was it only the fantasy of a moment, and then the moment is gone?

Pushing Back

These are some of the questions we find ourselves asking as we decide which fantasy, or rhetorical vision, to build our writing program upon—or, to think about things a bit differently for a moment—which principles to follow as WPAs. Any WPA, particularly one who has worked within public higher education, knows that as university or system leaders come and go (and as we have documented), the visions those leaders bring affect the work of the WPA. A certain amount of compromise is necessary, then, to do that work; however, it's also necessary, particularly in changing times, for WPAs to understand and articulate the principles from which they administer. Adler-Kassner has likened the turbulent situations in which WPAs can find themselves to a skyscraper in a storm: "Without a firm foundation, the skyscraper can't stand; it just won't hold up its own structure. On the other hand, a skyscraper also has to be fairly flexible on top of that foundation. If it's too rigid, it will break in strong winds. . . ." ("What Is Principle?" 395). To prepare themselves for the winds of change, WPAs should find a way to articulate their principles. To put it another way: while they may have no choice in the rhetorical visions new institutional or governmental leaders bring and in which they may find themselves cast, they should also decide what *other* rhetorical visions they want to participate in simultaneously, what *other* fantasy themes they want to echo, and what *other* dramas they want to play parts in. Because the WPA is also a *dramatis personae*, representing the university's mission.

To help us make these decisions, we find ourselves drawing on another, more durable rhetorical vision inscribed in the field of composition and rhetoric for the last thirty years: that of access and the right to a quality education. The 2014 CCCC conference theme, "Open Source[s], Access, Futures," attests to the staying power of that vision, which was established in 1977 with the publication of *Errors and Expectations* (Shaughnessy) if not before (Ritter), and lives on in the work of scholars and teachers too numerous to list here.[4] What underlies this vision is a range of assumptions: that students of all abilities and backgrounds deserve an advanced education; that those students' abilities are shaped by social forces and defined by educational systems; that sound student-centered pedagogy can and should help students gain self-efficacy within these forces and systems; and the belief that continuing to educate the public about all these matters is a worthwhile thing to do (Adler-Kassner, *Activist*). As publications in rhetoric and composition from the 1970s to the present remind us, our field supports the vision of a college education centered on the student as thinker and learner, rather than as a pawn in a state-sponsored plan for workforce production, and so do we.

These underlying elements of the vision of access and the right to a quality education help us decide when to give in to pressures brought about by other, contradictory, visions and when to push back. For example, when the BOR issued a directive to align our FYC curriculum with the Common Core State Standards, Lauren used the occasion to talk with faculty at a nearby community college and local high school teachers about their own goals for their students and how we might work with them to achieve those goals, while still complying with the mandate. In hiring peer tutors for the Writing Center and developmental writing classes, Rita maintains diversity as a goal, acknowledging that in addition to providing role models for our first-generation students and students of color, a diverse group of tutors is experienced in shuttling between different discourse communities (Grimm 88-89). Furthermore, Public Act 12-40 has threatened Eastern's system of directed self-placement. Our provost, citing a need for "multiple measures," has used the law to dictate that we place students on the high and low ends of the SAT Critical Reading spectrum using those scores, rather than according to the essay they write as part of the DSP process. We are pushing back against this imposition because it eliminates our students' ability to select a course that is right for them, by advocating with members of the PA 12-40 implementation committee for true "multiple measures" and by ensuring that our pedagogy is still accessible to all. Lastly, Rita, as a faculty representative on our University Senate, has helped spearhead efforts to resist the BOR president's efforts to homogenize our four campuses. We recognize that there is no neat wrap-up to this story, that our proposed solutions are only provisional and part of an ongoing situation. Yet while we recognize that our resistance may ultimately be futile, our field's rhetorical vision calls us to keep trying.

Notes

1. "Regional comprehensive institution" is, as many readers will know, a Carnegie Foundation classification that is no longer officially in use (for details of the reasons for the change, see Di McCormick and Zhao). However, it still has currency in conversation. Eastern, because it has several graduate programs, is now classified as a Master's College/University (smaller program) (Carnegie Foundation).

2. 1340.

3. See Schwalm's discussion of transfer articulation and course delivery (134).

4. See, for instance, the February 2014 issue of *College Composition and Communication*, with its editor's introduction titled "The Pursuit of Promise" (Yancey), as well as a review section that considers recent books on the intersections of social class and postsecondary education (Mitchler; Dilger, Hum; Mahle-Grisez).

Works Cited

Adams, Henry. *The Education of Henry Adams: An Autobiography.* NY: Heritage Press, 1918. Print.

Adler-Kassner, Linda. *The Activist WPA: Changing Stories About Writing and Writers.* Logan: Utah State UP, 2008. Print.

—. "What Is Principle?" *A Rhetoric for Writing Program Administrators.* Ed. Rita Malenczyk. Anderson, SC: Parlor Press, 2013. 394–406. Print.

Bormann, Ernest G. "Fantasy and Rhetorical Vision: The Rhetorical Criticism of Social Reality." *Quarterly Journal of Speech* 58 (1972): 396–407. PDF file..

Connecticut Board of Regents for Higher Education. "Transform CSCU 2020." Conneticut State Colleges and Universities, 5 March 2014. Web. 20 March 2014.

Dewey, John. *Democracy and Education*. NY: Free Press, 1916, 1944. Print.
Dilger, Bradley. "The Unseen Weight of Class." *College Composition and Communication* 65.3 (2014): 464–72. Web. 8 July 2014.
Donofrio, Beverly. *Riding in Cars with Boys: Confessions of a Bad Girl Who Makes Good*. NY: Penguin, 1992. Kindle edition.
Eastern Connecticut State University. "Vision Statement." Eastern Conneticut University, n.d. Web. 19 April 2014.
Fain, Paul. "Getting More Complete." *Inside Higher Ed*. Inside Higher Ed, 15 Nov. 2012. PDF file.
—. "Forks in the Road." *Inside Higher Ed*. Inside Higher Ed, 24 July 2012. Web. 8 July 2014.
Grimm, Nancy M. "Retheorizing Writing Center Work to Transform a System of Advantage Based on Race." *Writing Centers and the New Racism: A Call for Sustainable Dialogue and Change*. Eds. Laura Greenfield and Karen Rowan. Logan, UT: Utah State UP, 2011. 75–100. Print.
Hum, Sue. "When Institutions and Education Reproduce Social Class Inequities: What Else Factors In? Or, the Problem of Stinky Skin." *College Composition and Communication* 65.3 (2014): 472–78. Web. 8 July 2014.
Lambeck, Linda Conner. "Malloy Proposes Merging CSU with Community College System." *Stamford Advocate*. Hearst Media Services Conneticut, 9 Feb. 2011. Web. 13 April 2014. http://www.governor.ct.gov/malloy/cwp/view.asp?A=11&Q=473716.
Mahle-Grisez, Lisa. "For Whom Does It Profit?" *College Composition and Communication* 65.3 (2014): 478–85. Web. 8 July 2014.
Marx, Anthony. "Amherst College Commencement Address." *Amherst College*. Amherst College, May 2004. Web. 4 March 2014.
McCormick, Alexander C., and Chun-Mei Zhao. "Rethinking and Reframing the Carnegie Classification." *Change* (Sept.-Oct. 2005): 51–57. Web. 16 April 2014.
Mitchler, Sharon. "The Persistence and Complications of Class." *College Composition and Communication* 65.3 (2014): 459–64. Web. 8 July 2014.
Ritter, Kelly. *Before Shaughnessy: Basic Writing at Yale and Harvard, 1920–1960*. Carbondale, IL: Southern Illinois UP, 2009. Print.
Rodriguez, Richard. *Hunger of Memory: The Education of Richard Rodriguez*. Boston: David R. Godine, 1982. Print.
Schwalm, David E. "What Is Transfer Articulation?" *A Rhetoric for Writing Program Administrators*. Ed. Rita Malenczyk. Anderson, SC: Parlor Press, 2013. 131–42. Print.
Shaughnessy, Mina. *Errors and Expectations: A Guide for the Teacher of Basic Writing*. NY: Oxford UP, 1977. Print.
Stacom, Don, Hilda Muñoz and Jesse Leavenworth. "More Than 3,000 Awarded Degrees at Six Connecticut Colleges." *Hartford Courant*. Hartford Courant, 23 May 2010. Web. 13 April 2014.

State University of New York at Geneseo. "Viewbook." *Nxtbook Media*. Nxtbook Media, 2013. Web. 19 April 2014.

Symonds, William C. "Campus Revolutionary." *Bloomberg Business Week Magazine*. Bloomberg LP, 26 Feb., 2006. Web. 4 March 2014.

The Carnegie Classification of Institutions of Higher Learning. Carnegie Foundation, n.d. PDF file.

Vander Lei, Elizabeth, and Melody Pugh. "What Is Institutional Mission?" *A Rhetoric for Writing Program Administrators*. Ed. Rita Malenczyk. Anderson, SC: Parlor Press, 2013. 105–17. Print.

Villanueva, Victor, Jr. *Bootstraps: From an American Academic of Color*. Urbana, IL: NCTE, 1993. Print.

Yancey, Kathleen Blake. "From the Editor: The Pursuit of Promise." *College Composition and Communication* 65.3 (2014): 401–05. Web. 8 July 2014.

10 Negotiating Institutional Missions: Writing Center Tutors as Rhetorical Actors

Andrea Rosso Efthymiou and Lauren Fitzgerald

Writing program and writing center administrators at institutions with specialized missions need to attend to these missions as well as the values of the larger communities that they reflect. At religiously affiliated institutions in particular, where such stakeholders may share explicit and implicit communal values of a certain religious group, writing center and writing program administrators have the potential to "develop a rich understanding of the institution's ongoing purpose, and . . . find an opportunity to better align the mission statement of the institution and the mission of its writing program" (Vander Lei and Pugh 108). Following Elizabeth Vander Lei and Melody Pugh's advice, we encourage administrators to view their centers and programs in conversation with the greater institutional mission and to investigate this conversation.

We offer this advice based on our collective twenty-five years of experience at Yeshiva University (YU), the first and largest US institution of higher education under Orthodox Jewish auspices. For instance, during the first half of her career at YU, Lauren wrote or co-authored several pieces that, tightly focused on this institutional context, at least implicitly aimed to demonstrate that the classes she taught and programs she directed aligned with YU's mission and cultural values of the community it served. Doing so was important for a number of reasons. This research helped her gain knowledge about both the university and the community it served so that she could do her job more effectively—for example, by alerting new writing colleagues to the impact of the Jewish holiday schedule on when students can complete their work ("*Torah U'Madda*") or to show how seemingly straightforward notions of plagiarism and academic integrity are complicated and enriched by this religiously informed context, but not necessarily in the moralistic ways some might expect (Fountain and Fitzgerald). Moreover, this research produced much-needed publications for her tenure file that would, she hoped, speak to her own appropriateness and relevance to the institution and its mission, something she felt no little anxiety about as an obvious outsider. (She earned tenure and the programs are still going strong, so this plan seems to have worked.)

Influenced by Lauren's work at the Wilf Campus Writing Center of YU, Andrea too has researched the institution's undergraduate mission to better understand how this mission does and does not dovetail with YU's Beren Writing Center. As the Associate Director of the Beren Writing Center, Andrea occupies a position that is strongly administrative yet offers her the privilege of working closely and daily with tutors who vocally engage with YU's institutional mission inside and outside of the writing center. This research has oriented Andrea with the Jewish Orthodox mission of the institution, while also offering ample opportunity to document the rhetorical activities of tutors in and around the writing center. This work documenting tutors' rhetorical activities as a way of engaging with institutional mission has happily become Andrea's dissertation research.

Prompted by Andrea's dissertation research, we've learned something else that we want to focus on here—that along with attending to institutional mission, we should listen to those other crucial stakeholders in both our institutions and programs: students. Perhaps especially because of our work administering writing centers, sites that have long been noted for their student-centeredness especially when they are staffed by students (Bruffee; Kail and Trimbur; Trimbur), we have found that student tutors' collective and individual views of themselves and their communities don't always align with the stated mission of the institution, and these views in turn have important bearings on the work of our programs. Though our two writing centers operate separately, five miles apart and affiliated with the university's two quite distinct undergraduate colleges—Stern College for Women and Yeshiva College (for men)—we've found that the rhetorical activities of tutors on the two campuses engage with YU's institutional mission in ways that have given us new perspectives on the relationships of writing programs and institutional mission.

In understanding our tutors in terms of how they both listen to YU's institutional mission and engage with that mission in their writing center work, we see them as rhetorical actors—communal agents who engage in a variety of socially situated contexts. As rhetorical actors, tutors' rhetorical activities offer alternative models of interpreting and performing institutional mission to their colleagues in the writing center. Our work shows tutors communicating with each other and with other students, thinking of mission outside of their local context in the writing center, and extending their experiences at a religious, mission-driven institution to their communities and in their professional lives. A work that helps us frame how undergraduate tutors, as novice educators, engage with institutional rhetoric is Jessica Enoch's archival study *Refiguring Rhetorical Education: Women Teaching African American, Native American, and Chicano/a Students, 1865-1911*. Enoch offers us useful ways of thinking about how our tutors "create a rhetorical education that encourages students to interrogate the rules of rhetorical decorum and to consider what it would mean not to follow these rules but to break them" (71). While rhetorical education can be historically situated as a classical education in rhetoric and communication intended to prepare students for civic life (Glenn vii), we extend this definition, as Enoch does, to consider how an educational institution publically represents itself and how students at this institution mediate these institutional messages through their rhetorical activities within the institution. In other words, two questions we are asking are: how does institutional mission, as one form of public representation, serve as a reflection of the education an institution of higher education offers? Further, how do undergraduate students rhetorically, or publicly, perform adherence to and resistance of institutional mission?

As Andrea's work demonstrates, one tutor's resistance of a communal practice in the writing center—a breaking of a "rule of rhetorical decorum"—offers an alternative performance or presentation of such communal practice. Lauren's work shows that tutors on the Wilf Campus have developed a language for talking about difference that exceeds YU's undergraduate mission. Consistent with Enoch's presentation of the teachers in her archival study, tutors in our centers perform two complicated tasks at once: they perform institutional mission in ways sanctioned by that mission, while simultaneously engaging in "resistant pedagogical practices" (169) in the writing center. In so doing, tutors can be seen as engaging in "underlife" activities, a sociological concept made famous in composition studies in the late 1980s by Robert Brooke, who drew from Erving Goffman. With such activities, Brooks holds, "individuals . . . show that their identities are different from or more complex than the identities assigned them by organizational roles," in part by "distanc[ing] themselves from the surrounding institution" (142, 144). It is perhaps significant that the location for the underlife activities we see YU students engaging in as rhetorical actors is writing centers, which like Brooke's idealistic, if dated, vision of composition studies are also hailed as "disruptive" and off-the-grid sites of writer self-actualization (Brooke 150-51; Boquet 32, 67, 83; Grutsch McKinney 35-56).

Reading Institutional Mission as Shaping Rhetorical Education

At Yeshiva University, our mission, *Torah Umadda*, is to bring wisdom to life through all that we teach, by all that we do and for all those we serve.

- Our students learn and go forth, as both educated and ethical people, to share their own special talents with society
- Our faculty's research, academic work, and scholarly writings help bring wisdom to many of the most pressing social, political, medical, legal, and human rights issues facing the world today
- Our University serves as a platform to bring Yeshiva's collective wisdom to the world through our community outreach, publications, seminars, and broad range of academic programs

For Undergraduate Students

We bring wisdom to life by combining the finest contemporary academic education with the timeless teachings of Torah. It is Yeshiva's unique dual curriculum that teaches knowledge enlightened by values that helps our students gain the wisdom to make their lives both a secular and spiritual success.

—YU's Mission Statement, institutional website

Consistent with the research on institutional mission statements in higher education, YU's mission statement upholds the more universal conventions of the genre. For instance, in such phrases as "bring wisdom to life," "special talents," and "knowledge enlightened by values," as Christopher C. Morphew and Matthew Hartley describe in mission statements generally, the language here is "either excessively vague or unrealistically aspirational or both" (457). However, YU's mission stands out from others in the work that it does defining its specific audience. In its first sentence, this vagueness takes a specific form in the Hebrew phrase *Torah Umadda*, which is identified as *th*e mission of YU.[1] This phrase is not translated into English, one effect being that the mission becomes not merely vague but unintelligible for the non-Hebrew-speaking reader. To a reader with no discursive context for understanding *Torah Umadda*, the metaphor of "bring[ing] wisdom to life" can be further disorienting, in that the metaphor's meaning is unclear.

Though *Torah Umadda* is not translated, the undergraduate tutors that Andrea interviewed for her study access a specific translation of the term in their discussions of YU's mission. Tutors define *Torah Umadda* literally as "Bible and science" or "Bible and the secular world," a translation that reveals how the term *Torah Umadda* is not about transparency; rather, the institution's use of *Torah Umadda* is intended to draw rhetorical lines, fostering particular *identifications* (Burke 55) among an institution's stakeholders, lines that include members of a certain discourse community familiar with Hebrew and American Modern Orthodox Judaism. The discourse community implied by tutors' access to a definition of *Torah Umadda* reflects how, according to James Paul Gee, "Discourses . . . are ways of behaving, interacting, valuing, thinking, believing, speaking, and of reading and writing that are accepted as instantiations of particular roles (or 'types of people') by specific *groups of people* . . . Discourses are ways of being 'people like us.' They are 'ways of being in the world'" (viii). Considering *Torah Umadda* as functioning to define a discourse community, then, serves to highlight how YU's mission has a specific rhetorical function distinct among institutions of higher education. Gee's reading of Discourse identifies the multiple *topoi* that characterize discourse communities, many of which—like dress, prayer ritual, and language patterns—are particularly visible at a religious-driven institution like YU.

Understanding *Torah Umadda*—Bible and the secular world—as defining a discourse community begins to lay the groundwork for our understanding of how YU establishes a particular rhetorical education for its students. Although the institutional mission's invocation of *Torah Umadda* can disorient a non-Hebrew-speaking audience, the mission later becomes more explicit and accessible for a larger audience in its articulation of how the education YU offers its undergraduates "bring[s] wisdom to life": "We bring wisdom to life by combining the finest contemporary academic education with the timeless teachings of Torah. It is Yeshiva's unique dual curriculum that teaches knowledge enlightened by values that helps our students gain the wisdom to make their lives both a secular and spiritual success" (Yeshiva). YU's undergraduate dual curriculum, a concrete representation of *Torah Umadda* in a dual Judaic and liberal arts curriculum required of all students on the undergraduate level, is intended to educate the undergraduate women and men of YU's two campuses consistent with communal values and practices of Modern Orthodox Judaism in America. Consequently, YU's students are educated to understand and rhetorically communicate their religious identity within their community of peers. As will become evident below, many of YU's Modern-Orthodox Jewish students have lived lives that involve implicitly, if not explicitly, negotiating *Torah Umadda* as part of their day-to-day experiences. The undergraduate dual curriculum, then, is designed to provide a constant way to buttress students' religious education at an American institution of higher education, while furthering observant students' understanding and living of the mission. Our research finds that tutors revise the rhetorical education established at YU through moments where they both identify with and push against the undergraduate mission of the institution.

Writing Center Tutors Revising Rhetorical Education

Andrea's forthcoming dissertation, "Rhetorical Education in a Jewish Women's Writing Center," documents the rhetorical activities of undergraduate writing center tutors at YU's Beren campus, Stern College for Women, and argues that these rhetorical acts revise the institution's rhetorical education by offering alternative ways for understanding and performing institutional mission. One tutor, "Tara," who graduated in May 2013 with a Jewish Education major and an English minor, appropriated the space of the writing center for public negotiation of Yeshiva University's institutional mission. Through the rhetorical act of publically negotiating institutional mission, Tara's activity in the writing center and her later reflection on that activity in an interview with Andrea, serves as resistance of YU's rhetorical education.

In December 2011, during the moments before a writing center staff meeting, Tara appropriated the meeting—a space usually devoted to reflecting on tutoring sessions with student writers—to share with the staff her choice as a recently married woman to cover her hair. Covering one's hair after marriage is common for observant Jewish Orthodox women, and this practice extends from readings of the Torah that signify family law in Orthodox Judaism. In that December meeting, Tara, married only the month before, told the staff "how weird it is" to wear a *sheitel*, the Yiddish word for wig that some Orthodox Jewish women wear to cover their hair once they are married. The staff at *that* meeting on *that* day was composed solely of undergraduate tutors who were interested in following Tara's lead by taking up her hair covering as a line of conversation before the meeting started. The staff excitedly bombarded Tara with questions about her *sheital*, asking how it feels on her head and if it generates lots of heat, all the while offering compliments about how great her new hair looks. Throughout the conversation, Tara smiled, fingering her long, dark, glistening *sheital*. One staff member asked about the maintenance of Tara's wig, and Tara replied: "I always have a clean one to wear out. [The sheitel] gets dirty just like real hair. Not stinky like gym clothes, but dirty, just like any hair. So I have to wash it every few days. I even had to get it cut and styled. This *sheital* thing is serious." After more laughter and banter around Tara's wig, Andrea shifted the conversation towards administrative announcements for the writing center, and the staff moved to addressing whatever topic about peer tutoring that was on the agenda for that day. Through Tara's transaction with her tutor-colleagues, the writing center staff meeting that was typically a space for tutor education shifted its pedagogical focus to implicitly engage religious facets of the *Torah Umadda* mission of the institution.

What is latent in this exchange about Tara's *sheitel*, the wig she has chosen to externally represent her observance of family law in Orthodox Judaism, is that she performs a break from the conventions of her discourse community. In this rhetorical transaction in the writing center between Tara and her tutor-colleagues, all of whom are familiar with the religious practice of a married woman covering her hair, Tara identifies the "rules of rhetorical decorum" (Enoch 71) by both subtly invoking the institutional mission and resisting it. In one of my interviews with Tara, two years after this staff meeting, I asked her to recall this conversation about her *sheital*. In that interview, Tara connected the discussion about her hair covering to the religious identity of the institution. She told me that, at YU, "nobody talked about the culture of marriage in Judaism." Consistent with the work of scholars like Andrea Lieber and Tamar Ross whose research identifies the way Orthodox Judaism defines women's religious practices in terms of the private, rather than public, sphere, Tara revealed how the silence she felt as an observant Modern Orthodox Jew is specific to women. Tara also claimed that this private sphere of women's religious practices is amplified by the secrecy she perceived around the body of religious laws and practices that she didn't fully understand prior to becoming engaged to be married. Tara says: "I found out, when I got married, that nobody was talking. Nobody talks here. . . . You don't even learn that much about family law—and there's a lot of it—before you get engaged. You get engaged, and then you meet with a teacher; one specific woman, for however long it is that you're engaged." This piece of data points to the Judaic curriculum that is the cornerstone of YU's institutional mission. When Tara states that "you don't even learn that much about family law," she is indirectly pointing to the shortcomings that she sees in the Judaic core curriculum required of all students at YU. Part of this Judaic requirement on the women's campus involves a course in marriage law, a course that, according to Tara, didn't offer her enough of a satisfying picture of the way marriage laws would affect her life. Tara views this lack of education around marriage laws at her Jewish college as constructing a silence that is isolating; she even talked about feeling "pissed" that no one was talking. So in her transaction with tutor-colleagues, Tara strives to publically disrupt the silence she perceived around marriage laws in Modern Orthodoxy at YU.

Tara's linking of her conversation about covering her hair at a staff meeting with her frustration with the silence around marriage laws two years later reveals that her audience of peer tutors, although perhaps a small part of the institution in numbers—after all, our writing center employs about fifteen undergraduates each semester out of a student population of just over one thousand—in fact constitutes a "public." In an attempt to move beyond the familiar characterization of tutors as writing center stakeholders (Geller et al.), the data that features Tara figures tutors as institutional stakeholders, ones that listen to the mission and seek to push against it, pointing to ways that the mission falls short (Janangelo, Malenczyk and Rosenberg this volume).

The data from Tara's interview reveals other familiar characterizations for discussing writing center work as well, but also offers ways to complicate these characterizations. Tara connects her work as a peer tutor to her rhetorical act in the writing center when she says: "When I get to the writing center, everyone finds it hilarious that I'm bitching about the hair. *It's hot. It's itchy. I have so much hair on me right now.* It was so nice to be able to talk about it. . . . It's an openness." This openness points to a well-established characterization of writing centers as safe spaces (so common is this description, in fact, that an entire writing center conference was dedicated to questioning that metaphor in 2010). While there is certainly value in the comfort Tara felt sharing her experience covering her hair, it's worth noting how the familiar conception of writing-center-as-safe-space-between-student-and-tutor (see Grutsch McKinney 20-34) is refigured with this data. Tara's hair covering is both an external marker of religious identity and a public representation of an element of the institutional mission of the Jewish Orthodox college that Tara attends. In claiming a writing center staff meeting as a public forum, Tara is an undergraduate writing tutor who engages the institutional mission in ways she felt she could not outside of the writing center, particularly in her courses the institution has established for the sole purpose of furthering her religious education. And in her disruption of silence, Tara models an alternative for her tutor-colleagues who themselves might soon choose between silence and disruption of silence in their own observance of marriage laws.

As a final way to punctuate how Tara's rhetorical activity revises the undergraduate rhetorical education offered by YU, Tara connects her disruption of silence to her work in the writing center. When Tara explained the loneliness that she had felt silently dealing with marriage laws, Andrea asked her if her desire to talk about marriage laws was in any way related to her work in the writing center. Here's Tara's response:

> I think it's also having the encouragement. A big thing in the writing center is that a lot of times people know exactly what they want to write. They know exactly what they want to say, but they're not feeling confident enough. It's a lonely experience. [The writing center offers] companionship and shared experience. It's having the tutor be like, "Yes! I like that. That's good. You could do that." Having peer tutors also [. . .] say, "Yes, I took that class. I remember I did that paper." [Knowing someone] survived it, it's pretty nice.

Here Tara echoes how loneliness can frame both religious observance and the writing process. Yet she also articulates that, like her motivation to disrupt the silence around religious practice in an effort to share her feeling of isolation, working in the writing center complements the way she values "shared experience." This again frames the writing center as a safe-space, but also frames Tara's pedagogical goals: her work in the writing center, like her engagement with the institutional mission, demonstrates her communal values, her attempt to redefine the experience of college writing for students who come to the writing center and to redefine for tutors ways of upholding the religious values of the institutional mission.

WRITING CENTER TUTORS EXPANDING THE MISSION

> At the Wurzweiler School of Social Work, our mission is reflected by our history. We opened our doors at Yeshiva University in 1957 as America's only graduate social work school under Jewish auspices in a university setting.
> Throughout our history and with the full support of the University, we have reached out to an ever-widening constituency.
>
> —YU's Wurzweiler School of Social Work Mission Statement

Probably the most striking example of the way in which *Torah Umadda* is enacted in the writing center Lauren directs on the men's campus is in the one-with-one learning that is the cornerstone of writing center work. In traditional Judaism, a crucial means by which students (and, for many years, predominantly male students) engage in religious practice is in another kind of one-with-one learning, *havruta*, the paired, collaborative method of studying religious texts that is perhaps the oldest form of institutionalized collaborative pedagogy. Because most of the undergraduates who work in this center are deeply familiar with this process, engaging in it for the religious studies they participate in during their entire time in college, they come to the job usually already knowing very well what it's like to sit with someone else to discuss a text and the value of two heads rather than one in doing so. And despite essential differences between *havruta* partnerships and writing center peer tutoring—most importantly that the text that tutor and writer work on together is not divine—year after year, tutors and writers note the similarities

(Fitzgerald "Torah Is"). Perhaps partly as a result, our center is extremely popular, serving over a third of YU's undergraduate men.

However, this narrative—as well as others that Lauren has told about the alignment of the programs she has directed with the institutional mission—doesn't reveal the whole story. There is another, about the misalignment of institutional mission and program practice, about difference and diversity. For one thing, not all of the writers Wilf Writing Center tutors work with are undergraduates or familiar with *havruta* partnerships or even Judaism. This writing center also serves graduate students, including those from many of YU's non-sectarian graduate programs, most notably the Wurzweiler School of Social Work (WSSW).

The mission—and consequently the student body—of WSSW is markedly different from that of YU's undergraduate programs. This mission also signals a duality, but a different one from *Torah Umadda*. On the one hand, the school aligns itself with the university and its history: "We opened our doors at Yeshiva University in 1957 as America's only graduate social work school under Jewish auspices in a university setting." On the other, it acknowledges the school's increasing openness to a diverse student body: "Throughout our history and with the full support of the University, we have reached out to an ever-widening constituency." Though many students who attend WSSW are former YU undergraduates, many are not.

Initially, Lauren wondered if serving this "ever-widening constituency" would come into conflict with her need to show the Center's adherence to YU's undergraduate mission, which she understood to be about amplifying, if not enforcing, identification within the Orthodox community. During her first year on the job, for example, a student tutor was visibly upset after working with a WSSW student, declaring that he was "shocked" by her lack of skills as someone who had been admitted to graduate program. At the time, Lauren wondered if the tutor was also shocked by the identity differences he and the writer had to traverse—he, a Caucasian, Orthodox young man who had been in school practically his entire life (including his religious life); she, an older, African American woman who had been out of school between college and graduate school, and both working together at an institution that imposed gender segregation in all religious and several educational settings. This particular dyad, Lauren surmised, certainly would not have included the kind of comfortable, mutual identification typically found in *havruta* partnerships.

In part because of this assumption, Lauren decided to hire part-time faculty tutors (MAs and MFAs from other institutions) to work with social work students. However, doing so, ultimately if inadvertently, helped address this perceived conflict. Faculty tutors steadily increased the number of social work students who came to the Center. As a result, rather than segregating the undergraduate tutors from these graduate student writers, the groups mixed and mingled. To fulfill their tutor education program requirement of observing other tutors' sessions, undergraduate tutors sometimes sat in on faculty tutor sessions with social work students. More important, when the faculty tutors' appointments were booked up, social work students made appointments with undergraduate tutors and sometimes became repeat customers. Probably most important of all, undergraduate tutors began saying that they looked forward to these appointments and wanted more, even if the sessions weren't always comfortable and were sometimes even "shocking" because of the deeply personal and political nature of much of the writing social work students are asked to complete, whether related to their own lives or those of their clients.

Many of these undergraduate tutors wanted to work with social work students because they were planning ahead for graduate and professional schools and jobs that were not within the Orthodox community and for which they needed to be able to work comfortably and professionally, face-to-face and side-by-side, with people whose backgrounds and identities are different from their own. But these tutors also knew they needed to learn how to do so. And this is where the faculty tutors proved most instrumental, helping to institute an aspect of the Center's tutor education program that has been subsequently co-led and finally taken over by undergraduate tutors themselves. This training includes helping tutors acknowledge the identity differences they need to work across and to prepare for content very different from what they usually see from their peers. With former faculty tutors Tasha Kohl and Liesl Schwabe, Lauren and the Center's former Assistant Director, Allison Smith, coauthored an article on the initial stages of this program (Fitzgerald et al. 4).

The tutoring sessions that undergraduates have with social work students continue to be uncomfortable and even shocking, likely for all concerned; as Allison points out in the coauthored article, both undergraduate tutors and social work students might well have preconceptions about each other based on race, class, age, gender, ethnicity, and religion (Fitzgerald et al. 2). But, at the same time, tutors are developing a language and body of knowledge handed down from one generation of undergraduate tutors to the next. This new perspective has shaped the Center in important ways, "including how the Center, the tutors, and its writers are represented and how tutors and writers communicate with each other and reflect on their work" (Fitzgerald et al. 5). One way that this representation has shifted, for example, is in what Lauren now writes in recommendation letters for tutors. At the urging of one of these candidates, she points out that though outsiders might assume that YU's student population is entirely homogenous, it is not, and that the Center itself "is a crossroads for much of the diversity of the larger student body," which undergraduates participate in when they work with social work students.

Had Lauren listened only to the aspects of YU's undergraduate mission that ring on communal identification, had circumstances not conspired to give student tutors the chance to work with social work students, and had these tutors not voiced again and again their desire to reach beyond the undergraduate context and across identity differences, the formation of many, sometimes long-term and often mutually beneficial, if not always comfortable, professional relationships between these groups might have never been formed. Instead, and due to the student tutors, a writing center that outsiders (including Lauren herself) might have assumed would be too homogenous, conservative, and parochial to do so, is now engaging in the larger professional conversations about identity and anti-racism work taking place in writing centers across the country (Geller et al. 87-106; Greenfield and Rowan; Suhr-Sytsma and Brown).

Conclusion

Our two narratives are testimonies to the effectiveness of undergraduate peer tutors as rhetorical actors that writing center scholars have long extolled (Bruffee, Brown et al.; Hughes et al.). Nancy Grimm, for example, has argued that tutoring puts undergraduates in a unique position to engage in institutional change because it allows them "to participate in an authentic practice" of academic institutions, in contrast to other activities typically designated for undergraduates, which "are, at best, facsimiles of the authentic work of the institution" (97). Partly as a result of such participation, peer tutors at YU have served as insightful cultural informants to Andrea and Lauren as outsiders, filling us in on the ins and outs of the institution and its values—much as Grimm points out peer tutors ideally do for students "who are newcomers to a discourse or a culture" (77). One implication of this observation, then, relates to tutor education. How might we make institutional perspective more intentionally part of staff development so that tutors can be even more conscious of how their writing center experiences are rhetorical and public?

There is another implication as well. As unique and important as we believe writing centers are, we want to suggest that the special insight peer writing tutors gain from their work might well extend to many students on campuses of religiously affiliated and other special-mission institutions (Hansen, Hoppe, Janangelo, this volume). After all, even if they make up only a small percentage of a student population at a given time, peer tutors are, and by definition must be, students. It might well be that along with—or perhaps even instead of—the writing center's granting students special perspective on the institution, students with a specific set of interests, ones who appreciate the opportunity "to participate in an authentic practice" of academic communities, self-select to apply to work in writing centers in the first place (Hoppe, this volume). YU undergraduates, for example, most of whom do not work as tutors and many of whom might well never set foot in our writing centers, engage in a range of activities that, like those of the tutors, expand on and even resist YU's undergraduate mission, including initiating and leading community outreach activities such as providing tutoring and workshops for disadvantaged public high school students and countless other events that YU might or might not sanction but that students nonetheless feel are part of their mandate as active, twenty-first-century Orthodox Jews. After all, before they are students, they are people with particular identities and beliefs. These people would also no doubt have many rich insights into the workings of the institution that faculty, whether insiders or not, would benefit from. What would be possible with forums for engaging in such dialogue? Analogous to many of composition classrooms across the country, asking such a question presumes that tutors are engaged citizens—within their institutions and within their communities—and that it would benefit us to approach our work as writing center administrators invested in "citizenship-driven writing center[s]" (Wilkey and Dreese 173).

If we were to engage in such discussion, it's quite possible that many of the people who attend YU as undergraduates would tell us that they see YU's mission, and particularly *Torah Umadda*, as being flexible enough to withstand their resistance and expansion. Indeed, Andrea and Lauren's colleague Shalom Carmy, himself a former YU undergraduate, has argued that *Torah Umadda* is always-already a site of debate, between those who see the concept

> as a means to reconcile the tensions between traditional Judaism and mainstream American society, and those who believe that a genuine engagement with the liberal arts is as likely to sharpen the inevitable conflicts between the service of God and the values of man as to smooth them over. Both groups are equally committed to liberal arts study, and the latter may even be more willing to undertake the study of disturbing material. But their orientations are different: where the former seek harmony, for the latter, *Torah Umadda* does not bring peace but, so to speak, the intellectual sword. (33-34).

Because there is a strong tradition of diverse, often contradictory, interpretations of *Torah Umadda*, the student-tutor-people we've discussed here might well see the mission of the institution as allowing for resistant rhetorical practices as they talk about marriage laws or as they tutor students from other communities in our writing centers.

While tutors at YU might very well be emblematic of the *Torah Umadda* mission as the institution intends, as Carmy suggests, they are also performing the mission of the liberal arts as well. Specifically, the tutors whom we highlight here "sharpen the inevitable conflicts" that Carmy identifies as endemic not simply to religious institutions, but to the liberal arts more generally. When read and listened to carefully, Tara's connection between breaking a silence about a religious practice with the writing center staff and the encouragement she offers students she works with in the writing center, a seemingly mundane constellation of interactions, exemplifies the values of a liberal arts education. Tara's ability to "connect," as defined by Hughes et al., to her tutor-colleagues and to students in the center reflects "a deep concern for humanity—for connections among people—and argument for the importance of communication within a liberal arts education" (16). Lauren's research further emphasizes that tutors in the writing center she directs also want to "connect" and to communicate broadly. To attend to our tutors and students as rhetorical actors—to listen to them as they listen to their institutions—can offer us, as writing center and writing program administrators, models of how to productively engage these missions as well, perhaps also showing us ways to, as Vander Lei and Pugh put it, "contribute to the continuing evolution of the mission" (106).

Notes

1. An English transliteration of a Hebrew phrase, *Torah Umadda* can be represented variously, including, as we do here, *Torah U'Madda* and *Torah uMadda*.

Works Cited

Boquet, Elizabeth H. *Noise from the Writing Center*. Logan, UT: Utah State UP, 2002. Print.

Brooke, Robert. "Underlife and Writing Instruction." *College Composition and Communication* 38.2 (1987): 141–53. Print.

Brown, Renee, Brian Fallon, Jessica Lott, Elizabeth Matthews, and Elizabeth Mintie. "Taking on Turnitin: Tutors Advocating Change." *The Writing Center Journal* 27.1 (2007): 7–28. Print.

Bruffee, Kenneth A. "Peer Tutoring and the 'Conversation of Mankind'" *Writing Centers: Theory and Administration*. Ed. Gary A. Olson. Urbana: NCTE, 1984. 3–15. Rpt. *The Allyn and Bacon Guide to Writing Center Theory and Practice*. Ed. Jacob S. Blumner and Robert W. Barnett. Boston: Allyn and Bacon, 2001. 206–18. Print.

Burke, Kenneth. *A Rhetoric of Motives*. Berkeley, CA: U of California P, 1969. Print.

Carmy, Shalom. "Orthodox Judaism and the Liberal Arts." *Academe* 87 (2001): 32–37. Print.

Enoch, Jessica. *Refiguring Rhetorical Education: Women Teaching African American, Native American, and Chicano/a Students, 1865–1911*. Carbondale, IL: Southern Illinois UP, 2008. Print.

Fitzgerald, Lauren. "'Torah is Not Learned but in a Group': Talmud Study and Collaborative Learning." *Judaic Perspectives in Rhetoric and Composition Studies*. Ed. Andrea Greenbaum and Deborah H. Holdstein. Cresskill: Hampton, 2008. 23–42. Print.

—. "*Torah U'Madda*: Institutional 'Mission' and Writing Instruction." *Negotiating Religious Faith in the Composition Classroom*. Eds. Elizabeth Vander Lei and Bonnie Lenore Kyburz. Portsmouth: Boynton/Cook Heinemann, 2005. 141–54. Print.

Fitzgerald, Lauren, Natasha Kohl, Liesl Schwabe, and Allison Smith, "Opening the Doors to Diverse Populations—and Keeping Them Open." *Writing Lab Newsletter* 33.6 (Feb. 2009): 1–5. Print.

Fountain, T. Kenny, and Lauren Fitzgerald, "'Thou Shalt Not Plagiarize'? Appeals to Textual Authority and Community At Religiously Affiliated and Secular Colleges." *Pluralizing Plagiarism: Identities, Contexts, Pedagogies*. Eds. Rebecca Moore Howard and Amy Robillard. Portsmouth: Boynton/Cook Heinemann, 2008. 101–23. Print.

Gee, James Paul. *Social Linguistics and Literacies*. 2nd ed. London: Taylor and Francis, 1996. Print.

Geller, Anne Ellen, Michele Eodice, Frankie Condon, Meg Carroll, and Elizabeth H. Boquet. *The Everyday Writing Center: A Community of Practice*. Logan, UT: Utah State UP, 2007. Print.

Glenn, Cheryl. "Rhetorical Education in America (A Broad Stroke Introduction)." *Rhetorical Education in America*, Eds. Glenn et. al. Tuscaloosa, AL: U of Alabama P, 2004. vii-xvi. Print.

Greenfield, Laura, and Karen Rowan, Ed. *Writing Center and the New Racism: A Call for Sustainable Dialogue and Change*. Logan, UT: Utah State UP, 2011. Print.

Grimm, Nancy M. "Retheorizing Writing Center Work to Transform a System of Advantage Based on Race." Greenfield and Rowan 75–100. Print.

Grutsch McKinney, Jackie. *Peripheral Visions for Writing Centers*. Logan: Utah State UP, 2013.

Hughes, Bradley, Paula Gillespie, and Harvey Kail. "What They Take with Them: Findings from the Peer Writing Tutor Alumni Research Project." *The Writing Center Journal* 30.2 (2010): 12–46. Print.

Kail, Harvey, and John Trimbur. "The Politics of Peer Tutoring." *WPA: Writing Program Administration* 11.1–2 (1987): 5–12. Print.

Lieber, Andrea. "A Virtual *Veibershul*: Blogging and the Blurring of Public and Private among Orthodox Jewish Women." *College English* 72.6 (2010) 621–37. Print.

Morphew, Christopher C., and Matthew Hartley. "Mission Statements: A Thematic Analysis of Rhetoric Across Institutional Type." *The Journal of Higher Education* 77.3 (2006) 456–71. Print.

Ross, Tamar. *Expanding the Palace Torah: Orthodoxy and Feminism*. Lebanon: Brandeis UP, 2004. Print.

Suhr-Sytsma, Mandy, and Shan-Estelle Brown. "Addressing the Everyday Language of Oppression in the Writing Center." *The Writing Center Journal* 31.2 (2011): 13–48. Print.

Trimbur, John. "Peer Tutoring: A Contradiction in Terms?" *The Writing Center Journal* 7.2 (1987): 21–28. Print.

Vander Lei, Elizabeth, and Melody Pugh. "What Is Institutional Mission?" *A Rhetoric for Writing Program Administrators*. Ed. Rita Malenczyk. Anderson, SC: Parlor, 2013. 105–17. Print.

Wilkey, Christopher, and Donelle Dreese. "Institutionalizing Ethical Collaboration Across Difference in Writing Centers." *Marginal Words, Marginal Works?: Tutoring the Academy in the Work of Writing Centers*. Eds. William Macauley and Nicholas Mauriello. New York: Hampton, 2007. 169-182. Print.

Wurzweiler School of Social Work, Yeshiva University. "Mission and History." *Yeshiva University*. Yeshiva University, n.d. Web. 31 May 2014.

Yeshiva University. "Mission Statement." *Yeshiva University*. Yeshiva University, n.d. Web. 31 May 2014.

11 People Make the Place: Using an Evolving Mission as a Secondary School Teacher and Program Development Tool

Andrew Jeter

This narrative will detail the construction of an evolving mission statement for an academic literacy program for a large, public, suburban high school. The teacher-led program sought to address the academic needs of students and the professional needs of teachers in a school district with an administration with a meager track record for power sharing. At its height, the program, based on the writing center model conceived by Kenneth Bruffee in his seminal 1978 article "The Brooklyn Plan: Attaining Intellectual Growth through Peer-Group Tutoring" and now ubiquitous on college campuses across the United States, was staffed by approximately 15 faculty members and 250 peer tutors. It served an average of 219 students a day and recorded more than 30,000 discrete tutoring sessions each year.

Besides these remarkable figures, the program was also distinctive in that it favored teachers over administrators by empowering the teachers to take administrative control over a school-wide program. It reversed the decades-old model of top-down administrator-as-teacher-leader model and in its place allowed the people involved in the day-to-day education of students to make procedural, curricular, and pedagogical decisions. As the coordinator of the program, I served as a staff member whose original role was to facilitate the work of my colleagues who came from various departments and who worked in the Center at varying times during any given day. Eventually, being the primary spokesperson for and defender of the mission would be added to my responsibilities.

During the eight years that the program was operational, there were many attempts by the administration to reign in the power of the teachers through requests for the program to take on work that would have undermined our design and function. The work administrators required was always couched as "what's best for students," but this work also frequently ran counter to the Center's research-based design and function, which were described in our mission statement. Administration sought short-term gains on test scores and GPAs, we sought long-term academic rigor and stability for students.

The mission statement became, over the years, the single most important tool for protecting our program (DelliCarpini, DeRouen this volume). This mission acted to shield us from the whims of a constantly changing group of administrators who were most frequently concerned with short-term, boutique interventions, often focused on one specific remediation (e.g., reading, truancy, study skills) for a very limited number of students, over long-term, research-based educational programs open to the entire student body. Of course not all of the administrators who worked in our school during the lifetime of this program sought to undermine it. For the purposes of this chapter, the term administrators will be used to primarily indicate people in administrative positions, usually assistant principals or higher, who used their power to advance their own agendas while disregarding the advice and concerns of teachers. In 2013, the administration took control of the program and reversed much of the work detailed below. Mission statements are powerful things, but they exist at the purview of those with power.

A Place for People

When, in 2003, my colleagues and I set out to create a literacy center for our school, we knew, above all else, that it had to be a place for people. Very often, it seems, large public institutions can forget about the people who populate them. Institutions become more concerned with their procedures and protocols, movements of people through a system and toward outcomes like curriculum completion and achievement scores, and the ever-worrying graduation and/or retention rate. Our administration has also spent years propagating programs and then leaving them to flounder. In one case, the administration had created a guided study hall for students who had earned multiple Ds and Fs in a quarter. The program quickly became likened to a storage area for struggling students because the school refused to hire adequate teachers to staff the program. Similarly, just a couple of years prior to the creation of the Literacy Center, the administration decided to extend the middle school model into the high school for any freshman and sophomore who had earned below a certain score on the reading portion of the state's standardized test for eighth graders. Not only was the program created without the knowledge of teachers, but also only non-tenured teachers, those devoiced and vulnerable new teachers, were assigned to teach in the program. Calls for modifications to the program by the teachers and the school's reading specialist to address serious problems went unconsidered and the program was generally ignored until it was disbanded a few years later.

Seemingly more for the notch on their collective administrative belt than for systematic change, these flash-in-the-pan boutique programs have been our administration's preferred route to addressing student needs and padding resumes. And while all of these systems of control and *ad hoc* remediations can be important or useful to an institution, frequently lost in this kind of focus are the people for whom all of these protocols, procedures, and programs were created. This is as true for the teachers in a school as it is for students, neither of whom, at the secondary level, is often invited into the process of crafting or managing these protocols and programs.

In our local context, GPA and ACT scores had become the yardstick against which everything else was measured. Because of this, or perhaps to enhance this focus, our writing center was only hiring AP Literature seniors to tutor other students, and the school had created a reading center that provided remediation for students who scored under a particular cut score on a state-issued standardized test taken during eighth grade. Students would be assigned to the reading center until they could increase their score on the test. Both decisions, to only hire the most successful student-writers based on a standardized format and to create a center for remediation based on required attendance, were made because a school culture had been nurtured wherein the most important consideration was to think about the end results of an intervention. No one, it seemed, was thinking about what was most likely to happen during the intervention between the people involved in the process. In almost every particular, our institution had focused on something other than the individual and the individual's ability to create and understand knowledge within the context of a people-centered matrix. This also created a school in which only the highest-scoring students and the lowest-scoring students were having their needs addressed. We had tracked classes with smaller class sizes for the AP, Honors, and Basic students. And we had highly focused intervention programs for the students who did poorly. Lost in the mix were the vast majority of students who were "regular."

What we needed was a place in our school that could honor what people did with each other, a place where we could embrace the key ideas Kenneth Bruffee put forth in "Peer Tutoring and the 'Conversation of Mankind.'" Bruffee explained that "knowledge is an artifact created by a community of knowledgeable peers and . . . learning is a social process not an individual one" (214). We needed to make room in our community for this kind of knowledge construction (DelliCarpini, this volume). Remembering that schools were supposed to be sites for this kind of activity, we decided to create a place where any student could become a tutor and any student would want to be a tutee. What we set out to build, with Bruffee as a framework, was inspired by John Dewey's assertion that the purpose of education was more education. We hoped for our students that we could create a place for them that would nurture what Dewey describes as a dispositional attitude of "open-mindedness," which he feels is required to be a truly reflective thinker. Dewey describes this liberalness of mind as the, "accessibility of mind to any and every consideration that will throw light upon the situation that needs to be cleared up, and that will help determine the consequences of acting this way or that," which leads to an understanding that "intellectual growth means constant expansion of horizons and consequent formation of new evpurposes and new responses" (206).

For all of our students to have this opportunity to grow, we knew we needed to create a place that was not only open to all, which allowed for "any and every consideration," but was flexible enough to meet the needs of any student (Efthymiou and Fitzgerald, this volume). Whereas the school had previously assumed that an AP Literature student was the best "almost teacher" to work with a struggling freshman, we instead wanted to make a space where a sophomore, fresh from her own struggles with the Freshmen English standard *Romeo and Juliet*, could be the guide and the reflective thinker who could relate to that struggling freshman.

So, as we met to design this new literacy center, a place where any student could receive support in any academic subject, we were acutely aware that we needed to redirect the institution's focus back onto the people, both students and teachers, who would be inhabiting and working in this new space in our community. We knew that to get buy-in from teachers and students that they would have to feel like they were a part of the community. In this instance, we utilized James Gee's definition of a discourse community: "a socially accepted association among ways of using language, of thinking, and of acting that can be used to identify oneself as a member of a socially meaningful group" (29). *For the teachers* to be able to identify themselves, to use the "language," they needed to have a voice not only in the construction of the program but also in how it operated, how it served, and how it evolved from simply being a writing center into being a community-building forum for students of diverse backgrounds. *For the students*, we wanted them to begin identifying themselves with a community that valued learning and critical thinking, not just "making the grade." *For both groups*, we wanted them to see that they were actually being engaged in a meaningful conversation about not just what to learn, but also *how* to become a better learner while being a full member of the community.

To achieve this goal, the design team decided that the program would be run by teachers, not administrators. Central to this goal was creating a mission that would achieve two things for our stakeholders. The first was that it would guide the work of the people in the teacher-led center, which included teachers, the peer tutors, and the tutees. The second thing we hoped the mission would do was to protect these groups from the demands of other community members to solve *any* problem. Purposefully omitted from the group of decision-makers for the program were the administrators.

As with most public schools, ours operates mostly in a top-down fashion where the administrators are on top and the faculty is on the bottom. This is problematic for several reasons, not the least of which is that many administrators have fewer years of teaching experience than do the faculty and that these same administrators rarely ask for input on major, or even minor, decisions about how to create the best learning environment for students. The problematic nature of this administrative approach is reinforced by the fact that there have been no requirements for their bosses, the elected members of the board of education, to have any experience in or knowledge of teaching theory, curriculum, or practice. Indeed, until recently, Illinois State Law mandated that board members had only to be citizens over eighteen who had lived in the township for at least one year, were registered to vote, and were not sex offenders ("(105 ILCS 5/) School Code.").

A recent change has added a four-hour professional development scheme for those duly elected board members that covers "education and labor law, financial oversight and accountability, and fiduciary responsibilities." Additionally, board members must now also go through a training course on the newly required teacher evaluation model the state has adopted. Conspicuously missing from these training sessions are discussions of educational theory, curriculum, and pedagogy. ("Mandatory Board Member Training") In the end, this has led to a formula for running a school that is solely predicated on poorly informed administrative decisions, which rarely sits well with experienced, dedicated teachers. Indeed, most of the decisions that led us to the place where there were precious few opportunities for students to receive the kind of academic assistance they really needed had been made by administrators. Change, we felt, was long overdue.

Creating a Mission

When the design team met to begin organizing our new program, many of my teacher colleagues were excited to jump right in. When I expressed an interest in writing a mission statement for our program, there were several people who saw this as unnecessary and too corporate-like for a school program. Weary from too many years of the corporate model being applied to schools, many of my colleagues eschew anything that even remotely signifies the business world. To these people, I made the following argument.

A mission is a program. It is the mind and the mouth, the heart and the soul. A mission is the conscience, spirit, and faith of a program because a mission statement explains what a program does and is and what it would like to do and like to become. It undergirds a program with a philosophical stance and a theoretical position. It says what participants value and why they have come to value those things. It has the power to name stakeholders and to locate a program within the context of a greater organization or institution (Kinkead, DeRouen, Hoppe this volume). And, by the very language it does *not* use, I argued, it can and will say what a program will not do, what it does not believe in, and who is not a stakeholder. This power of the negative is strong. The negative can isolate, exclude, alienate, and marginalize (Janangelo, this volume), but it can also leave space for a program to consider or reject demands from outside parties. Leave the wrong person off the list and you have potentially made an enemy for life. Be inclusive and you win friends. However, there is also a danger in including too many or being too broad.

In fact, I foresaw that our program's broad-based nature, serving any student with any academic concern, could be its "Achilles's heel." If we had crafted our mission with heady, unchecked optimism, we could have potentially opened our program up for doing a whole host of things that were not really what we had envisioned. We could become, as I have described elsewhere, "all things to all people" (40). As we opened up ownership to a wide range of stakeholders then, we would also open ourselves up to a wide range of expectations for what we do and whom we would serve. I envisioned administrators knocking on our door requesting that we assign students to the Center for remediation or assign student-tutors to assist special needs students in lieu of law-mandated one-to-one teacher support. We did not want to become the next boutique program.

It was actually only a few weeks into the new school year once we had opened our doors that the expectations to take on these kinds of responsibilities began. First was an expectation for us to set aside a table for students from our in-school suspension program. The administration demanded that we set aside this table so that students from in-school suspension could be sent to sit at it. If they needed academic help, it was explained to me, then tutors could be sent to the table to work with "the delinquents." We were to become an extension of the disciplinary deans' detention center. Then came the addition of four students' names on my rosters. Our rosters are kept in a computer program and, as a teacher, it is not uncommon for a new name to appear one day on a class roster. This frequently occurs when the school gets a transfer student who needs to be placed into classes. In this instance, my rosters were for the tutors who worked in our center and were used solely for attendance purposes. The four new students were not tutors, but instead were students who were receiving multiple Ds or Fs in their classes. The administration, without consulting the teachers, had placed them into the Center in lieu of a study hall. Essentially, they had mandated these students' attendance.

In both cases, the administrators responsible had attempted to violate our mission, which stated that student visits should be voluntary. It should be noted that these attempts to intervene for students who struggle were not in and of themselves bad. Those students needed help, however, there were other ways or other programs, offered by the school, for them to use. But because the Literacy Center was new, it was perceived by the administration as the newest boutique program. If it was new, the groupthink went, they should use it. Eventually, other demands like these would be made of our program and our mission would come to our rescue repeatedly.

These examples illustrate how our program was perceived as all things to all people. For students, however, the Center was, in many ways, actually all things. It was designed for every student to be able to use whenever he or she saw fit. This was the program's broad appeal and our mission had to take this into consideration. The population of a school is an ever-changing group of individuals. This raised another interesting challenge for the team writing the original mission—how to write the mission so that it would stay current for the constantly changing group of users it was attempting to serve. Besides the obvious change as individuals grow and mature, our community also experienced changes in ethnic, cultural, and religious groups. During the lifetime of the program, our school saw many changes to its student population. After the beginning of the war in Iraq, for instance, our population of Iraqi refugees increased rapidly. Students who had been living in refugee camps for years were not literate in their native languages, which made their acquisition of English even more difficult. We also, during this time, had an increase in students coming from religious schools in southern Pakistan. Their approach to education and the skills they arrived with were drastically different than what we had been accustomed to. During this time we also saw a marked increase in students who were living at or below the poverty line. They brought a different set of concerns and required the staff to change the ways we had hitherto addressed certain academic situations. For years, our school had been changing around us, and we knew we needed to be able to change with it. We decided we needed to write a mission that changed with our patrons and that evolved with our understanding of how best to address their academic needs. We needed a mission that would allow us to engage in a conversation, as Bruffee would describe it ("Peer Tutoring"), with the people we served.

The evolving mission statement of our program, as it came to be known, raised the ire of more than one administrator. For many years, in fact, I argued about it with the principal, who said things like, "You can't make it up as you go!" and "The mission is the mission, it's not supposed to change!" The business model for repeating success is deeply engrained in the approach administrators take to addressing problems in schools. When they encounter a problem, they create a program to address it. When the problem changes or the intervention no longer seems to work, they then create a new program to address the changed situation. This is how boutique programs have become so prevalent in our schools. But the problem is that this kind of behavior does not really engage the entire community in a conversation about what is actually happening with students. If anything, it creates a one-way conversation, so to speak, wherein the administrators, focused on end results, fix things without spending time considering and engaging with those whom they would fix. In so many ways, they spend their time clapping with one hand, rejoicing in their own cleverness while creating a stunning silence with their ineptitude at creating sustainable, meaningful educational models predicated on actual student need. For those administrators, Bruffee's argument that "learning is a social process" ("Peer Tutoring" 214) does not ring true because it does not mean that learning is something that should be imposed on students without including their voices or their concerns.

In the end, however, we *could* change and the mission *did* change. The teachers who staffed the Center set up an annual review of the mission, which coincided with our annual review of the job descriptions we wrote for ourselves for our work in the teacher-led program. At the beginning of the fall term, faculty on the Center's staff would receive a copy of the mission statement for review. They would submit revisions and craft questions for debate. We would meet to discuss the proposals, which ranged from changes in grammar and word choice to critiques of whole goals and beliefs. Early on, the staff came to recognize that there was no one, single definition of the word "literacy" being used throughout our school community. We addressed that by adding language that detailed that the three core academic literacies were critical thinking, reading, and writing. As this was a part of our mission, it allowed us to reject requests to do such things as mandatory test prep and computerized "course credit recovery" programs. In another instance, we discovered that some departmental directors were attempting to make our staff do things that we as a program had rejected. The idea was that if they could not make the program do what they wanted, then they would make the teachers working in the program do what they wanted. In the second year of the program we added a line to the mission that described it as "a safe place where teachers can be creative, take risks, evolve as educators, and *hold ownership over their professional experience.*" This is not to say, however, that all administrators had designs to bend the program to their will. The program was actively supported by a small group of administrators who were new to their positions and had recently been a part of either the program's teacher leaders or the program's design team. Each year the teacher leaders would discuss the mission, our students, and our work in the community. Changes were made. Classes came and went. The mission evolved. The students attended in record numbers. We had managed to create Bruffee's "community of knowledgeable peers" ("Peer Tutoring" 214) where social learning could and did happen.

The Evolution of Mission

The original mission, as written by the design team in 2005, was a concise two-paragraph testament to what we envisioned. It included as much as it possibly could, which spoke to its role as mediator for the different voices of the design team, while trying to clearly express the purpose and function and the desired outcome of the new program:

> The Literacy Center will offer opportunities for students and teachers to educate each other on the important learning strategies, meta-cognitive skills, and creative problem-solving that are necessary to succeed across the curriculum. Housed in an environment that is friendly to both students and teachers, the Literacy Center will help to promote a school climate that celebrates and values academic rigor by providing highly competent help, the safety to ask questions, and developing a common vocabulary and pedagogical practices that link the disciplines of learning.
>
> Students can turn to the Literacy Center for help in the area of high literacy, which includes critical thinking, problem solving, and application. Consequently, the student tutors have the chance to develop interpersonal skills while engaging in a highly rewarding experience. For teachers, the Literacy Center will be a place where the different content areas come together and connect learning. This will be a safe place where teachers can be creative, take risks, and explore mistakes.

The idea of collaboration is deeply imbedded here, as is the idea of students taking an active role in the program. In fact, in all of the different versions of the mission, the line "student and teacher to educate each other" was never altered or removed. It spoke to a community actively interested in Dewey's notion of education for education's sake. Another line that would go unaltered throughout the life of the program spoke to the teachers' desire to make the school a place where students *wanted* to be. "Housed in an environment that is friendly to both students and teachers, the Literacy Center will help to promote a school climate that celebrates and values academic rigor . . ." speaks to the desire of the teachers to make a space in our school that would be welcoming and where the idea of "celebrating" academic rigor would not be thought of as preposterous.

What was altered by the staff over the years also speaks to the nature of the mission, the program, and the staff's own evolving understanding of the power of collaborative learning and the role of teachers as leaders. By 2007, language had been added to the mission that spoke to this greater understanding. In particular, our understanding of literacy had changed. We saw reading and writing as serving academic literacy, not being separate from it. By including this definition of literacy in our mission, we were also redefining it for our community. We were up front and public in our declaration: critical thinking, reading, and writing are the three core academic literacies.

Our understanding of what our student tutors were getting out of the program also evolved. We knew that their own literacy skills would improve, but we had not really understood how they would be recognized around the community as leaders. To the list of things provided by the program, we added, "a community based on volunteerism and collaboration." We also saw our own roles and the work we were doing in a new light. We realized that we were enacting Dewey's call for democracy through education in a way the philosopher perhaps did not expect. We had taken the program and turned it into a model for how to run a school democratically. The term "democratically run, teacher-led initiative," which was added to the teacher section of the mission in 2007, would become so often repeated that it became synonymous for our program:

> For teachers, the Literacy Center is a *democratically run, teacher-led initiative* where the different content areas come together and connect learning and teaching. The Literacy Center will be a safe place where teachers can be creative, take risks, evolve as educators, and hold ownership over their professional experience. To promote ownership throughout the school, teachers agree to a term limit of two years of service at a time.

By the sixth year of the program, our understanding of what students, both tutors and tutees, were getting out of it had matured and that is reflected in the mission. As we saw more and more students begin to advocate for themselves, we started to equate the embracing of academic rigor with maturity. In 2011, the mission was revised to denote this new understanding. Originally, we had described students as seeking "high literacy" as in this section from the mission in 2007: "For students, the Literacy Center will be a place for developing high literacy which includes effective reading, writing, and critical thinking skills as well as 'the ability to use language, content, and reasoning in ways that are appropriate for particular situations and disciplines'" (Langer). It was altered by introducing the term "academic maturity" to our community: "For students, the Literacy Center is a place for developing academic maturity, which includes proficiency in the three core academic literacies, while learning the skills and joys of interacting appropriately with a wide variety of learners and teachers." Our mission evolved with our growing understanding of our students and our profession. It reflected and guided what we knew and valued (DelliCarpini, Kinkead, this volume).

Mission Becomes Professional Development

One outcome of having an evolving mission statement was that it became a kind of iterative, recursive professional development for teachers. Each year, teachers were asked to consider the needs of students and teachers from a school-wide perspective. We looked at the work we had done in the past and the goals we felt we had or had not met. Since we were the owners of the program, there was no one to avoid saying difficult things to and overly praising ourselves always felt a little self-centered. We took the opportunity every year to be brutally honest with ourselves because our review of our mission, and our job descriptions that were derived from it, required it.

In the beginning, or as new people would come onto the staff, there were moments when teachers would push back against this new kind of power and honesty. On several occasions, I had teachers say to me that they were not "in charge here" and so could not make the kinds of decisions the program required of them. It took a lot of convincing and time for the teachers to see that we really did change to meet the needs of students and teachers and that when we met to discuss the mission, the changes that were proposed usually did happen. This caused the buy-in we had hoped for, but also produced in the faculty members a more nuanced way of discussing and explaining the Center and its mission. Over time, the language of the mission, terms like "teacher-led," "volunteerism," "core academic literacies," and "across the curriculum" seemed to flow from teachers' mouths. Annually, the administration runs the faculty of our school through seemingly countless hours of "professional development," but it rarely feels recursive and it is usually only tangentially related to the actual teaching and learning that faculty live through on a daily basis. Our program, however, fleshed out daily examples of the kind of work we envisioned in our mission statement and in its annual review. To return to Bruffee, we had actually created "the sort of social contexts, the sorts of community life, that foster the kinds of conversations we value" (209). Indeed, we had achieved James Gee's "socially accepted association among ways of using language, of thinking, and of acting that can be used to identify oneself as a member of a socially meaningful group" (29).

Although I believe this speaks to the power of the evolving mission statement we used for our Literacy Center program, it should be noted that both the push-back and the eventual embracing of the program by faculty took place in a professional setting that traditionally devalued teachers' voices, experience, and expertise. Teachers were, and sadly still are, ripe for this kind of ownership and intellectual engagement in their academic lives. Some teachers are also not ready. Some teachers in our institution balked at ever participating in our teacher-led program. For some, they had the classes they wished to teach and that was enough. "Why take on new responsibilities if I do not have to?" I heard more than once. It is perhaps a truism that teaching is a *job*. Teachers are hired to do specific things: to teach a curriculum, to be at school between certain hours of the day, to act as *in loco parentis*, to fulfill the contractual obligations agreed upon. And for as much as the profession of teaching is a *calling* for so many of us, there are other concerns that people have in their lives: their own children, their mortgage, their health, their retirement. Teachers are, after all, people, and there was never any additional money set aside for participation in our program. It was not easier to be a part of the program's staff. It was easier, however, to come to work, teach your classes, and then go home. Struggling to create an articulate, rigorous teacher-led community was only a self-realizing reward, and one that came at the potential cost of alienating the administrators who were in charge of course and room scheduling. It would be unmerited and overly simplistic to say that teachers did not want to participate because of complacency, but a willingness to sustain the status quo was clearly evident. This willingness, we learned, cannot always be addressed by a well-crafted or well-meaning mission and is prone to thrive in a place where teachers' ideas and creativity are routinely repressed.

Evolving Mission as Foil

The program was designed to be owned and used by teachers and students. The program's mission engaged teachers in deep and meaningful reflection about the way we wanted teaching and learning to occur in our community. The program and the mission, however, existed within the confines of a larger institution and that institution's mission. Our mission gave the program the opportunity to distance itself enough from the monolithic school culture and its mission so that our program could try new and interesting things, like evolving, that might engage modern students. This is what Gordon MacKenzie called "orbiting the giant Hairball."

In 1910 Joyce Hall, a young man from Nebraska, began selling greeting cards out of a shoebox from his hotel room in the growing community of Kansas City. A hundred years later, Hallmark Greeting Cards, Inc. is a billion-dollar business and the largest employer of "creative workers" in the world. It is also widely known as one of the more monolithic, bureaucratic corporations to ever exist. It believes deeply in the tried-and-true method of repeating success by only doing what has been successful before, not the challenge of risk. In this place of rules and regulations, Gordon MacKenzie found his calling as a creative genius and marketing master. MacKenzie was the man responsible for irritating most of his supervisors in the giant, bureaucratic institution by always wanting to try new things and push the boundaries of control that the corporation could have on its creative employees. He is also the man they eventually let loose to be as creative as he could be. MacKenzie went on to create Shoe Box Greeting Cards, a brand which introduced funny and witty cards to the corporation and sealed its status as the leading greeting card company in the world. MacKenzie attributes his success to pulling away just enough from the corporate colossus, which he describes as a giant hairball, where "every new policy is another hair for the Hairball" (31), that his group could orbit it—free from the Hairball's policies, protocols, and procedures, while still remaining close enough to share in the Hairball's wealth and resources. New ideas and products enrich the Hairball, but can only be created by avoiding the policies and procedures put in place to restrict the inherent risk in trying new things.

Our mission allowed us to orbit the bureaucracy inherent to the hairball of our institution. We stayed close enough because we served the same students and required the resources and protection of the district, but we operated under different rules and through different processes to address the learning needs of students, which were not being addressed in the school or the standard classroom setting. We orbited around the hairball so that we could enact and live by the process-based standard for writing center work most famously articulated by Stephen North who said, "we aim to make better writers, not . . . better texts" (441) and by the collaborative learning paradigm envisioned in peer tutoring by Kenneth Bruffee ("The Brooklyn Plan"). Our mission dictated that we not only worked collaboratively but also shared the risks and rewards of running that program. Our focus was clearly on the students who came to our Center, not their academic work, and on their ability to do that work independently.

CHANGE IS POSSIBLE

The power of our mission was transformational. Students began advocating for their academic needs in unprecedented numbers. They felt like the school was not just speaking to them, but also listening to them. If nothing else, their attendance to the Center, with an average of 30,000 discrete tutoring sessions occurring each school year, indicated that they were comfortable in their school, it was a place they wished to inhabit. Similarly, teachers began to imagine that their expertise and experience was useful for more than teaching in individual classrooms. Their skills and their energy could be used to create and guide a school-wide academic program that really worked. Teachers became emboldened to suggest changes and to make demands on themselves and their colleagues to evolve alongside our ever-changing student body and within the context of prevailing educational theory and practice. Two such teacher-initiated changes were guided due dates for student papers, in which a part of the assignment took into account the need for multiple drafts with multiple visits to the Center for peer-to-peer revision sessions, and the Rent-a-Tutor program, in which teachers could request student tutors to come to their classrooms and participate in classroom activities. The Rent-a-

Tutor program was a direct result of teachers requesting a service that allowed the collaborative learning paradigm championed by the program to be inserted into the traditional classroom.

Our mission empowered us to do things that had never been seen before in our community. We orbited the giant hairball of our institution and managed to be creative and spontaneous and insightful. But the power of the mission was not enough to stave off the will of the administration. The hairball was their territory and the fact that we had specifically stepped out of their realm of control would eventually lead to the dismantling of the program. In a public address to the Board of Education, the superintendent said that she would be replacing the program's coordinator, the teacher tasked with upholding the mission, with an administrator who would have to follow her orders. The first action of the new administrator was to strip the mission of its language describing the program as a "teacher-led program." The second was to begin assigning students to the Center for remediation.

The removal of teachers from the decision-making process is symptomatic of the national movement to commercialize and dehumanize education for all but the extremely rich. With the continued shuttering of so many public schools across the country so that for-profit, charter schools can open utilizing public moneys, the disintegration of the notion of community continues unchecked by our politicians and administrators. Focused solely on the achievement of students as measured by standardized tests and immutable standards, these schools mark the rising tide which will, if unchecked, drown our public education system and the promise that it has always held for every child. The promise is one of experimentation, of risk. The promise is one of placing trust in teachers and students to strive for academic maturity for all students. But privatized, for-profit schools are not risk takers; they do not include disparate voices or give audience to ideas from far afield. They eschew change. The purpose of education is not more education; it is a score on a test, a benchmark. Change is unwelcome and unwanted. The hairball remains.

Perhaps the most compelling lesson from this experience and the mission it spawned is that change, if not wholly permanent, is possible. Teachers can find their voices and students can be recruited to participate willingly in their own education. Institutions can be challenged and policies and protocols put in place to stifle change can be confronted. These acts can be a boon to the institution, creating new ideas that will strengthen and fortify the whole. It behooves anyone, however, to remember that this kind of work needs to be focused, guided, and envisioned in a mission because the mission is truly the voice, the mouth, and the mind of a program, and regardless of whether or not a program like this can be sustained long-range, it is an experience worth trying, a risk worth taking.

Works Cited

Bruffee, Kenneth. "The Brooklyn Plan: Attaining Intellectual Growth through Peer-group Tutoring." *Liberal Education* 64.4 (1978): 447–468. Print.

—. "Peer Tutoring and the 'Conversation of Mankind.'" *The Longman Guide to Writing Center Theory and Practice*. Eds. Robert Barnett and Jacob Blumner. NY: Pearson Education, Inc, 2008. 206–218. Print.

Dewey, John. *Democracy and Education*. NY: Macmillan Company, 1930. Print.

Gee, James. "What is Literacy?" *Relations, Locations, Positions: Composition Theory for Writing Teachers*. Eds. Peter Vandenberg, Sue Hum, and Jennifer Clary-Lemon. Urbana, IL: National Council of Teachers of English, 2006. 29–39. Print.

"(105 ILCS 5/) School Code." *Compiled Statutes*. Illinois General Assembly, n.d. Web. 19 Apr. 2014.

Jeter, Andrew. "Building a Peer Tutoring Program." *The Successful High School Writing Center: Building the Best Program with your Students*. Eds. Dawn Fels and Jennifer Wells. NY: Teachers College Press, 2011. 39–50. Print.

Langer, Judith. A. "Beating the Odds: Teaching Middle and High School Students to Read and Write Well." *National Research Center on English Learning & Achievement Research Report No. 12014*. Albany, NY: University at Albany, 1999. PDF file.

MacKenzie, Gordon. *Orbiting the Giant Hairball: A Corporate Foul's Guide to Surviving with Grace*. NY: Viking, 1998. Print.

"Mandatory Board Member Training Spring 2014." *Illinois Association of School Boards*. Illinois Association of School Boards, n.d. Web. 16 Apr. 2014.

North, Stephen. M. "The Idea of a Writing Center." *College English* 46.5 (1984): 433–46. Print.

12 Same-Sex Marriage at a Jesuit University: Institutional Integrity and Social Change

Joseph Janangelo

In June, I read an article titled *"Father of the Bride 3* to Feature Gay Wedding." Apparently, "if negotiations prove successful," the film "will feature a gay plot" (Towle).

> The twist in this threequel is that Little Matty is now 29 and gay and getting married to a Navy SEAL's son. Father of the bride George is "thunderstruck and speechless" and has problems with the whole gay thing. So wife Nina kicks him out of the house, according to a pitch which Disney loved . . . "It's a timely idea," my source said, "I told Charles I just hope it goes forward before gay stops trending . . ." (Finke)

This chapter explains how "the whole gay thing" would not stop trending at one Jesuit university. It shows how public debates about hosting same-sex marriages on campus inspired a policy change that stimulated ongoing discourse about institutional integrity and fidelity. Regarding mission, the story traveled and featured a contested "twist." Responses to that twist reveal the complexity of moving forward while honoring traditional teachings. This chapter has two parts. Part one analyzes passionate debates. Part two records the interest and ire of a range of invested parties.

Part One: Fall 2013—A Storied Showpiece

Last fall, I took a graduate student to lunch to celebrate her wedding. She was married in our school's chapel and held her reception on school grounds. The chapel has received thoughtful redecoration and is a point of campus pride. This spring, it garnered public praise:

> In a recent poll by Best College Reviews, Loyola's very own, Madonna Della Strada, was named one of the most beautiful chapels on a university campus. Ranked at number 16, Madonna Della Strada, is a modern cathedral built for the Jesuit district and is located steps from Lake Michigan at Loyola's Lake Shore Campus. To learn more, visit . . .

Wanting to learn more I visited our Conferences Services web page, *Wedding Ceremonies at Madonna Della Strada*. Here is what I found:

> For members of our University community, Catholic weddings can be performed in the University's Madonna Della Strada Chapel on the Lake Shore Campus, an officially designated sacred place. University property and facilities are not available for other wedding ceremonies, whether civil or religious . . . . If you are interested in holding your Roman Catholic wedding ceremony at Loyola's Madonna Della Strada Chapel please contact . . . . Please note, either the bride or groom must have a direct affiliation with Loyola University Chicago and be Catholic in order to use the chapel . . .

Initially, this description seemed both welcoming and clear. It struck me as sensible and even innocuous for the school to stipulate that "in order to use the chapel" couples should have "a direct affiliation" with Loyola. Yet the specific wording belies a conversation about institutional fidelity and purview that reverberated across national and local news sites.

Day I: Seeding and Speeding Change

In September 2013, our school made national news due to a petition posted on Change.org by one of our students. The petition reads: "We call on Loyola University Chicago to end the discriminatory policy banning same sex ceremonies on campus." The article states that "this petition will be delivered to main officers of our university including the Chairs of the Council of Regents and Board of Trustees, as well as the President." The article then quotes petitioner, Christine Irvine, who states:

> As a recent transfer student, I spent my first week on campus enamored by all Loyola has to offer. I was particularly impressed with its expressed commitment to social justice rooted in the Jesuit tradition. I felt proud of my new home and excited about the next two years. That same week, my fiancé and I started to plan our wedding. Mary and I have been Edgewater residents for over two years and imagine celebrating our commitment with loved ones in the neighborhood, overlooking Lake Michigan. We were thrilled by the prospect of holding our ceremony at Loyola.

Those plans were derailed because "when I called to set up an appointment, I was told that Loyola doesn't allow same-sex ceremonies on campus and I was heartbroken." The student attributes this to bias: "Because of our sexual orientation, because we are gay, we are banned from celebrating one of the most meaningful days of our lives on Loyola's campus." In terms of institutional mission, the key flashpoints are *heartbroken* (think of student recruitment and retention, as well as LGBTI alumni and LGBTI-friendly donorship), *rooted* and *celebration*. Also, the words *banned* and *because we are gay* portend predictable trouble spots: the tension between fidelity to church teachings and the reality of social change, including a visible and vocal student demographic with needs and rights.

Trouble abounds when the student quotes from the (then) current Conferences Services web page: "The University boasts 'unique and elegant venues . . . to make your once in a lifetime event truly memorable,' but not for same-sex couples—not only in the Madonna Della Strada chapel but also in any of Loyola's event spaces." Trouble accretes as she adds, "By denying same-sex couples the privilege of celebrating our love and commitment on campus, the University communicates that the relationships of our heterosexual peers are more highly valued, accepted, and celebrated than our own." Trouble accelerates when Irvine suggests that the policy contradicts the university's mission statement: "Loyola claims to embrace social justice and attempts to be a 'home for all our students—embracing all races, sexes, gender identities, religions, ethnic backgrounds, socio-economic classes, sexual orientations, and abilities.'" This comment regarding integrity leads to the salvo: "We call on Loyola University Chicago to live up to these values and create a home for all, regardless of sexual orientation, by ending the discriminatory policy banning same-sex ceremonies on campus."

Regarding mission, I see three points. The first is that at least some undergraduates are becoming institutional policy critics and mentors. The second is that these community members are capable of orchestrating social media events that capture public attention and throw national focus on campus decisions. The petition shows that students have recourse beyond taking "no" for an answer. Undergraduates can stage a public conversation that offers lessons in terms of what (once scared, peripheral, and vulnerable) members want for and from *their* institution in terms of policy and action. The third is that far from expressing vulnerability and seeking protection from physical harm, LGBTI students rightfully see themselves as fully vested, valuable and thus entitled community members who can prompt their institutions to change.[1] The response to perceived exclusion and injustice can be advocacy and self-help as rhetors create a public outing that calls upon an institution to live up to its mission statement and other defining documents. Abetted by social media, these institutional critics are poised to do something galvanic.

Day II: Echoes and Reverberations

This issue was soon covered in our student newspaper the *Loyola Phoenix*, which is known as "The student Voice of Loyola University Chicago." Written by Jordan Berger, the article's title is "CIVIL UNION PETITION: Petition Calls for Same-Sex Ceremonies on Campus." Berger begins with the facts: "After junior visual communication major Christine Irvine, 26, said Loyola's Conferences Services denied a request to hold her same-sex civil union ceremony on campus, she started a petition in protest of Loyola's rejection." Berger then quotes the student: "'Imagine what it would feel like to be planning for an incredibly meaningful part of your life, and to one day be told that the school just doesn't do this thing, and it's because your partner is another woman,' Irvine said." Irvine goes on to explain her motive: "I was just trying to think of what we might do so no one else ever has to have that conversation." Yet after reading that "the online petition, which Irvine launched through Change.org on Sept. 11, has gained support from more than 750 people, including some Loyola students," we learn about her strategy: "Irvine said she chose to create a petition specifically with Change.org because she has seen the website produce the very thing it takes its name after: change." She is quoted as saying, "a petition is a helpful tool to rally support behind a cause," and that "I've seen other Change petitions be really successful in changing these kinds of local-specific issues." Finally, we are apprised of the endgame: "Irvine said she hopes her petition will open the door for discussion about—and more clarity in the language of—Loyola's policy."

Open has several definitions, including being receptive to change and vulnerable to wounds and disease (*Merriam-Webster*). The second positions institutional leaders as gatekeepers and protectors of tradition. That appears to apply when "Maeve Kiley, Loyola's director of communications, said in an email to The PHOENIX that the university, including Conference Services, would not partake in any direct interviews." Regarding sensitive issues, silence can signal a refusal to engage with critics and an attempt to foreclose conversation and stave off questions. Adding one qualification, Berger reports that

> . . . Kiley did, however, provide a statement of Loyola's current policy. "Currently, the university guidelines are that we allow marriages on campus that are recognized by the State of Illinois," Kiley said in the email. "But, the university welcomes all wedding receptions on campus, including same-sex marriages." According to the Conferences Services web page, campus facilities may also be available for "ceremonies" legally recognized by the state of Illinois.

If "but" may not bespeak support, it does suggest legal tether and the limits of institutional purview.

Berger then brings Irvine back, and she articulates a mission-related tension point: "I hope the school will come to terms with this policy that [it has] put into place, be clear about what it means, and have a conversation about whether or not it's really in line with [the university's] values of social justice and nondiscrimination, because I don't think it is." This is a reference to one of the university's central commitments. This articulate rhetor then frames her request in terms of public policy: "Irvine claims that because Section 212 of the Illinois Marriage and Dissolution of Marriage Act prohibits same-sex marriages in the state, she and her fiancée wanted to have a civil union ceremony, not a marriage, in Loyola's Piper Hall or Palm Court." We then learn that some facts that support the request: "Illinois legalized civil unions on June 1, 2011, when the Illinois Religious Freedom Protection and Civil Union Act took effect." We read that "as defined by Section 10 of the act, a civil union means 'a legal relationship between two persons, of either the same or opposite sex.'" Yet "Section 20 of the statute states that parties of civil unions are entitled to 'the same legal obligations, responsibilities, protections, and benefits as are afforded or recognized by the law of Illinois to spouses.'" For added credibility, there is a map of states that recognize same-sex marriage. The reporter notes, "Illinois is one of four states in the U.S. that provides for civil unions of same-sex couples" and adds that "the university would not comment on this distinction."

This information is followed by reactions from Loyola undergraduates. The panoply of voices reveals a range of perceptions about the role and purview of institutional mission (DelliCarpini, Malenczyk and Rosenberg, this volume). First, we read that "even though Illinois recognizes civil unions, some students like freshman human services and theology double-major Abbey Smith, 18, said Loyola's identity as a Catholic institution serves as an adequate basis for denying same-sex ceremonies on its campus." Smith outlines the contours of institutional authority. She argues, "You can't come to a Catholic institution and expect [it] to go against a principal Catholic belief." She adds, "It would be rather out there for [the university] to change the policy." The student contends, "It's more than just a school. It's the entire Catholic faith." Ceding authority to church teachings, she concludes, "It's not like it's the school's decision."

The idea that, as a Jesuit institution, the university must adhere to church teachings is echoed by a staff member: "Loyola's Director of Campus Ministry Lisa Reiter also said that in the university's decision to not host same-sex ceremonies, the school is upholding Catholic beliefs toward marriage." Here, the decision making reflects fidelity: "I think this is one of those policies where administrators at the university are really trying to use Catholic teaching to inform a decision, to help [the school] be faithful in its identity as a Catholic Jesuit institution, . . . " This suggests that being true to institutional identity can involve working within articulated parameters. Mission and identity sometimes remind us of what we are asked or required to stand for and against.

Such oppositional positioning reminds me of an idea philosopher Jacques Derrida advances in his essay, "The Law of Genre." Discussing literary practice, Derrida writes, "As soon as the word 'genre' is sounded, as soon as it is heard, as soon as one attempts to conceive it, a limit is drawn" (56). Describing the interplay of possibility and prohibition, he writes that in "making genre its mark, a text demarcates itself" (65). Simply put, the literary work can be only this (a poem), not that (a novel). A parallel between generic and institutional practice is that they are both subject to "precautions," "protocols" and prohibitions (58) that circumscribe artists' and campus leaders' choices. As Derrida notes, "Thus, as soon as genre announces itself, one must respect a norm, one must not cross a line of demarcation, one must not risk impurity, anomaly, or monstrosity" (57). In other words, strict fidelity to the *law* bespeaks what "thou shalt not" do or permit in terms of institutional or textual practice. Whether experienced as duty, calling, tether or tie, institutional mission can offer an equally strict rubric for defining what community members, however valued, should (not) get to do at a specific campus site. Adherence to mission can underwrite policies and priorities regarding protection, sanction, and celebration (DelliCarpini, this volume). It can also authorize saying no in the name of institutional fidelity (Hansen, this volume).

Such refusals have articulate adherents. One of them is "senior philosophy and psychology double major and seminarian Domenick Tirabassi IV, 21," who "said students that disagree with Catholic teachings should still be understanding of Loyola's decision against same-sex civil unions on campus." Tirabassi states that "Loyola has been highly understanding and accommodating to people of many faiths and ideologies, providing them with places of prayer and recognition on campus, . . . " He argues for reciprocity: "One would expect Loyola to receive the same understanding from those who disagree fundamentally with its moral teachings." One might expect a seminarian to defend the university's decisions. Furthermore, some critics might characterize "highly understanding and accommodating" as an overstatement bred of straight privilege. Yet the student's words underscore the challenge institutions face when navigating social change. In setting policy, one must ask: what is the greater fidelity, social justice or Catholic belief? What are the ethical definitions and limits to being understanding and accommodating? For some, policy change resembles redress: it is too little, too late or too much, too soon.

Berger cites yet another vision of mission: "In addition to Loyola's Catholic identity, junior, undecided major, Emily Poynton, 20, said Loyola should keep its policies in place as it sees fit due to its status as a private university." Poynton points out that this status constitutes a key portal of purview: "Loyola is a private Catholic university, so its policy is fine . . . " She adds, "it's not a public institution," and "it would be a totally different story if it was a public school." This perspective also receives counter-argument: "But senior communication and French double major Emily Taft, 21, said that despite Loyola being a private Catholic university, hosting same-sex ceremonies on campus would uphold the school's mission of social justice." Taft adds, "In recent years, Loyola hasn't been a university that just accepts traditional viewpoints and moves on its merry way," and states that, "It's very much in the Jesuit heritage to challenge social norms." The student sees an opportunity to be in the vanguard: "We've done a lot to challenge those norms, but I think we could go further. It'd be really cool if we could be one of the first universities to recognize a [same-sex] civil union ceremony on our campus." She also champions commitment: "Taft said that in recognizing civil unions on campus, Loyola would be furthering its dedication to social justice initiatives similar to those the university has already embraced." She offers an analogous example: "The Stritch School of Medicine is providing financial support for undocumented students," and argues, "That is something that may not be widely popular, but it stays true to the mission of social justice." Taft also heralds the exigent, ethos-building moment: "This is a time where we could say the church has an official standpoint, but we as a community disagree." In this scenario, supporting social justice is the primary force in revising institutional practice.

Berger then adds a voice that reframes the situation: "Senior philosophy major and president of Loyola's LGBTQU organization, Advocate, Paul Kubicki, 21, said that regardless of the university's intention behind its policy, it should always act in a manner that ensures equality for all people." Kubicki is quoted as saying, "It's hard to tell our students that we're an open, accepting and supportive campus when we do have policies that disproportionately affect specific communities and denigrate them to a different status. . . ." He adds, "That has to be changed, and I hope the university will work together with us." In this case *open* signals diplomacy and goodwill on the part of students and student leaders. But might it also suggest that when it comes to publicizing one's brand (e.g., Jesuit higher education), a school's marketing materials may not constitute full truth in advertising? Might such restrictive policies alienate a formidable demographic made up of prospective high school, transfer, and graduate students, not to mention LGBTI parents? Might such policies drive business away from private schools that count on tuition revenue and student satisfaction rankings? In appealing to the widest demographic, can a school afford to be perceived as alienating any constituency? Despite the diplomacy, I notice the imperative: "That has to be changed." I find it telling of the limited sway that contemporary community members, especially those who rightly feel they and their forbears have sustained injury, may grant traditional practice. Displeased students versed in social media can become formidable institutional critics.

Kubicki suggests that the proposed change accords with papal leadership.[2] He notes "In sentiment, [Francis] has done a lot that's really wonderful," and adds that "[his] sentiment of inclusion is exceptionally important for Loyola to consider." Yet this interpretation is contested by Tirabassi, who "said he believes Francis was simply reiterating statements of inclusion that already exist in Catholic social teaching." Tirabassi, who was quoted earlier in the article states, "Loyola has upheld precisely what the Holy Father is speaking about," adding, "The church is a home for all." Final word is given to advocates for change: "Both Kubicki and Irvine said that in the event that Illinois legalizes same-sex marriage, they hope Loyola sticks to its current policy, which could mean the university might host same-sex ceremonies on campus." The article concludes with a look forward: "Same-sex marriage may very well pass in Illinois in the next couple of years," Irvine said. "I wonder if Loyola will act on what [it is] saying in the policy if that happens?" "I wonder" offers a provocation. What will the institution do when it can no longer say no? Clearly "the student Voice" (Berger) comprises many visions of institutional rights and obligations. In this fidelity test case, multiple institutions (Jesuit school, private school, marriage) and ideas (mission statements, social justice, and the law) are in sensitive conversation by stakeholders who want different things to happen.[3] Offering hospitality to change is difficult when appeals are made in/secure by different kinds of evidence. Without a shared compass to validate desires and resentments, what is inflammatory and unjust to some seems obvious or right to others. This nexus of needs and concerns intensified when the story went viral.

PART 2: WINTER 2014—DISCOURSE TRAVELS

The conversation traveled to at least two more venues. The first is Matthew Archbold's "No Same-Sex Marriages in Loyola Chicago Chapel, Campus Open to Receptions," published on February 27, 2014, five months after the earlier discussions. The article was written for the Cardinal Newman Society. This is an especially interested audience as shown in its mission statement: "Founded in 1993, the mission of The

Cardinal Newman Society is to promote and defend faithful Catholic education."

Archbold sets the facts in telling context: "In light of the Illinois law legalizing same-sex marriage which is scheduled to go into effect in June of this year, Loyola University Chicago announced that it has changed its policies to allow only Catholic weddings on campus, according to ChicagoPride.com." Archbold, citing an LGBTI news source, shows that institutional stakeholders read broadly and purposefully. Having conducted research, he offers an explanation by the afore-mentioned Maeve Kiley: "Our policy reflects our desire to reserve and use our facilities and campuses for rituals and ceremonies that are congruent with our obligations and values as a Jesuit, Catholic institution. . . ." Kiley adds, "That is why we are limiting weddings to Catholic ceremonies in our Catholic chapel." Although congruence compels a respectful no, there is some compromise, "However wedding receptions 'regardless of religious or gender identification' will be permitted in any of the university's other venues including Loyola's Cuneo Mansion and Gardens, Kiley reportedly added." Note that in September Kiley was quoted as saying, "But, the university welcomes all wedding receptions on campus, including same-sex marriages" (Berger). To already dissatisfied parties, this change may signify small progress. To an institution, it may signal intentional learning, understanding, and outreach.

Addressing interested stakeholders, Archbold identifies a precedent-setting moment:

> At the time of the change to Illinois' same-sex marriage laws and its unclear religious exemptions, Loyola's requirement for marriage ceremonies occurring on campus was only that they were legally recognized by the state. With the new law having the state legally recognize same-sex marriages, Loyola's policy would have allowed for same-sex marriage ceremonies to take place on many campus venues other than Madonna Della Strada chapel.

"Would have allowed" shows that institutions, however resistant, must sometimes obey legislation. Archbold is writing with a purpose: to inform readers who may face similar test-case situations. Addressing colleagues at Catholic institutions, he gives this "community of concern" a heads-up about what could happen on their campus (Daloz Parks 131).

Outlining the backstory, Archbold adds a quick flashback: "Late last year, the University administration announced it was discussing changes to its policy." He adds that "around that time, the editorial board of *The Loyola Phoenix*, Loyola University Chicago's student newspaper, publicly pleaded with the Jesuit institution to allow same-sex marriages to be performed on campus as a way of honoring the university's 'Jesuit values of inclusion and social justice.'" He then delineates a bigger picture:

> *The Chicago Tribune* reported in November that while the law does not require clergy to perform same-sex weddings or force churches to host same-sex ceremonies "it also does not permit people or religious institutions to deny a same-sex couple the opportunity to rent any other venue for a same-sex marriage ceremony or celebration, if the venue is otherwise available to the public." The Cuneo Mansion and Gardens is open to the public for rental and would likely not qualify for an exemption.

By identifying a resonant fault line, Archbold alerts readers who need to think ahead and steward their institution's future.

On March 3, 2014, the story traveled to *Queerty*, a news outlet whose mission features two fragments: "Free of an Agenda" and "Except that Gay One." Dan Tracer's headline is alliterative and accusatory: "NUPTIAL NONSENSE: University Adopts New Policy to Keep Gay Weddings off Campus Grounds." Tracer immediately ascribes motive: "Ahead of Illinois' gay marriage law going into effect in June, Loyola University Chicago has adopted a new policy that will restrict same-sex couples from wedding on campus." He frames the policy change as a preemptive strike and surmises the purpose of its strategy: "The university is refusing to comment and distancing itself from seeming antigay by also restricting wedding access to *any* couple who isn't Roman Catholic-sanctioned and has ties to the school." Sensing deception, Tracer discerns something sketchy and strategic: "But the timing sure is convenient. The move comes only months after student Christine Irvine filed a petition to persuade the school to honor the state law by allowing same-sex ceremonies." He then quotes Irvine: "It's really disheartening," she told the *Windy City Times*," an LGBTI news source that prides itself on "CELEBRATING 28+ YEARS OF Lesbian Gay Bisexual and Transgender NEWS." She remarks, "It's a sign of the non-acceptance and non-tolerance of the LGBT students on campus . . . a sign of disrespect of our love compared to our peers."

Rather than discuss fidelity to church teaching, Tracer identifies an institutional parrying he deems self-serving and self-limiting: "It's also a backwards-thinking move at a time when 58 percent of American Catholics *approve* of gay marriage (higher than the national average)." Unlike Archbold, Tracer is addressing a critical audience. Yet rather than upbraid the school, he shows understanding while registering critique: "We get that change is hard to fathom for deep-rooted institutions, but the wave of gay marriage has already begun to swell and universities of all places should be riding it to shore before it crashes over their heads." As a policy critic, Tracer offers two important lessons. The first is that "backwards-thinking" increases institutional vulnerability. The second is the risk of resisting change: a wave can swell to engulf those who would, or could, not move.

Conclusion: Testing Mission's Mettle

This fidelity test case features competing perceptions of institutional integrity and intransigence. It shows that the claims made by mission matter, and have consequences in epideictic and deliberative, pathos-driven spheres. As a test case, this story teems with stakeholders who describe what *their* school should do regarding openness, adaptation, purview, and principled policy change. These debates about what should (not) happen at a particular campus space offer leadership lessons for stewards working to move their institutions "forward" (Finke). Here are the main ones I see:

Mission-Related Policy Decisions Can Transcend In-House Conversation. They can quickly become and remain everyone's business.[4] As such, they are a topic of community and public opining, speculation, and critique. Especially on the Internet, everyone may have a public say. That means policy decisions and revisions are subject to instantaneous and ongoing input, advice, approval, and dissent.[5]

Undergraduates Can Become Articulate Policy Analysts and Critics. When speaking to or about disenfranchised community members (e.g., LGBTI students, staff, or faculty), don't confuse historical injury with contemporary vulnerability. Don't equate having been scarred with being too scared to speak up. Instead, anticipate ardent and iterative public pushback by policy critics who, versed in social media, remain unfazed by a well-reasoned "no." Rather than sustain continued denigration, these networked stakeholders may seek redress by bearing voluble witness to perceived injustice. They will speak eloquently by offering grand and granular readings of institutional policies, texts, and paratexts. Moreover, these public rhetors will find readers who deem their arguments persuasive, at least to a point.

"Community" Has No Fully Predictable or Unilateral Contours. Members of affiliation groups have varied perspectives, reactions and desires. They may not express agreement or even substantial accord. For example, in the *Queerty* discussion thread, we see one reader agree with the reporter and state, "You would think that these businesses and organizations would learn that digging in on bigotry never works for them." Yet that view, in that LGBTI forum, is challenged by someone who asserts:

> While the Roman church has an unbroken history of doing whatever it can to damage the lives of homosexuals, but, really, this is the one kind of thing that they should be entitled to do. Since they consider their "university" a religious institution, its services can legitimately be restricted to the church's members who have not offended it in some way. If not that, then religious freedom is really threatened . . . (Tracer)

Although this individual excoriates several church practices, he still defends that particular decision. His nuanced thinking underscores the complex, "all things considered" approach that community members can take.[6]

Institutions Should Review Their Policy Statements for Their Emotional Effect. It is important for institutions to assess the rhetoric of their policy statements to learn how it may be interpreted by community members, particularly those who perceive themselves as disadvantaged.[7] At a pragmatic level, this can mean using focus groups to review drafts and versions of wording. That would help schools discern the perceived rhetoric of the appeal and the, perhaps, limited appeal of the rhetoric.

Institutions Should Reconsider the Value of Composing Airtight Policy Statements. Both Archbold and Tracer suggest that the policy's specific wording protects the institution's interests and brand.[8] But is it possible to protect one's brand to one's detriment? Here I refer to Philip E. Smith II's "The Mission of Rhetoric and the Rhetoric of Mission Statements." Smith defines mission statements as rhetorical documents that describe and defend departmental actions and aspirations. Having reviewed many samples, he concludes, "All the statements I collected, extensive or brief, were composed in rhetorical modes that were meant in one way or another to be found bulletproof by their intended audiences of administrators, assessors, and accreditors" (33). Evidently, the go-to strategy involves using invincible wording and airtight rhetoric to deflect criticism and disable resistance.

That strategy is found in policy statements, as well. I wonder if, in composing contemporary policy and mission statements, other rhetorics (e.g., perhaps of inclusion and capaciousness) could be more effective? For example, airtight language is suspect (Tracer). "Bulletproof" (Smith) rhetoric can make institutions look defensive, as if we are bracing for a counter-attack after launching the first volley. Worse, it may look as if we do not value critical stakeholders' input. Most of all, bulletproof texts can further alienate community members who can often see a "no" coming their way. They may associate such rhetoric with sketchy stratagems. Historically injured constituencies remember injury quite well. Thus seemingly innocuous wording can evoke chains of historically-referenced inequity. Silence also sends a message. Consider how "the university would not comment on this distinction" (Berger) can look to young people hungry for conversation. Rather than starting trouble, institutional critics may not be importuning or shooting ideological bullets. They may be sharing emotions, voicing considered opinion, and asking important questions of their school. That leads to my final point.

When Acting in Character and Commitment, Institutions, Like Community Members, Have a Right to Resist and Persist. The ongoing work of institutional fidelity involves having, prioritizing, and acting on commitments (Behm, DeRouen, DelliCarpini, Jeter, Kinkead, this volume). To lead is often to disappoint. That thought can and should fuel extended, time-intensive debates. Regarding any controversial policy decision, someone loves or loathes it. All parties may have unsuspected resources and adamant allies. Finding no solace in the decision, alienated community members may go away and stay away. They may not become donors or recommend the school to prospective students.

Yet responsible leadership overrides the dislike or fear of alienating community members who have known unjust disappointment. It also discourages riding a timely "wave" to profitable and palliative ends (Tracer). Acting on such impulses connotes pandering and cowardice. Our biggest work is with the timeless. As such, behavioral limits pertain.

Discussing my chapter topic, a colleague observed, "There was only one way this story could end." That may be true at this point in time. But from an institutional perspective, it is always this point in time . . . until the next time[s]. By that I mean institutions live at a threshold of now and soon. Their tipping points are indomitable and resilient. Often new and/or cause-worthy to someone, they are poised to make a strong campus and public comeback.

My belief is that sensitive critique can inspire institutional intake and learning. There is almost nothing sentimental about this. My point is that taking an observant (in all its connotations) view helps us realize that "our" institution is never ours alone and that a worthy idea never "stops trending" (Finke). I wish to conclude by suggesting that revisiting and revising institutional policies—perhaps into passionate, painstaking perpetuity—is an understudied brand- and ethos-building project. However vexing in practice, it is worth noting that, whatever policies we revise or revoke in order to be open to change and true to mission, we are not the only ones defining our work and identity. An acid truth of institutional stewardship is that *someone is always promoting your brand.* It is how, why, and to what effect that should concern, but not compel, institutions as they move forward.

Notes

1. Such change is often discussed in terms of curricular revision. For example, in "Criteria for the Selection of Young Adult Queer Literature," Stephanie R. Logan, Terri A. Lasswell, Yolanda Hood, and Dwight C. Watson offer perceptive ideas for LGBTIQ inclusion. They write, "In reviewing the literature and developing the selection criteria, we chose to place an emphasis on those novels that fall into the queer consciousness/community framework, believing that it is important for educators to delve into contemporary texts and move beyond simple coming-out narratives to engage readers in thinking emphatically and critically" (31).

2. Berger explains, "Irvine's petition comes around the same time Pope Francis published remarks that the Roman Catholic Church has grown 'obsessed' with moral doctrines like gay marriage." Berger also notes, "On Sept. 19, he [Pope Francis] expressed his vision of a church that is inclusive and a "home for all," according to the *New York Times*."

3. In "Being Gay at a Jesuit University," Wade S. Taylor and Kevin J. Mahoney show how complicated decision-making can become when an institution feels it should draw a line between offering support and issuing endorsement. The authors discuss the creation of an LGBTQ Resource Center at George-

town University. They link the Center's work to a central Jesuit value, "the care of the whole person (*cura personalis*) and the need to provide necessary resources for all students including at-risk populations" (45). In discussing institutional understanding and outreach, the authors explore the complications that can ensue when "some student groups may want to use the LGBTQ Resource Center as a platform to push a particular perspective about sexuality that may or may not be in concordance with the Catholic Church." They explain that "At the university, some students wanted the resource center to endorse a 'Sex-Positive' week, which was hosted by GU Pride, United Feminists, and the Georgetown Solidarity Committee." They report "that the resource center chose not to endorse this agenda." Taylor and Mahoney then reveal a key compromise, adding that the center "did, however, continue its mission by providing resources and education, when necessary, for those students, faculty and staff associated with or affected by 'Sex-Positive' week" (47). This mission-related outreach has its supporters. For example, in "Students Speak: The Integrated Catholic Gay Student," Georgetown alumni Zack Pesavento calls the Resource Center "a natural expression of its [Georgetown University's] ongoing mission to educate the whole person" (34). See Kevin Clarke's "How to Build a Better Student" for a discussion of how Jesuit higher education contributes to students' character formation.

4. The story has received extensive coverage. One article is "Loyola University Chicago Petitioned to Allow Gay Wedding on Campus." Some of the other articles include: Derrick Clifton's "Loyola Bans Same-Sex Weddings in New Policy," Andy Kossak's "Christine Irvine Seeks to Have Same-Sex Marriage on Loyola University Campus," Paul Kubicki's "Loyola Marriage Policy is Unjust," Dominic Lynch's "University, Petitioners Both Wrong," Alexandra Schmidt's "As Chicago, Cook County Make Progress towards Marriage Equality, Loyola Does Not," James Stancliffe's "Religious Freedom or Social Injustice?" and Benjamin Woodard's "Loyola University Limits Campus Weddings in Wake of Same-Sex Marriage Law."

5. The communicative potential is multiplied as online texts beckon more discourse. Consider the following invitation: "For Change.org Multiply Your Impact: Turn your signature into dozens more by sharing this petition and recruiting people you know to sign. YOU YOURFRIENDS THEIR FRIENDS 10,000 approx." ("Loyola University Chicago: End"). Another example is Tracer's article, which is tagged "Gay Marriage, Illinois, Loyola." The host site, *Queerty*, also invites readers to "Share on Twitter Share on Facebook" and "Email." Finally, notice the request appended to Archbold's article: "When reprinting/reposting, please include the author's name, a link to our website, and the following text: 'Originally published by Catholic Education Daily, an online publication of The Cardinal Newman Society.'"

6. Community members can be unpredictable when drawing limits. For example, a reader who supports Tracer's argument may not for a number of

reasons, including internalized homophobia, appreciate the article's paratext: a photo of a transgender woman with the linked caption, "Cuba's Vibrant Transgender Community Revealed." My point is that we cannot assume any precise degree of buy-in by perceived community members or stakeholders.

7. In "LGBT Legal Issues in Jesuit Higher Education," Bryce Hughes argues that, "Due to their relationship with the Roman Catholic Church, Jesuit universities are faced with the complex issue of balancing their need to provide student support with their need to maintain Catholic identity" (15). Despite these complications, he states that "Overall, it is important for Jesuit universities to address LGBT legal issues by validating those members of their institutions who identify as LGBT" (20). Hughes asserts that "It is not enough for Jesuit colleges and universities to adhere to the law, nor is it enough for them to simply assent to Catholic Church doctrine." He contends, "Jesuit colleges and universities are called on to do more by reaching out and affirming all people who come to their doors, and by doing so with a sense of mission and justice behind their work" (20). For Hughes, "Affirming the experiences of LGBT individuals at Jesuit colleges and universities is beneficial not only to the LGBT people they impact but also to the greater campus community by demonstrating an institutional commitment to hold a higher standard of care for the whole person." He concludes that, "In doing so, these institutions maintain their fidelity to the Jesuit tradition of higher education which inspires their work" (20).

8. I am reminded of Hughes's idea that "Generally, policy-makers at these institutions consider these issues within the framework of protecting the university, both with respect to creating a safe and welcoming environment for all members of that community, and the institution's public image" (20). Aware that schools are sometimes watched and discussed publicly as they do their work, Hughes contends, "There is also a dialogue happening on Jesuit campuses about what it means to be Jesuit" and adds, "This has important legal implications regarding how the general public perceives the institution's exercise of religion, particularly how strict it adheres to religious doctrine in its policy and practice." Hughes concludes with a gesture of reflection and anticipation: "This was the case for Georgetown in *Gay Rights Coalition*, and could easily be the case for any other school if sued for discrimination on the basis of sexual orientation" (20).

Works Cited

Archbold, Matthew. "No Same-Sex Marriages in Loyola Chicago Chapel, Campus Open to Receptions." *The Cardinal Newman Society*. The Cardinal Newman Society, 27 Feb. 2014. Web. 15 June 2014.

Berger, Jordan. "CIVIL UNION PETITION: Petition Calls for Same-Sex Ceremonies on Campus." *Loyola Phoenix*. Multi NEWS, 26 Sept. 2013. Web. 2 June 2014.

Clarke, Kevin. "How to Build a Better Student: Can a 16th-Century Discipline Improve Modern Scholarship?" *America: The National Catholic Review*. America Press Inc., 16 May 2011. Web. 1 June 2014.

Clifton, Derrick. "Loyola Bans Same-Sex Wedding Ceremonies in New Policy." *Windy City Times*. Windy City Media Group, 26 Feb. 2014. Web. 3 June 2014.

Derrida, Jacques. "The Law of Genre." Trans. Avital Ronell. *Critical Inquiry* (1980): 55–81. Print.

Finke, Nikki. "*Father of the Bride* Turns Gay." *NikkiFinke.com*. N.p., 15 June2014. Web 16 June 2014.

Hughes, Bryce. "LGBT Legal Issues in Jesuit Higher Education." *Magis: The Jesuit Journal of Student Development* 2 (2008): 15–22. Print.

Irvine, Christine. "Loyola University Chicago: End the Discriminatory Policy Banning Same-Sex Ceremonies on Campus." *Change.org*. Change.org, Inc, 11 September 2013. Web. 5 June 2014.

Kossak, Andy. "Christine Irvine Seeks to Have Same-Sex Marriage on Loyola University Campus." *Opposing Views*. Render Media, 14 November 2013. Web. 2 June 2014.

Kubicki, Paul. "Loyola Marriage Policy is Unjust." *Loyola Phoenix*. Multi NEWS, 25 February 2014. Web. 1 June 2014.

Logan, Stephanie R., Terri A. Lasswell, Yolanda Hood, and Dwight C. Watson. "Criteria for the Selection of Young Adult Queer Literature." *English Journal* 103.5 (2014): 30–41. Print.

"Loyola University Chicago Petitioned to Allow Gay Wedding on Campus." *Huffington Post*. TheHuffingtonPost.com, Inc, 13 Nov. 2013. Web. 1 June 2014.

Lynch, Dominic. "University, Petitioners Both Wrong." *Loyola Phoenix*. Multi NEWS, 25 September 2013. Web. 4 June 2014.

"Madonna Della Strada Named One of the Most Beautiful College Chapels." *Loyola University Chicago*. Loyola University Chicago, n.d. Web. 3 June 2014.

"Open." *Merriam-Webster*. Merriam-Webster, Inc., n.d. Web. 6 June 2014.

Parks, Sharon Daloz. *Big Questions, Worthy Dreams: Mentoring Emerging Adults in their Search for Meaning, Purpose, and Faith*. Revised Tenth Anniversary Edition. San Francisco: Jossey-Bass, 2011. Print.

Pesavento, Zack. "Students Speak: The Integrated Catholic Gay Student." *Conversations on Jesuit Higher Education* 34.1 (2008): 51. Print.

Schmidt, Alexandra. "As Chicago, Cook County Make Progress towards Marriage Equality, Loyola Does Not." *Loyola Phoenix*. Multi NEWS, 26 Feb. 2014. Web. 3 June 2014.

Smith, Philip E. "The Mission of Rhetoric and the Rhetoric of Mission Statements." *ADE Bulletin* 121 (1998): 31–6. Print.

Stancliffe, James. "Religious Freedom or Social Injustice?" *Loyola Phoenix*. Multi NEWS, 25 Sept. 2013. Web. 12 June 2014.

Taylor, S. Wade, and Kevin J. Mahoney. "Being Gay at a Jesuit University." *Conversations on Jesuit Higher Education* 41.1 (2011): 41–47. Print.

Towle, Andy. "*Father of the Bride 3* to Feature Gay Wedding." *Towleroad: A Site with Homosexual Tendencies* 16 June 2014. Web. 20 June 2014.

Tracer, Dan. "NUPTUIAL NONSENSE: University Adopts New Policy to Keep Gay Weddings Off Campus Grounds." *Queerty* 3 March 2014. Web. 4 June 2014.

"Wedding Receptions: WEDDING CEREMONIES AT MADONNA DELLA STRADA." *Loyola University Chicago*. Loyola Universiy Chicago, n.d. Web.

Woodard, Benjamin. "Loyola University Limits Campus Weddings in Wake of Same-Sex Marriage Law." *DNAinfo Chicago*. DNAinfo, 26 Feb. 2014. Web. 4 June 2014.

Afterword

Steve Price

In his "Introduction" to this book, Joseph Janangelo describes institutional mission (IM) "At its best." He notes how IM "is a motor for action," how it "can set an institution apart from others," "can become a rhetorical tool that trumpets a school's deliverables," and "can also issue a mandate for institutional work." All true, certainly. If we take "mission" literally, then embedded in the statements are our goals, our purposes, an indication of our convictions and callings. As Janangelo and others in this collection illustrate, mission statements can be powerful pronouncements that articulate what we value, guide our actions, and promote our ongoing care for and attention to our programs and initiatives.

My own experiences with IMs, however, have not always shown them "At [their] best." Our English Department Mission at Mississippi College, for instance, failed to inspire much reaction in me, other than apathy, when I first read it as a new assistant professor back in 1999:

> Within the broad reference of Christian education, the Department of English undertakes in its freshman work to give each student a grasp of the tools of written communication with the aid of the latest word processing technology. On the sophomore and advanced levels, the department introduces the student to the great heritage of Western literature placed against the rich background of classical and Christian humanism. The study of literature is looked upon as the exploration of the best that has been thought and said in the world, and consequently, of those documents of the past and present most worthy of study. (*English Department*)

I'm sad to say that our Mississippi College English Department mission—still in place today—represents aspects of IM "at its worst." In part the meaning of the departmental mission fails to offer much substance. The laudatory language might initially spark enthusiasm in the casual, and probably supportive, reader. In truth, though, statements like "the great heritage of Western literature" and, especially, "the rich background of classical and Christian humanism" mean little in practical terms. They fail to indicate—to the department itself, to students, to off-campus stakeholders—what specifically might be taught or valued. Similarly vague, the concluding statement about the value of studying literature ("the exploration of the best that has been thought and said in the world") is circular while pointing to little that the department actually values, like literature of the American South. These descriptions and parameters were favorites of a past chair long gone from the school, I'm told today, but say little about what might actually be taught in my department. The current mission fails to acknowledge our new writing program or our interest in social justice and so is hardly a true "mission" of the department. And, we can only sheepishly lament that we're still proudly proclaiming that our students will work "with the aid of the latest word processing technology," which in the early 1990s progressively pointed to newly available desktop computers but today hardly speaks to the department's interest in digital media, web genres, and electronic texts as a distinct discourse. In *A Critical Look at Institutional Mission*, we see examples of IM anchoring curriculum (DeRouen), facilitating expansion of curriculum (Kinkead), and helping to negotiate curricular challenges (Malenczyk and Rosenberg). At Mississippi College, however, the content of our departmental mission is nothing more than a static curiosity, an archived text to pull off the shelves and cynically chuckle at how things used to be.

Just as problematic in the Mississippi College English Department Mission, maybe even more so, is the lack of a process involving the mission and the lack of shared investment in its maintenance. Not only has our departmental mission been largely overlooked and not accessed, but it also was neither collaboratively shaped nor collectively rethought. Reading between the lines of our unwritten departmental history, a previous chair was probably told that he needed a mission statement, and he dutifully and privately penned our grand, yet hollow statement, which was promptly forgotten. Without a collaborative process and collective revisiting of the departmental mission, we're left merely with disconnected, meaningless words, a common-enough problem with IM, which Jason Hoppe identifies in this collection, noting the potential for a weak IM to "feel somewhat far from the work of individual programs and departments, not to mention any given classroom."

The process of collaboratively investing in and creating and shaping an IM can be immensely powerful, though. In this collection, Andrew Jeter shows how developing a mission can facilitate the growth of a program, rally long-term investment of local stakeholders, and motivate challenging, even risky, work as the mission is continuously revisited and revised. Missions need not be sent to die a slow death on the vine of an institutional webpage, the faculty at Niles West High School remind me.

In the Mississippi College English Department, unfortunately, we've missed opportunities with our mission statement, in both the content and the process. Our static, long-forgotten and rarely used document fails to represent what we value, to describe clearly what we do, and to communicate with stakeholders outside the department. We clearly could use *A Critical Look at Institutional Mission*.

My own department is certainly not alone in mishandling IM. In this current collection, for instance, Dominic DelliCarpini points out how competing tensions on campus can lead to unintended mission creep and how missions are prone to overexpansive or vague language; Jeter talks about cynicism toward IM in general; and DeRouen notes the challenges of turning lofty language "into the lived experiences of the students." Also, DeRouen, and Malenczyk and Rosenberg describe their successful uses of IM in implementing curriculum changes at a small liberal arts college and at a public comprehensive institution. The "liberal arts" concept is just as frequently misused, though, invoked when convenient for the appropriate marketing audience without acknowledging and negotiating the curricular tensions (which can be productive) produced by competing pre-professional programs at those same institutions.

My own discipline—writing centers—may be one of the most frequent offenders of IM. With frequent turnover of directors, a thread tends to emerge each year on the WCenter listserv, asking for examples of mission statements that can be borrowed. Inevitably, directors are quick to share examples and links. A recent search of the WCenter archive for "mission," for instance, shows threads beginning in April 2011, May 2012, January 2013, and June 2013 (*WCenter Archive*). One director writes, representative of the recurring search-for-a-mission post genre: "I'm in the process of developing a mission statement for the center, and I was wondering if anyone had advice about what absolutely must be included, what distinguishes a writing center, and what should be left out." I don't mean to critique the director here or to disparage her use of mission; I think her post is all too indicative of how many of us, uninformed about the potential and power of IM, would react. Rather, what jumps out at me in this post is the tendency of so many to see mission as "one size fits all," the assumption that one writing center can be described the same way as another. I do cringe a bit reading the post, envisioning a new director cutting and pasting different statements and ultimately creating a document that might generally describe her center but that lacks the nuances and details of her own work, that fails to celebrate how her center addresses local conditions and reaches out to local stakeholders. Absent in the mission statement she creates, and in the missions of all of the others who take this unnecessarily iterative approach, is the spirit of her program, metaphorically described in this collection by Jeter as "the mind and the mouth, the heart and the soul. A mission is the conscience, spirit, and faith of a program." By merely borrowing IM, rather than engaging in a process of examining our own local context and shaping a statement that reflects our goals and actions and expectations, we risk creating hollow platitudes that might fill space on a flyer or webpage but offer little else. For all that IMs can do, they also illustrate abundant and frequent missed opportunities.

In his "Introduction," Janangelo notes that "The term institutional mission . . . has become central to contemporary academe." The reach of IM is even greater than just the use of the term, though, as illustrated in this collection. Today, IM is frequently enacted, influencing curriculum, policy, interpersonal interactions, and the actions of faculty, staff, undergraduates, alumni, and other stakeholders. In this collection alone, for instance, we see how IM becomes action in a range of schools and contexts, including liberal arts and religiously-affiliated institutions, a military academy, a land-grant institution, a public high school, and a two-year college. From the assortment of institution types alone, it's clear that a mission statement can't simply be plucked from an outsider's website in any useful manner. With the growth of parallel trends in assessment, accountability, the growing expectation of transference of skills from elementary school through graduate school, demands that we show the impact of our educational programs, and so on, it's increasingly important that IM be done well. We need IM "At its best" because our missions become our starting points, and so much more, as illustrated in this collection.

My first major takeaway from *A Critical Look at Institutional Mission* is foundational, a definition, which for me represents the "possibilities" mentioned in the "Introduction" and captures many of the things that a strong IM offers. As I peruse my notes, I'm struck by the number of talking points that jump out at me, in my own words and the words of authors from the collection, reminding me of what IM can do. For example, IM:

- is a "focal point . . . for curriculum development"; it "can tether us"; it's an anchor or starting point;
- "defines an organization's relationships with external constituencies and stakeholders";
- is a "counter-balance" to mission creep;
- can create "productive tension";
- can protect and help us to build, like when we "reach out beyond the traditional"; it can be "a shield";
- can "ease . . . frictions";
- can motivate action, can untrench us; and,
- can provide us with language for our programs, "language that mirrors that already ratified by our institution."

Andrew Jeter captures many of these same elements in his extended definition of a mission statement:

> A mission is a program. It is the mind and the mouth, the heart and the soul. A mission is the conscience, spirit, and faith of a program because a mission statement explains what a program does and is and what it would like to do and like to become. It undergirds a program with a philosophical stance and a theoretical position. It says what participants value and why they have come to value those things. It has the power to name stakeholders and to locate a program within the context of a greater organization or institution. And, by the very language it does *not* use . . . it can and will say what a

program will not do, what it does not believe in, and who is not a stakeholder.

Jeter chooses an apt, substantive metaphor of the body—the entire body—in all its complexities, from "the mind and the mouth" to the "heart and the soul" to the "conscience [and] spirit." He reminds us that a mission statement must represent us, must serve as a statement of our identity, who we are and what our program is, from a variety of perspectives. Jeter also alludes to mission construction as an exercise in selection, noting that we must pay attention to the language and the traits that we do not include. As Jeter points out, "This power of the negative is strong." What we choose to announce in our mission must be carefully chosen, taking into account values, goals, audience, language, and always grounding these choices in our local context. Jeter positions missions here as complex texts that require thinking both about the content as well as the rhetoric of the statement itself.

My second major takeaway is actually my favorite aspect of the collection, that the authors feel a responsibility to address the "provocations" (Janangelo) associated with IM. If we're realistic and accurate in our missions, then with power and potential comes, sometimes, tension and conflict. For me, the full value of a collection like *A Critical Look at Institutional Mission: A Guide for Writing Program Administrators* comes not only from its definitional qualities but also from its willingness to complicate and to see the full picture of IM, including the messiness. Tension and conflict, the terms I'll use in a positive way to denote the power of IM to prompt not only agreement but also disagreement, debate, questioning, and even, perhaps, confusion, take many forms in this collection. For instance:

- Behm discusses how IM can help his colleagues to grapple with issues of "community, collegiality, openness, transparency, and trust in each other";
- DelliCarpini notes that multiple voices, including those in the community, can tangle with IM, creating a "productive tension";
- DeRouen encourages stakeholders to "grapple with sacred cows";
- Rosso Efthymiou and Fitzgerald show at length how students can "both identify with and push against" IM, creating a site of productive resistance and "debate";
- Hoppe identifies competing missions that create "a struggle" and force him, and his students, to "synthesize ostensibly op-

posed interests and perspectives in a holistic course of intellectual development";
- Malenczyk and Rosenberg describe the "binds and pulls" of competing missions—the "apparent contraction[s]" and the "complicated scenario" we face in an institutional environment and must "negotiate" and,
- Janangelo identifies "the tension between fidelity to church teachings and the reality of social change, including a visible and vocal student demographic with needs and rights."

"Provocation" abounds in this collection. Note that no author even remotely suggests that IM-inspired tension or conflict is a reason to avoid mission-based work. Rather, the authors—here in this collection and at home in their local institutions—embrace the ways that IM can disrupt and challenge. In that messiness—competing ideas, varying perspectives of stakeholders, varying and evolving and multiple missions, and so on—is a landscape for growth, the potential for new ideas to emerge. As Janangelo reminds us, "Sensitive critique can inspire institutional intake and learning." Provocations, as another aspect of IM, can be as productive and useful as the positive possibilities. *A Critical Look at Institutional Mission: A Guide for Writing Program Administrators* captures the full complexity of institutional missions in both theoretical and practical ways.

Works Cited

English Department Program Goals. Mississippi College. Mississippi College, n.d. Web. 18 August 2014.
WCenter Archive. Lyris. Lyris, Inc., n.d. Web. 23 August 2014.

Contributors

Nicholas N. Behm is Associate Professor of English at Elmhurst College in Elmhurst, Illinois. He studies composition pedagogy and theory, writing assessment, and critical race theory. He is a former member of the CWPA Executive Board and served on the committee charged with revising the CCCC Statement on Preparing Teachers of College Writing. With Greg Glau, Deborah Holdstein, Duane Roen, and Ed White, he is co-editor of *The WPA Outcomes Statement—A Decade Later*, which won the 2013 "Best Book Award" from the Council of Writing Program Administrators. With Duane Roen and Sherry Rankins-Robertson, he is co-editor of *The Framework for Success in Postsecondary Writing: Scholarship and Applications*.

Anita R. Cortez is Director of the Office of Undergraduate Research & Creative Inquiry as well as the Administrative Director of the Developing Scholars and Edgerly-Franklin Urban Leadership Scholars Program at Kansas State University.

Dominic DelliCarpini is Naylor Endowed Professor of Writing Studies and Dean of the Center for Community Engagement at York College of Pennsylvania. He also served for five years as Chief Academic Officer and thirteen years as Writing Program Director. DelliCarpini's recent research interests include writing and civic engagement, undergraduate research in writing studies, and faculty development. He currently serves as Vice President of the Council of Writing Program Administrators, with his presidential term for that organization to run from 2017-19.

Andrea Rosso Efthymiou is Assistant Professor of Writing Studies & Composition at Hofstra University, where she also directs the Writing Center. She researches tutors' rhetorical activity and civic engagement.

Anita M. DeRouen is Director of Writing & Teaching and Assistant Professor of English at Millsaps College in Jackson, MS.

Lauren Fitzgerald is Professor of English and Director of the Wilf Campus Writing Center at Yeshiva University, where she also serves as Chair of the Yeshiva College English Department. With Melissa Ianetta, she edited *The Writing Center Journal* (2008–13) and wrote *The Oxford Guide for Writing Tutors: Practice and Research* (Oxford UP 2015).

Kristine Hansen is Professor of English at Brigham Young University, where she teaches undergraduate courses in professional writing, rhetorical style, and the history of rhetoric, as well as graduate courses on rhetorical theory and research methods. She has directed the English Department's composition program; and as Associate Dean of Undergraduate Education from 1998-2004, she directed the university's writing-across-the-curriculum program. She has served on the Executive Board of the Council of Writing Program Administrators and on the editorial board of its journal.

Jason Hoppe is Associate Dean at the United States Military Academy and founding Director of the West Point Writing Program and Mounger Writing Center. His research broadly engages American literature, composition studies, and the history of higher education and the public humanities. He is currently completing a monograph on the antinomian literary networks of major nineteenth-century women writers.

Andrew Jeter teaches composition and is the former Literacy Center Coordinator at Niles West High School in Skokie, IL. He is the current Research Director of the Idea Lab and President of the Chicagoland Organization of Writing, Literacy, and Learning Centers.

Joyce Kinkead is Professor of English at Utah State University; she served as Vice Provost for Undergraduate Studies & Research, Associate Vice President for Research, Acting Dean, and Associate Dean. Her experience includes directing writing programs and writing centers. She is the author or editor of a number of books: *Researching Writing: An Introduction to Research Methods* (2016); *Farm: A Multimodal Reader* (2014); *Undergraduate Research Offices & Programs* (2012); *Advancing Undergraduate Research: Marketing, Communications, and Fund-raising* (2011); *Undergraduate Research in English Studies* with Laurie Grobman (2010); *Valuing and Supporting Undergraduate Research* (2003); and *The Center Will Hold* with Michael Pemberton (2003). In 2013, the U.S. Professors of the Year Program honored her as the winner for the state of Utah. In 2012, she was named a Fellow of the Council on Undergraduate Research, an award that recognizes her national reputation for promoting undergraduate research, the first humanist to be so honored. As a Fulbright Senior Scholar, she worked at the University of Stockholm and for the Ministry of Education in Cyprus.

Jeffrey Klausman is Professor of English at Whatcom Community College in Bellingham, Washington, and has served on the executive committees of the Two-Year College English Association, the Conference on College Composition and Communication, and the Council of Writing Program Administrators.

Rita Malenczyk is Professor of English and Director of the Writing Program and Writing Center at Eastern Connecticut State University. She is immediate Past President of the Council of Writing Program Administrators. Her work on the rhetoric and politics of writing program and center administration has appeared in a range of journals, including *WPA: Writing Program Administration* and *The Writing Center Journal*, and numerous edited collections, including Kelly Ritter and Paul Kei Matsuda's *Exploring Composition Studies: Sites, Issues and Perspectives* (Utah State UP, 2012) and Heidi Estrem et al.'s. collection *Retention, Persistence, and Writing Programs* (Utah State UP, forthcoming 2017). With Susanmarie Harrington, Keith Rhodes, and Ruth Overman Fischer, she co-edited *The Outcomes Book* (Utah State UP, 2000), and her edited collection *A Rhetoric for Writing Program Administrators* (Parlor Press) has just appeared in a second edition (July 2016).

Steve Price is Professor of English Writing and English Secondary Education at Mississippi College, where he also directs the Writing Center. He is a co-editor of *The Writing Center Journal* and a faculty editorial board member for *Young Scholars in Writing*. His scholarly interests include research methods in writing center studies and the implementation of undergraduate research.

Lauren Rosenberg is the author of *The Desire for Literacy: Writing in the Lives of Adult Learners* (CCCC/NCTE 2015). Her literacy research extends to a current project on the writing practices of military veterans while in service and in university settings. Rosenberg's writing on literacy issues has appeared in *Community Literacy Journal* and *Reflections, A Journal of Public Rhetoric, Civic Writing, and Service Learning*; she has also co-authored book chapters and articles on feminist rhetorical practices and writing program administration, including a co-authored piece with Rita Malenczyk in the *Writing Lab Newsletter*. Rosenberg is Associate Professor, Writing Program Director, and Associate Department Head in the English Department at New Mexico State University. She was coordinator of the first-year writing program at Eastern Connecticut State University from 2008 to 2015.

Farrell J. Webb is Dean in the College of Health and Human Development at California State University Northridge. He was the Academic Director of the Developing Scholars and Bridges to the Baccalaureate Program while a Professor at Kansas State University.

Index

AAC&U (Association of American Colleges and Universities), 38, 134, 139, 147
academic discourse, 87
academic freedom, 45, 82
academic marketplace, xii
Academically Adrift (Arum and Roksa), 11, 20
accountability, xiii, 191, 227
ACT, 118, 188
adjunct, 42, 78, 88, 90
adjunct labor, 42, 78, 88, 90
Adler-Kassner, Linda, 44, 55, 57–58, 157, 160, 164–166
administration, xi, 24, 36, 41–43, 71–72, 80, 89, 120, 153–154, 162, 186–188, 192, 198, 201, 213
Advanced Placement, 118, 129, 188–189
alumni, xii, 71–72, 93, 116, 125, 127, 205, 218, 226
Amherst College, 91, 157–158, 167
Anderson, Paul, 39, 147, 166–168, 185
Arizona State University, xi, xv
assessment, xii, 6, 40, 42–47, 49, 52, 53, 54–56, 90, 99, 107, 134, 139, 146, 227; strategic, xii, 6, 40, 42–47, 49, 52–56, 90, 99, 107, 134, 139, 146, 227
Association of American Colleges and Universities (AAC&U), *see AAC&U*
audience, 13, 57, 156–157, 173–174, 176, 201, 211, 214, 225, 228
autonomy, 45

baccalaureate colleges, 25
Bartholomae, David, 87, 90
best practices, xii
boards of trustees, xi, 86, 116–117, 155
Bormann, Ernest, 151, 155–156, 158, 161, 164, 166
Bousquet, Marc, 89–90, 93, 110
Boyer Report, 27; *Reinventing Undergraduate Education; A Blueprint for America's Research Universities*, 27
branding, xii, 78, 105, 146; rebranding, xii, xiii
Brigham Young University (BYU), xiii, 112–129
Bruffee, Kenneth, 170, 181, 184, 186, 189, 193–195,

235

198, 200, 202
budget, 6, 81, 86, 90
Kenneth Burke,, 107
Burke, Kenneth, 107
Business Week, 128, 157–158, 168

Carnegie Foundation for the Advancement of Teaching, 37, 73, 115, 166, 168
Catholicism, xi, xv, 34, 127, 204, 208–209, 211–212, 217–220
chairs (department), 36
change agents, xiii
Chiseri-Strater, Elizabeth, 28, 39
Chronicle of Higher Education, xi, xv, 36, 80, 91, 154
civic engagement, xii, 5, 9, 13, 19–21
civil unions, 207–210
class size, 189
collaboration, 32, 95, 195–196
collaborative, 15, 17, 20–21, 31–32, 55–56, 136, 178, 196, 200–201
College Board, 118, 129
College English, 91, 185, 202, 224–225
Common Core State Standards, 151, 165
commonplaces, 12–13, 15–18
community colleges, 27, 31, 41, 44, 66, 79–80, 84, 151, 154, 162, 165
community engagement, 3, 6, 7, 13–15, 21, 140
competency-based education, 89
completion rates, 82
composition theory, 55, 87
computers, 224
Condon, William, 185
Conference on College Composition and Communication (CCCC), 29, 30, 86, 165
conventions, 28, 104, 173, 175
creative writing, 32
credibility, 56, 208
critical thinking, 17, 21, 47, 63, 94, 136, 190, 194–197
curriculum, xiii, 5, 10, 14, 28, 32, 42, 45, 83, 92, 94, 107, 117, 121–123, 130–136, 138–147, 162, 165, 172, 174, 176, 186–187, 190–191, 195, 198, 217, 224–227
Cushman, Ellen, 10–13, 20, 22

decision-making processes, xii, 41, 89, 201, 217
deliberative rhetoric, 12
Derrida, Jacques, 208, 220
Developing Scholars Program, 59
development, program, 102
directorship (of writing programs), 109
disciplinarity, 136, 141, 144
disciplinary expertise, 45, 50
discrimination, 219
Downs, Douglas, 28, 37, 39
DSP (directed self-placement), 59–65, 68, 71–73, 165
Duke University, 125

Duncan, Arne, 81, 91
dynamic criteria mapping, xii, 40, 43–44, 46–47, 50–57

Eastern Connecticut State University, 13, 152, 167
education, general, xiii, 24, 42, 118, 130, 132, 135, 137, 145
efficiency, 106, 151, 155, 162
Elmhurst College, 40–42, 44, 46, 50, 56–57
Elon University, 28, 38
engagement, xii, xiv, 5, 7–8, 12–16, 18–19, 21, 34, 50, 52, 95, 138, 140, 145–146, 178, 183, 198
ethics, xi, 32, 52, 63, 88
ethnicity, 60, 180
ethos, xii, 5, 12, 210, 217
Evans, David, xi, xv
Evergreen State College, 15–16
exordium, 19

faculty scholars programs, 121–126
faith-based colleges, xi, xiv, 16
fantasy theme analysis, 156, 159, 164
first-year composition, 21, 83, 152, 165
first-year scholars programs, 43, 45–52, 54, 56–57
first-year writing, 20, 28, 30, 32, 83, 141
first-year writing program: funding, 5, 33, 36, 71–72, 84, 86, 116–117; space, 6, 11, 36, 49, 138–140, 143, 145, 161, 174, 175, 189, 190–191, 196, 214, 226; staffing, 136, 143
Fleming, David, 93
format, 29, 188
four-year college, 79
Franklin & Marshall College, 17
funding models, 5, 33, 36, 71–72, 84, 86, 116–117
future scholars programs, 112

gay, 202, 204, 216–217
gay marriage, 211
Gee, James Paul, 173, 184, 190, 198, 202
gender issues, 64, 66, 179–180, 205, 212
genre, 81, 209
Gettysburg College, 17
goals, xii, xiii, 4, 5, 7, 13–14, 16, 18–21, 35, 45–46, 62, 70–71, 73, 102–103, 113, 117, 126, 136, 155, 157, 165, 178, 194, 197, 223, 226, 228
grammar, 57, 194

habits, mind, 6, 7, 9, 13–14, 17, 18, 20–21, 45
Harrington, Susanmarie, 44, 57
Harris, Muriel, 37, 109, 111
Harvard University, 8, 61, 115, 118, 160, 167
HBCU (Historically Black Colleges and Universities), xi, 24, 33–34

hiring practices, xii, 117, 128
Historically Black Colleges and Universities, see HBCU
Howard, Rebecca Moore, 39, 184
Huot, Brian, 55, 58

ideology, 209, 216
information literacy, 83
innovation, xii, 4, 41, 53, 100, 109, 140
Inside Higher Education, 36, 80, 91, 154, 167
institutional history, xi
institutional mission, xi–xiv, 3, 6, 12, 14, 16, 18–20, 24–25, 30–31, 36–37, 40–41, 43–44, 46–56, 92, 101–103, 113, 127, 130, 151, 162–163, 169, 170–171, 173–175, 177–179, 205, 208–209, 223–229
intellectual heritage, xi
interdisciplinary, 15, 43, 132
internship experiences, xii, 153
interviews, 91, 114, 152, 157, 159, 162, 175–177
investment, 158–159, 224, 225
ivory tower, 8
Ivy League Schools, xi, 87, 110

Janangelo, Joseph, and Adler-Kassner, Linda, 42
Jesuit Colleges, xiv, 34–35, 203, 204, 205, 208, 210–213, 217, 219–221
Johns, Ann, 100, 109

Johnson, Kristine, 6, 18
Johnson, Robert R., 6–7, 12, 22, 33, 38
Judaism, 173–175, 178–179, 183, 184

Klausman, Jeffrey, xiii, 28, 63, 77, 85, 93, 127, 137, 153, 161
knowledge, rhetorical, 8

Lafayette College, 17
land-grant institutions, 24–25, 27, 226
language, 12, 80, 86–88, 103, 119, 133, 140, 144–146, 159, 171, 173, 180, 190–191, 194, 196–198, 201, 207, 216, 224–225, 227–228
Lanham, Richard, xi, xv; *The Economics of Attention*, xv
Larson, Richard, 80, 91
leadership, xii, 16, 34, 43, 46, 61, 71–72, 80, 84, 86–89, 109, 110, 131, 152, 161, 211, 214, 216
legislatures, 81, 84, 151, 157
LGBT legal issues, 218
LGBTI, 207, 214
LGBTQI, 204, 205, 209
LGBTQU, 209
liberal arts, xi, 13–17, 28, 33, 41, 45–46, 80, 94, 131, 151–154, 157–164, 174, 183, 225–226
linguistics, 125
literacy, 25, 30, 35, 186–187, 189, 194–197

literacy centers, 187, 189
literacy education, 25, 35
literature, 9, 36, 44, 82, 86–87, 94, 109, 152, 217, 223, 224
Loyola University of Chicago, 127, 204–213, 218–221
Lu, Min-Zhan, 81, 86
Lumina Foundation, 81, 86

Malenczyk, Rita, xiv, 21, 22, 39, 79, 93, 133, 151, 166–168, 176, 185, 208, 224–225, 229
marketability, xi, 35, 41, 80, 84, 199, 210, 225
Marx, Anthony, 157
mechanics, 78
media, xi, 83, 158, 206, 211, 214, 224
microaggression, 66, 69
millennial students, xii
mission statements, xi–xii, 13, 18, 80, 103, 109, 131, 140, 155, 173, 211, 215–216, 223, 225
Modern Language Association, 87, 91
Muhlenberg College, 15–16
multidisciplinary, 135

National Conference on Peer Tutoring in Writing, 30
National Survey of Student Engagement (NSSE), 27–28
National Writing Project, 22
NCTE, 22, 168, 184
NPR (National Public Radio), 100

objectives, xiii, 35, 42, 45–46, 99, 102
orthodoxy, 176, 185
outcomes, 17–19, 46, 53, 56, 69–70, 136–138, 146, 187; program, 10
outcomes, learning, 14, 18–20, 44–47, 52, 55, 102, 133, 135–138, 140, 144, 146

pedagogy, xi, xii, 5–7, 13, 20, 25, 31, 41, 44, 93–95, 99–100, 165–166, 171, 175, 178, 186, 191, 195
peer tutoring, 175, 178, 200
placement, 62, 81, 83, 87, 90, 143, 145, 151
portfolios, 7, 16
Powell, Malea, 58
power, 10, 17, 29, 40, 41, 70, 98, 165, 186–187, 191, 196–198, 200–201, 226–228
PowerPoint, 63
prestige, xi, 69, 72
Prezi, 63
Princeton University, xv, 73, 110, 115, 125, 129
professional development, 53, 86, 109, 191, 197–198
Puritan rhetoric, 157

Queerty, 212, 214

racial issues, 60, 64, 180
recruitment, xi, xii, 27, 68, 205
reform, curricular, xiii, 130
remediation, 62, 187–188, 192, 201

research institutions, 70, 117
research, secondary, 32
retention, xi, xii, 27, 45, 62, 118–119, 146, 187, 205
revision, curriculum, 133
rhetoric, 3, 10, 20, 29, 78–79, 82, 102, 141, 144, 158, 164, 165, 171, 215–216, 228; *deliberative*, 9, 12–14, 17–18, 214; *epideictic*, 214
rhetorical acts, xiv, 5, 170–174, 177, 181, 183
rhetorical knowledge, 8
rhetorical practice, 183
rhetorical visions, 151, 155, 157, 160, 161, 164
Richard Young, xiii, 29–30, 38, 39, 112, 114, 116, 129, 217, 220
Rose, Shirley, 22, 23
rubric, 54, 209

same-sex marriage, 203, 207, 211–213
SAT, 153, 154, 165
self-placement, 83, 165
service learning, 3, 5, 7, 8, 20, 36
Shaughnessy, Mina, 165, 167
situation: rhetorical, 100
small liberal arts colleges, 130, 137, 225
Smith, Dorothy, 180, 184, 208, 215–216, 221
social change, 20, 205, 209, 229
stakeholders, xi–xiii, 3, 5, 42, 53, 55–56, 95, 169–170, 173, 176, 190–192, 211, 212, 214–216, 219, 224–229
standards, 63, 104, 114–115, 118, 128, 153, 201
statement, policy, 215, 216
strategic goals, 132, 145
strategic planning, 133, 136–137
strategic plans, 95, 130–137, 139, 146, 153
syntax, 17

technology, 44, 56, 98, 103, 223–224; access, 29, 35, 60, 63, 79, 139, 152, 154–155, 165, 173, 213
Thomas, Susan, 7, 8, 22, 37, 74
topoi, 12, 173
Torah Umadda, 172–175, 178–179, 182, 183, 184
transparency, 46, 173, 228
tribal colleges, 24
tuition increases, 116, 210
two-year colleges, xi, xiii, 31, 77–82, 86–89, 226

undergraduate research, xii, 25, 27–32, 35–37, 61, 68–69
underprepared students, 162
underrepresented students, 61–62, 65, 69, 71
United States Military Academy, xi, 92, 111
United States of America, xi, 34, 74, 78–79, 92, 93, 108–109, 111, 128, 157, 186
University of California Berkeley, 61, 110, 125, 184

University of North Carolina at Chapel Hill, 29

vision statements, 133, 135, 157
voice, 8, 73, 143, 190, 202, 210–211

Wardle, Elizabeth, 28, 37, 39
Wayne State University, 14
Webb, Farrell J., 66, 69
Webb, Farrell J., and Cortez, Anita R., 61, 62, 63
West Point, xiii, 92–96, 100–106, 109–111
White, Edward M., 60, 100
Wilson, David McKay, 115, 129
Windy City Times, 213, 220
World Wide Web, xv, 22, 38–39, 57, 73–74, 90–91, 110–111, 129, 147, 166–168, 185, 202, 219–221, 229
writing: authentic, 3, 6, 18, 19
writing across the curriculum, 20, 135, 142, 144
writing assessment, 53, 55
writing centers, xiii–xiv, 31, 169–171, 174–179, 181–183, 186, 188, 190, 200, 225; tutors, xiv, 30, 104, 165, 170–183, 186, 190, 192, 195–197, 200
writing process, 63, 99, 104, 178
Writing Program Administration (journal), 21–23, 142, 147, 185
Writing Program Administrators, Council of, 22
Writing Studies, 29, 31, 36–38, 90

Yancey, Kathleen Blake, 55, 58, 142, 147, 166, 168
Yeshiva University, 169, 172, 174, 178–179, 185
Young Scholars in Writing, 29–30, 39

About the Editor

Joseph Janangelo is Associate Professor of English at Loyola University Chicago and Past President of the Council of Writing Program Administrators. With Michele Eodice, Joe directs The CWPA Mentoring Project, which he co-founded. The Mentoring Project offers graduate students, adjunct, and full-time faculty at two- and four-year colleges professional development opportunities related to teaching, administration, and scholarship.

Joe's books include *Resituating Writing: Constructing and Administering Writing Programs* (with Kristine Hansen) and *Theoretical and Critical Perspectives on Teacher Change*. His work has appeared in a range of journals, including *WPA: Writing Program Administration, The Writing Center Journal, College Composition and Communication, College English, Teaching English in the Two-Year College,* and *Kairos: A Journal of Rhetoric, Technology, and Pedagogy.*

Joe volunteers at Chicago House, which serves children and adults impacted by HIV and AIDS.

www.ingramcontent.com/pod-product-compliance
Lightning Source LLC
Chambersburg PA
CBHW030537230426
43665CB00010B/923